Astream

American Writers on Fly Fishing

EDITED BY ROBERT DEMOTT
Foreword by Howell Raines

Skyhorse Publishing

Skyhorse Publishing books may be purchased in bulk at special discounts for sales promotion, corporate gifts, fund-raising, or educational purposes. Special editions can also be created to specifications. For details, contact the Special Sales Department, Skyhorse Publishing, 307 West 36th Street, 11th Floor, New York, NY 10018 or info@skyhorsepublishing.com.

Skyhorse® and Skyhorse Publishing® are registered trademarks of Skyhorse Publishing, Inc.®, a Delaware corporation.

www.skyhorsepublishing.com

10 9 8 7 6 5 4 3 2 1

Library of Congress Cataloging-in-Publication Data is available on file.
ISBN: 978-1-61608-215-4

Printed in the United States of America

To

Nick Lyons, angler for all seasons,
with affection and gratitude.

"The angler—
the focus of all this rather

than a subordinate element,
one who has come to know how it is done,
but not how it comes out—"

—John Engels
"Painting of an Angler,
Fishing the Source," from *Sinking Creek* (1997)

"He imputed to the world of fly fishing, which he loved deeply, a sense of character and tradition and wit; he saw it as a human activity, full of wonder and excitement, far beyond the mere catching of fish—an activity that enlivened the heart and sparked the imagination. It had the power to bring out the best in men—and some of the worst. He told us about the stupidity of much high-pressured 'sport' and the fun we might have on our fishless days. He was far more than what he'd admit to. . . . He was a superb writer, who will be read a hundred years from now, and a great-hearted, humorous, and perfectly remarkable man."

> —Nick Lyons, describing Sparse Grey Hackle (a.k.a. Alfred W. Miller), in "Winter Dreams with Sparse," from *Confessions of a Fly Fishing Addict* (1989)

Art by Mari Lyons

Contents

Preface and Acknowledgments

"Good fishermen are likely to be good readers. . . ."

—Odell Shepard, *Thy Rod and Thy Creel* (1930)

*A*stream: *American Writers on Fly Fishing* is a sequel—perhaps companion is a better term—to *Afield: American Writers on Bird Dogs*, which I co-edited two years ago with Dave Smith, my close friend, longtime hunting partner, fellow English professor, esteemed Southern poet, and avid bird-dog man. *Afield* gathered prose narratives by twenty-three poets, novelists, short story writers, and essayists, all of whom addressed aspects of upland bird and waterfowl hunting with trained pointing and flushing dogs. Pulitzer Prize–winning novelist Richard Ford's masterful Foreword put icing on the cake. This volume, too, springs from a conviction that many creative writers not associated with the specialized hook-and-bullet press are also serious outdoorsmen and outdoorswomen. While hunting is sometimes treated as a politically incorrect vice, the closeted wild child of atavism, fly fishing seems to be another matter entirely among writerly people, who are quick to share its many dimensions and are especially praiseful about its allure and qualities. I've heard Arnold Gingrich's quotation—"It's the most fun you can have standing up"—more often than I can recall, to which I counter that the most fun you can have sitting down is reading about fly fishing. The stained glass window above Izaak Walton's gravestone in Winchester Cathedral pictures the old boy taking his ease against a tree trunk on the bank of the nearby Itchen. His rod is close at hand but he isn't fishing; he's reading a book.

In our time, vehicles for conveying angling yarns have changed drastically. As with our culture at large, hegemony has yielded to diversity. The incalculable number of touring fly fishing movies, online angling blog sites, web-based discussion threads, and cyber magazines (which foreground digital art and photography and embedded videos over the written word) has altered the dimensions of Fly Fish Nation. Given the speed of technological progress, that's an inevitable transformation, and nearly everyone I know applauds the democratic shift toward inclusiveness. The swerve away from elitism has made access to previously specialized information easy, affordable, and direct, no matter our economic status. Indeed, few things signal a major paradigm shift in our acquisition of knowledge more than displaying fly fishing applications on our smart phones, even as we wade river X or cruise estuary Y. (Orvis recently announced that their fly fishing app for iPhone, iPad, and Droid devices was selling at an unprecedented and unanticipated rate and had already become one of the "most widely downloaded outdoor apps in use.") Our current spectatorial appetite is aided and abetted by ubiquitous, easy-to-use digital and mobile phone cameras, so that it isn't too much of a stretch to say that we inhabit a visual age in which instant gratification and feedback is the norm rather than the exception. Videographers and digital shutterbugs rule the roost. Nothing jacks up our dreaming quotient or brings a tingle to our skin like a stunning picture of a pristine fishing scene. A picture is worth a thousand words, but paradoxically it takes words to say that, which is where this collection comes in. Reader, at the risk of sounding like a fuddy-duddy, be warned: Even if you read this on your Kindle or your Nook, you hold a throwback in your hand.

No one knows precisely how many books on angling have been published in the past 500 years in English. Certainly there are enough to qualify angling as the most frequently written about sporting activity in the world. And among those many thousands of titles, there are more anthologies of fishing essays than a person can shake a fly rod at. I have read stacks of them—enough to know that compiling one is as shifty and tricky as fishing itself. Russell Chatham's Silent Seasons (1978), David Seybold's Seasons of the Angler (1988), Holly Morris' A Different Angle (1995), Ted Leeson's A Gift of Trout (1996), John Cole and Hawk Pollard's West of Key West (1996), with its superb paintings by Peter Corbin and David Harrison Wright, and the Yale Anglers' Journal editors' retrospective collection, Tight Lines (2007), with prefatory material by Nick Lyons and James Prosek, set a high standard for angling appeal and literate content. Even these exemplary volumes, however, frequently rely on reprinted material. The ideal is a collection of wholly original essays never before printed in any other publication. However, that is as elusive as joining the informal "10-20-30 Club" of West Virginia's Elk River (10x tippet, 20 inch trout, size 30 fly). It can be done, but not on a regular basis or on demand. Every variable imaginable has to fall into place. Sometimes coming close to the mark is all we can ask. I aimed for a completely original gathering, but, as usual, the best intentions of fish and men have a way of falling short. Nearly all the essays published in Astream were written for this anthology, though a few, which have since been revisited by their authors, had prior lives and are used here with permission.

Guy de la Valdène's "Remembering Woody" appeared in different form as "Woody" in West of Key West: Adventures and Reflections Fishing the Flats from the Contents to the Marquesas, John Cole and Hawk Pollard, eds. (Mechanicsburg, PA: Stackpole Books, 1996), pp. 163–174.

Jim Fergus's "Let's Do It Again Next Year" appeared in shorter form as "The Trout Reunion" in Field and Stream, volume CXVI (May 2011), pp. 68–71, 78.

Pam Houston's "In the Company of Men (Redux)" appeared as "In the Company of Fishermen" in A Little More About Me (New York: W. W. Norton, 1999), pp. 103–112.

Sydney Lea's "Epic and Idyll" appeared in shorter form as "Brown, Gilbey's, Happy Ending" in Rise Forms (http://riseforms.com) in 2010.

Thomas McGuane's "Seeing Snook" appeared in Sports Illustrated, Vol. 101, Issue 1 (July 5, 2004), pp. 80–86.

Craig Nova's "A Shell Game" appeared in a shorter version as chapter six in the revised edition of Brook Trout and the Writing Life (Hillsborough, NC: Eno Publishers, 2011), pp. 83–90.

In "The Art of Fiction," first published in 1884, eminent American novelist Henry James, who knew more than most about the ups and downs of the writing process, said that art "lives upon discussion . . . upon variety of attempt, upon the exchange of views and the comparison of standpoints." While I can't imagine that august late-Victorian gent ever tying on a fly, much less baiting a hook, it does not strike me as too far a reach to say that his basic metaphor applies here: Fishing, too, feeds upon discussion and conversation, to which I would also add curiosity, attentiveness, patience, and passion. On the water, or at our writing desks or tying stations, what are we fly fishers, anyway, but people on whom, as James encouraged, "nothing" should be "lost"? I am pleased to acknowledge that all the following persons, places, and things, far from being lost, have lent their part to the conversation that brought this collection to print.

Tony Lyons, president of Skyhorse, was enthusiastic about this collection from the get-go. My talented editor, Jennifer McCartney, did everything possible to bring Astream to presentable form, as did every member of that firm, and April Rondeau for her fine copyediting job. I am indebted to the entire Skyhorse staff for jobs well done.

Special thanks go to Guy de la Valdène, Chris Dombrowski, Ron Ellis, Jim Harrison, Craig Mathews, and Paul Schullery for advice, encouragement, suggestions, discussion, and friendship; to Anna Collins-Proper of Belgrade, Montana, who graciously allowed the use of a chapter from her late husband's unpublished book manuscript; Howell Raines of Henryville, Pennsylvania, who carved out time from a busy life and writing schedule to provide the Foreword; and to Bob and Mary Hendrix of Santa Monica, California (Mary's fly image is used as a spacer throughout this book). Thanks also to Kent Clements, Rodger Gaulding, Dennis Hess, and Lars Lutton, all of whom shared an immodest amount of stream time with me in the past couple of years as this project was being launched and who spurred me on with their interest and enthusiasm.

I profited from contact and conversations with Dan Lahren, Livingston, Montana; Roger and Janet Ornduff, Gravois Mills, Missouri; Patrick Daigle and Bucky McCormick of Blue Ribbon Flies, West Yellowstone, Montana; Greg Gress, manager of Longhorn Ranch, Ennis, Montana; Leon Sagaloff,

Frontier Anglers, Dillon, Montana; John Sampson, Ruby Springs Lodge, Alder, Montana; Dave Breitmeier and Loretta Fortney, Elk Springs Resort and Fly Shop, Monterville, West Virginia; Lea Chatham, Chatham Fine Art Gallery, Livingston, Montana; Rich Beckwith and Dave Carpenter of Angler's Xtream, Parkersburg, West Virginia; Earl Du Back, Ledyard, Connecticut; Professor Marsha Dutton, Chair, English Department, Ohio University, Athens, Ohio; and Kim Allen Scott, Special Collections Librarian, Merrill G. Burlingame Special Collections, Montana State University Library, Bozeman, Montana. I also thank Connecticut attorney Pete Hauser, whose interest in fish-lit anthologies helped plant a seed several years ago, and fellow members of my Trout Unlimited group—the Blennerhassett Chapter of Parkersburg, West Virginia—many of whom (especially Ted Brunson, Mark Byron, Dave Fulton, Roy McCammon, Steve Saluk, and Joe Webb), because they love to talk fishing and swap stories, seemed to me to be part of this book's ideal audience.

To the *Astream* contributors I have fished with in Montana and elsewhere—Bennett, Fox, Harrison, Leeson, Lyons, Mathews, Nova, and Schullery—many thanks for good cheer and exceptional memories. Tom Montgomery of Jackson, Wyoming and Stephen Collector of Boulder, Colorado generously provided photographs of Charles Gaines and Jim Fergus, respectively. To them and to all *Astream* contributors: my deepest gratitude for sticking with me on this project, for working at what could only be called below-minimum wage, and for conspiratorial help in keeping the true nature of this collection a secret as long as possible from Nick Lyons. You will all be amply rewarded in angling heaven. Those who also lent a hand and words to *Afield*—de la Valdène, Ellis, Guernsey, Harrison, Lea, Mathews, McGuane, Nova, and Raines—your rewards will be doubly beyond measure.

Not all fishing is done in water. Even an edited anthology requires building what novelist John Steinbeck once called a "wall of background." My dry land excursions, undertaken to build a foundation in primary angling literature, started many years ago but accelerated a decade ago when I taught an undergraduate seminar at Ohio University on "The Literature of American Fly Fishing" (highlighted by a visit from Jim Harrison, who told students that "writing about fishing is as difficult as any other kind of writing"). Prior to, and since then, my curiosity about and fascination with what Arnold Gingrich called "the fishing in print" has rivaled my zest for fly fishing itself and has led me to some true honey holes: Beinecke Rare Book and Manuscript Library, Yale University, New Haven, Connecticut; Jerry Bartlett Memorial Angling Collection at the Phoenicia Library in Phoenicia, New York; Datus Proper and Nick Lyons Archives in the Bud Lilly Trout and Salmonid Collection at Burlingame Special Collections, Montana State University's Renne Library, in Bozeman; National Sporting Library in Middleburg, Virginia; Anglers' Club of New York in Manhattan; Carl Otto Kretzschmer von Kienbusch Angling Collection at Princeton University's Firestone Library in Princeton, New Jersey; Catskill Fly Fishing Center and Museum in Livingston Manor, New York; and last, but not least, the American Museum of Fly Fishing in Manchester, Vermont. Travel to these archives and repositories has been aided by awards from Ohio University's English Department and College of Arts and Sciences, and by discretionary research funds from my Distinguished Professorship.

The Dean family's Elk Springs Resort in Monterville, West Virginia; Rodger Gaulding's Rivers of the West cabins in Cameron, Montana; and Gil and Mary Willis's Elk River Inn in Slatyfork, West Virginia have been especially congenial work sites, which is to say they have not only fostered contemplation and reflection but have also been handy to great fishing on, respectively, the fabled Madison River and the less well known but equally satisfying Elk River and Slaty Fork of the Elk.

"The good fishing starts when a river imposes itself on an angler," Verlyn Klinkenborg claims in his introduction to John Inglis Hall's *Fishing a Highland Stream* (1993), "never the other way around." Indeed, rivers teach us all kinds of things and serve up all kinds of surprising experiences: The salmon fly and caddis hatches, for example, of the Madison and Yellowstone are well known and widely documented in contemporary sporting literature. But a person would be hard pressed to find a hatch as startlingly prolific and bountiful as the Elk's May sulphur extravaganza. To be in its midst, especially at dusk as emergers trail off and spinners begin to fall—a coffin fly mixed in here and there like a piece of scrumptious white cotton candy—gives the impression that no matter what else is haywire in your life, it is still possible to achieve bliss, even if only briefly. Although it is far less well known abroad and is not widely written about, it's an event that redefines the meaning of "super hatch." Anyway, digression aside, it was to those waters in West Virginia and Montana I rushed as soon as my notebook was closed and my computer switched off for the day.

"Angling," Harry Middleton rightly remarks in *The Bright Country* (2000), "is about a lot more than fishing." To Mari Lyons, Nick's Queen of the Waters, and to Kate Fox, owner of Textual Healing, LLC, and Parmachene Belle of my heart, not one scintilla, not one iota, not one smidgen of this book would have been possible without you.

RD
Athens, Ohio
January, 2012

List of Illustrations

Foreword

Howell Raines

When I was invited to write the foreword to a new edition of *The Compleat Angler*, I quoted Tom McGuane on why we revere Izaak Walton, that endearing old royalist pontificator and—according to some literary detectives—incurable plagiarist. Walton doesn't really teach the canny reader how to fish, according to Tom, but rather "how to dream." As I made my way through the pages before you, I had the same thought about *Astream: American Writers on Fly Fishing*. It's a book for that vast army—in which we all serve—of people who, while obeying the payroll masters of this great and good Republic, sit at our desks and dream of having a rod in hand and a fair chance at being humiliated by a trout. Or a tarpon. Or a panfish.

Izaak Walton is far from alone among writers in seeing the fishing we do astream and the fishing we do in our heads as being of a piece. One of our writers, Greg Keeler, expands the thought by linking our need for angling stories to the "dreaming places" revered by aboriginal Australians. In passing such a place, Keeler notes, an individual is obligated to tell the story of what happened in that spot to him or others. I submit that the same impulse gives rise to this collection of essays by anglers determined to share the stories of the individual dreams they've each carried home from their own places.

As a writer and reader, I've always been a little suspicious of anthologies. To begin with, if it's a subject you've explored and you're not invited to the party, you feel jealous. If you're included, you're apt to feel jealous, too, when you see your piddling effort printed alongside the work of a master like Nick Lyons. On balance, though, I've become a fan of anthologies of sporting literature. Fishing and hunting have the most extensive catalogs in the field of sporting literature, and a collection like this serves the valuable role fulfilled in the college curriculum by the "survey course" in American or British literature. Let's face it: In one lifetime, most of us can't read everything from *Beowulf* to *Moby-Dick*, covering all the greater and lesser masterpieces along the way. So there's value in having a buffet set by an editor with wide knowledge and a demanding critical eye. It's fitting that this volume is dedicated to Nick Lyons, for he best sums up what unites the writers and readers of fishing tales. "All the fishing I ever did lives in me," Nick points out, and so does all the reading of works by Roderick Haig-Brown, John Inglis Hall, Ted Leeson, "and a hundred more that all live inside me and release a sentence or two when I least expect and most need them."

The English major in me wants to discuss these pieces one at a time, but there's nothing worse than a guide, whether in a museum or a bonefish skiff, who doesn't know when it's time to step aside and let the thing under contemplation speak for itself. Yet I can't resist throwing up a few trail markers for you, not necessarily because one piece is better than another, but as a tip of the hat to this or that writer who brightened my day, just as your own list will brighten yours. One thing you'll find is that the famous bylines herein do not have a monopoly on the well-turned phrase. Take, for example, the actor Michael Keaton, whose memories of a Pennsylvania boyhood are highlighted by the observation that on their outdoor adventures his father "smelled like Old Spice and work." A number of these pieces can help you recapture what Joseph Monninger calls "that other country . . . the land of our youth."

Yet who can cast a fly or bring to hand a bluegill on a worm without contemplating mortality? Le Anne Schreiber's description of seeing snapping turtles mating among lily pads reminds me of all the wonderful things I may never see because none of us in one lifetime can read enough, travel enough, or cast far enough. There's always something around the next bend of the stream.

So I must say a word about the presence in this collection of an unpublished essay by Datus Proper. His *What the Trout Said* helped educate me and my boys during our novitiate adventures on the Rapidan and other Blue Ridge streams he loved. He died, much too early, a fisherman's death by an accidental fall on the Montana stream he describes so delightfully in these pages. So let's give Datus Proper the last word on what happens when we read about our sport and pastime. In reality or imagination, "you kneel by the river, shoot your line, and hit the ring of the rise. You and fish and fly meet where you have always met, in that window between stream and sky."

Introduction
Writers Fishing, Fishers Writing

Robert DeMott

". . . next to fishing itself, there is nothing better than a good fishing book."

—Steve Raymond, *The Year of the Trout* (1995)

1

My fly fishing enthrallment started one May day in 1956 on Connecticut's Saugatuck River when a brightly colored foot-long male brook trout took a Grey Ghost streamer I had tied myself—inexpertly, I should add— loosely following Carrie Stevens's recipe, with an improvisational mix of feathers plucked from my grandparents' Barred Rock chickens. The brookie looked like a hand-painted ceramic tile, its colors almost neon in their brilliance. I don't recall much else about that day, but I remember that fish, its deliberate grab in deep water and its give-and-take throb that traveled up my arm all the way to my heart. Corny as it sounds, I can't say whether I hooked that fish or it hooked me. It was a sweet moment because I had missed most of school that year, recuperating from corrective surgery on both feet. While my seventh-grade classmates were following their normal regimen of boisterous early-teen activity, knee-high plaster casts kept me immobile for months on end. I was housebound, scuttling around like a crab, neglecting homeschooling assignments in favor of watching Hopalong Cassidy movies on television with my grandfather, devouring outdoor magazines and

Herter's catalogs one after another, and keeping boredom at bay by the trial-and-error process of learning to tie flies.

Though there were moments when I wasn't sure I'd ever walk again and thus would never be able to use the flies I was creating, I kept at it with a kind of bulldog determination, figuring that being close to a fishing-related process was better than not fishing at all. In that I was only partly correct, but given the right dose of optimism, there is nothing like repetitive activity to kill time, tedium, and ennui, all of which I had in spades. By mid-April, freed from cement boots, I was back in junior high school during the week and fishing on the weekends with impetuous abandon, trying to make up for what I'd lost and dimly guessed even then that I would never get back. To make room for more stream time, I even quit tying flies on a regular basis, a perverse overreaction I have always regretted.

I made it to the Saugatuck that day by pestering my mother into chauffeuring me to Weston and then passing her time with a book while I worked a stretch of the stream around Cartbridge Road with my swap shop outfit. It was a clunky fiberglass fly rod, a dinged-up Pflueger Medalist reel with a pocked, grainy level line, to the end of which I had affixed a short leader of plain four-pound test monofilament cribbed from my spin outfit. In the large scheme of the day's global geopolitical events, landing that trout was among the most minor of minor occurrences.

And yet, though I could not have said why or how at the time, my life changed. Some shift, some axis tilt, some compass realignment, nearly imperceptible at first, took place that day and gradually intensified in the following decades. I don't fool myself that it was a full-blown, game-changing conversion (those came later in life and had nothing to do with fishing), but a door definitely opened and I walked through it toward a life—or at least an aspect of life—that seemed not necessarily better than the one I owned but different, perhaps more intriguing and tantalizing. Somehow, a life with fly fishing in it seemed a cheery prospect, and I doubt that back then I could have been more articulate about its appeal. But angle is everything, and although it was a long time before I caught another trout on a fly, that first one lit me up in such a way that I eventually weaned myself from spin fishing and bait casting (at which I had become deadly) in fresh water ponds and lakes and brackish estuaries and saltwater reaches of my home state. Plying creeks, brooks, streams, and rivers in southwestern Connecticut and southern Vermont with a fly rod was what I felt most moved to do, often at the expense of other, more pressing facets of my life, especially school, about which I was fairly indifferent.

Discovering fishing at a young age is not unusual. Neither is passing from one style or form of fishing to another, nor is becoming a passionate, even obsessive practitioner—such moves are among our piscine Ur-stories, our mythic angling evolutions. Almost every angler I know went through a similar experience, earlier or later, then or now. In those days, however, before the advent of Trout Unlimited and when the Federation of Fly Fishers was not even a gleam in anyone's eye, my fly fishing was entirely self-taught, which is to say it was a frustrating process of trial and error. My father did not fish or hunt on a regular basis, so I could not turn to him for anything but a hearty pat on the back and his encouragement to "Keep at it."

One relative of ours and one family friend fished with fly rods and spoke of its pleasures, but neither offered to give me a casting lesson or to take me along to a stream. My mother's brothers, who mentored me in other meaningful outdoor ways, were seasoned fishermen, true adepts with a Mepps Aglia spinner or a C. P. Swing on light spin tackle, but not yet with fly gear. The sporting goods stores in Norwalk, my hometown on the north shore of Long Island Sound, sold fishing gear, but most of it was aimed at the heavy duty surf casting, trolling, and down rigger saltwater trade, of which there was plenty in those bountiful waters. I did not know such a thing as a fly shop existed, had never witnessed a full-blown caddis or mayfly hatch, and, because we kept and ate the fish we caught, I was totally ignorant about catch-and-release ethics. I certainly did not know any angling experts personally and, even if I had, as a child of working-class parents there was little enough discretionary money for guidance, casting lessons, or special equipment.

That winter and early spring, life inside my hothouse bubble lent itself to tolerable escapes, however. When I wasn't tying flies or fantasizing about fishing adventures, I was reading, a habit of mind that took hold so deeply it became a defining factor in my life. (It was not for nothing that I became an English teacher.) Gradually, by keeping up with *Field and Stream*, *Sports Afield*, and *Outdoor Life* I came to recognize some legendary names—A. J. McLane, Ted Trueblood, and Joe Brooks, my absolute favorite. I gleaned whatever I could by paying attention to the men who paid attention. There are people from my generation who claim that Ernest Schwiebert's *Matching the Hatch* (1955) was the signal book of that era, but for me it was Brooks's *Complete Book of Fly Fishing* (1958), which came out a couple of years into my hit-and-miss apprenticeship. I checked out a copy from the Norwalk Library and pawed through it until my fingers and eyes bled. Illustrated with pages of workaday drawings, charts, and black-and-white photos, Brooks's practical advice and clear instructions were critical to my development (such as it was), and I tried out many of his pointers and strategies as often as I could on the perch, bluegills, bass, and chain pickerel at Hailey's Pond and Wood's Pond, my neighborhood fishing venues and personal Waldens, or on the pale-hued rubbery hatchery rainbow trout stocked in the semi-urban Norwalk River, which I could reach by bicycle in a few minutes of hard peddling.

Brooks was a globe-traveling angler who fished in parts of the planet I knew even then I would never have the money or leisure to visit. Yet his was also a democratic, blue-collar sensibility, characterized by a plain prose style that spoke to a wide audience about tactics in a familiar, accommodating manner. Even when I stumbled in my learning curve, when I wanted to pick up my spinning rod again and throw a Mepps or Dardevle for trout or Hula Popper for bass, Brooks's reassurance that "with a little practice, fly fishing is, not easy, but quickly learned, and that once learned, it pays dividends such as no other type of fishing can offer" sustained me and gave me courage to step up. Later, with money saved from caddying at East Norwalk's Shorehaven Golf Club, I bought my first split bamboo fly rod, a used two-piece 7½ foot Sewell N. Dutton "Angler's Choice." A bargain basement, bottom-rung wand all the way, but my most prized possession, nonetheless—a lovely honey-brown lightning rod for conducting every angling dream and hope I had. There was, I consoled myself as I threw yet another tailing loop or struck too late on a trout rising to a dry fly, a better day coming.

The twin seductions of fly fishing and reading—both solitary activities tailor-made for an only child—came to me at the same time (writing came much later), so I cannot overestimate what Brooks meant to me at that juncture of my angling life when I was keen for practical instruction to buttress on-stream experience. As I became more proficient with fly gear, my desire—the shape of my hunger—changed and I did what so many others have done when instructional appetite begins to wane: I began seeking out the kinds of texts aimed at imagining angling experience more deeply and vividly. There were huge gaps in my reading curriculum, but along the way in that formative period I encountered William Faulkner's "The Bear" and Ernest Hemingway's "Big Two-Hearted River," which altered forever the way I thought about outdoor subjects. Later, I discovered astonishingly good literary sporting pieces by John Graves and William Humphrey and by a couple of my near contemporaries—Jim Harrison and Tom McGuane—in *Sports Illustrated* and elsewhere. Their fiction and essays seemed to exist in a category of attitude separate from anything I'd seen before; their language, torqued down for maximum grip, seemed more real than experience itself. I was primed for change, and eventually ran into Nick Lyons, another writer who was breaking the whole field wide open back then.

The way fly fishing burgeoned as an industry in the 1970s was exciting and scary. New technologies, new techniques, new information, new attitudes, new publications, new voices: It seemed that all of a sudden a fresh world opened up that accelerated progress and stretched the sport's horizons in ways unthinkable fifteen years earlier. It was a cautionary moment, as well, and an end to innocence, because it meant that many of us well-meaning part-timers might always remain out of the loop, out-stripped or intimidated by the growing legion of newly elevated experts, authorities, pundits, and celebrities. Anyway, before the tide shifted for good, my angling life had already started to subside. College, marriage and family, and graduate school, followed by seventy-hour weeks getting my teaching life at Ohio University off the ground, established a set of priorities destined to disqualify me as a trout bum.

I kept reading, however, and I drew on the work of some of the new class of cutting-edge pros (specially Doug Swisher and Carl Richards) when, as a kind of a lark to see if my work life and hobby life could be bridged, I wrote a scholarly article on how and why American expatriate poet Ezra Pound (whose famous mantra "make it new" not only revolutionized Modernist poetics but also seemed tailor-made for fly fishing) quoted recipes for tying the Blue Dun and Grannom patterns from Charles Bowlker's *The Art of Angling* (1774) in his own "Canto LI" in *The Fifth Decad of Cantos XLII–LI* (1937). The essay, which came out of a graduate seminar on American literature I was teaching, appeared in 1972 in *Paideuma,* a respected but esoteric publication where it might have remained interred in its own ivory tower dust if it were not for a series of surprise moves (engineered by a kindly stranger, W. M. Frohock, a fly fishing Harvard professor and noted literary critic), which ended in the article's being reprinted five years later in an issue of *Fly Fisherman*, fully dressed right down to the last stuffy footnote.

In its second go-round, the essay was vetted by Nick Lyons (I learned much later), who besides being a contributing editor to *Fly Fisherman*, also wrote its "Seasonable Angler" column. By then, of course, I had read just about everything Nick had published—his was one of the emerging voices of the era that was especially congenial to my ear. Lyons put a face on fly fishing that looked a lot like the rest of us. Not long after *Fly Fisherman* appeared in the spring of 1977, I received a cordial note from Nick (though many years would pass before I met him in person). I responded to the effect that no matter what else I ever achieved in my academic life, nothing would ever top publishing on Ezra Pound—the world's most controversial, allusive, and cranky poet—in a popular angling magazine. I don't know if my university colleagues saw the absurdity of that juxtaposition (they gave me tenure anyway), though I suspected that Nick surely did.

2

So in honor of his eightieth birthday, and in appreciation of his incomparable, decades-long career as fly fishing author, editor, publisher, and all-around instigator, facilitator, and mentor who has touched the lives of more anglers and writers than anyone can tally, *Astream* is dedicated to Nick Lyons, on whom, thankfully, in true Jamesian fashion, nothing was ever lost. (Should anyone doubt that, visit the Lyons archive in the Merrill G. Burlingame Special Collections department of Montana State University's library. Collection 2475, the Nick Lyons Ephemera Collection, covers 1932 to 2005 and fills forty-two boxes that take up almost seventeen feet of shelf space [http://www.lib.montana.edu/collect/spcoll/finfdaid/2475.html]. It is a must stop online or in person for anyone interested in learning more about the cultural and material history of fly fishing in our time.)

Lyons's comment about Sparse Grey Hackle, which serves as an epigram to *Astream*, applies equally to Nick himself: "He imputed to the world of fly fishing, which he loved deeply, a sense of character and tradition and wit; he saw it as a human activity, full of wonder and excitement, far beyond the mere catching of fish—an activity that enlivened the heart and sparked the imagination." Like so many other people during the past forty years, I have benefitted directly from Nick's "various lives," as he calls them in *My Secret Fishing Life* (1999)—not just his multifaceted skills, but his ask-for-nothing-back generosity, his friendship, and especially his marvelous habit of mind and intellectual demeanor. I am certain I speak for many, many people—both in and out of this volume—when I say that Nick's life and career are utterly deserving of celebration. I say that knowing full well that he is uncomfortable in the spotlight and will probably be embarrassed by all the fuss.

One of my most enjoyable fishing experiences occurred several years ago when Nick shared the mysteries of his infamous pellet fly, which he whittled from a wine cork and developed through trial and error to fool the huge, finicky rainbow trout in his friend's spring-fed pond near Woodstock, New York. (Nick tells of a more recent big trout encounter with his friend, literary agent Knox Burger, in "Indian Summer of a Fly Fisher" in this collection.) We were slumming that day, no question about it, but stooping low—metaphorically anyway—with chum to illicitly increase our odds gave a kind of surreal tint to the day. Nick Lyons, former University of Pennsylvania basketball star, renowned fishing author, celebrated member of prestigious angling clubs and societies, legendary book publisher, respected Hunter College faculty member, poised with wispy fly fishing gear in one hand and grubby liver pellets in the other; it was another exquisitely weird moment too delicious not to be cherished.

When every traditional fly we offered had been spurned, as Nick knew they would be, hoity-toity finesse went out the window. "Watch this," he said gleefully, broadcasting handfuls of processed fish food. In a few minutes, dinner bell clanging loudly, trout the size of torpedoes began boiling—no, erupting—at the surface. One cruiser (we guesstimated its weight at eight pounds) ate the cork fly (probably accidentally) and, after an electrifying straight-line run into the next county, broke us off with less effort than it would take a bear to swat a mosquito. Best of all, its loss didn't matter. As two life-long English professors who had made a fetish of teaching *Moby-Dick*, we could have viewed losing that rainbow as Ahabian, which is to say, as tragic, but instead the whole venture veered toward Ishmaelian comedy and self-deflation. It was joyous, riotous fun, a carnival of fly fishing impropriety and misadventure. But then anyone who has followed Nick's books, from *The Seasonable Angler: Journeys Through a Fisherman's Year* (1970) to *The Gigantic Book of Fishing Stories* (2007), which he edited; followed his hundreds of magazine columns and essays in *Fly Fisherman, New York Times, Field and Stream, Fly Rod and Reel, Fish and Fly,* and elsewhere; and followed, as well, his countless generous forewords and introductions to others' fly fishing books, knows that he writes with poetic passion and earthy clarity infused with wit, whimsy, irony, and humor that marks him as an enemy of self-aggrandizement, pretentiousness, and look-down-your-nose preciousness. That day at Bill's Pond, I like to think, life and art conjoined.

In *Walden*, Thoreau devotes an entire chapter to the act and art of reading and says it behooves us to read books "as deliberately and reservedly as they were written." Books create pathways to follow, as they did last summer when Kate Fox and I (and later Rodger Gaulding and I) fished a section of Odell Creek near Ennis, Montana, where Nick's wonderful memoir, *Spring Creek* (1992), and the shorter, equally lyrical *Sphinx Mountain and Brown Trout* (1997) are set. Both volumes are illustrated by Mari Lyons in her signature impressionistic style, thereby adding yet another layer of readerly enjoyment.

I am a sucker for visiting geographic places upon which books and paintings are based, and I've made a quirky hobby of gauging representational relationships—usually complex and fraught—between physical venues and their textual counterparts. I've pursued this oddball fascination for decades from Maine to California, and I have never been disappointed with my findings, never become tired of viewing what author X or artist Y saw at a given place that started their juices flowing. Mine too, because as I prefer spring creeks to any other kind of water, the pastoralist in me was already salivating as we drove north from our digs in Cameron toward Ennis. What is water—flowing, still, or tidal—but a blank sheet on which to inscribe our aspirations? "Give us this day our daily fish," says the great Chilean poet Pablo Neruda. To which the only reasonable response is "Amen."

It was exhilarating to stand on a south-facing plateau of the Longhorn Ranch and take in Sphinx Mountain to the east, rising nearly 11,000 feet in the Madison Range, its chiseled features a kind of grey sidebar to the green-going-brown benchland and the blue-tinted East Branch and West Branch of Odell sparkling in morning light. Nearly everything had its real or imagined counterpart in Nick's texts and Mari's drawings, right down to the same rutted two tracks we traveled overland that morning to reach the creek. The stream isn't as comely as it was in the halcyon days when Nick fished its water and Mari painted its surrounding landscape. Some areas have shallowed and could stand judicious restoration to remove silt, narrow runs, and deepen holes, but many goodly fish are still present in the pools Nick immortalized—Second Bend, Farrago, Paranoid, and all the others.

There are rare days when the tiniest things seem linked to the whole shebang of earth, sky, and water. All we need for pleasure and satisfaction is laid at our feet, and our hope is that we do our part well enough not to screw up the outcome. I was on a pilgrimage that day and in the right frame of angling mind, so it was impossible to be disappointed in that little simulacrum of paradise. Finicky and shy, tucked beneath treeless meadow cutbanks to escape summer's sun, which drifted like a giant yellow indicator in the August sky, the trout—gorgeously marked and colored-up wild browns—came intermittently to hand on various small dries tied on 6x and 7x tippet, each fish, I liked to think, a descendant of those alligators Nick, Craig Mathews (who reports on those days in "In the Nick of Time" in this collection), and ranch owner Herb Wellington and his other guests caught and released more than twenty years ago. I came to understand, in a way I never quite had before, Thoreau's metaphysical proclamation in *Walden* that we fish all our lives without knowing that it isn't fish we are really after.

As far as I know, it was the late Datus Proper who first dubbed Nick "godfather," and in the sense that he has been a formidable and exacting, but generous and companionable, guide to so many of us in the late-twentieth and early-twenty-first century world of fly fishing, the sobriquet is thoroughly earned. For those who favor a more spiritual tag, Peter Kaminsky, in *The Fly Fisher's Guide to the Meaning of Life* (2008), says Nick is our "Saint Paul, the spreader of the creed, the grand communicator. . . ." His nomination is equally true. Pay your money and make your choice. Either way, whether we wield a pen or a fly rod or both, we all oscillate in Nick's orbit. Viva Nick Lyons!

3

For a skeptical reader, wondering what in 2012 A.D. could possibly be said that is new about fly fishing, a method of angling that in its rudimentary form dates back millennia, the thirty-one essays collected here, different as they are from one another, indicate that a lively conversation among men and women about what we value is still possible and salient, even centuries after two inspiring texts—*A Treatise of Fishing with an Angle*, attributed shakily and perhaps mythically to Dame Juliana Berners, composed around 1450 and first printed in Wynkyn de Worde's *Book of St Albans* (1496), and Izaak Walton's bucolic pastiche *The Compleat Angler* (1653)—established the happy efficacy of fishing not just as a utilitarian practice, satisfying personal pursuit, and spiritual endeavor, but as proper literary subject matter. Both are primarily bait-fishing texts, but given their influence on fly fishing consciousness and decorum across the ages, that seems not to have mattered. Our mother and father who art in fishing: We look for our predecessors wherever we can.

I'll wade deeper here and say that nearly every brother or sister of the angle has since walked in their shadows. Most of our scribbling in English about fly fishing in the past 500 years has been a sustained commentary—pro and/or con, instructional and/or philosophical, technical and/or theoretical—on these two worthies, with perhaps a third thrown in for good measure: Charles Cotton, who added his twelve-chapter fly fishing treatise, *Instructions on How to Angle for a Trout or Grayling in a Clear Stream* to the fifth edition of Walton's book in 1676. In my darker moments I sometimes think that in striving for originality, we don't often do much more than signify on foundational texts, whether by Berners or Walton, Cotton or Bowlker, Skues or Halford, Gordon or Wulff, Haig-Brown or Lyons, McGuane or Gierach. Of course I am overstating the case, but then it's not for nothing that Joan Wulff opens her acclaimed instructional casting video, *Joan Wulff's Dynamics of Fly Casting* (1985), by dressing in cowled garments, a funky allusion to Dame Juliana. And at the risk of sounding cheeky, what is Norman Maclean's *A River Runs Through It* (1976) but a kind of Western frontier rebuttal to Walton's and Cotton's escapist idyll? And how about William Humphrey's *My Moby Dick* (1979)? What's that but an ironic riff on Melville's epic tale, itself the grandfather of all the one-that-got-away yarns? Given enough time and the long arc of history, what goes around comes around. And sometimes, goofy or not, stays with us.

In his prefatory note to *The American Angler's Book* (1864), Thaddeus Norris, the home-spun Yankee Walton, claimed that despite the "many books on angling by British authors . . . few American works on the subject have yet been offered to the reading public; and this in the face of the fact that we are an angling people." Norris need not have worried. A lively angling tradition exists in America among its creative writers. Consider fiction writers, for example: from Washington Irving to Zane Grey, from Ernest Hemingway and Philip Wylie to William Humphrey and Richard Brautigan, from John Hersey, Norman Maclean, and William G. Tapply to Rick Bass, Kevin Canty, Anthony Doerr, David James Duncan, Carl Hiaasen, John Larison, John Nichols, Annie Proulx, and the dozen or so novelists included in this book, there's more than enough to allay Norris's fears.

Indeed, fly fishing seems to be the sport (and subject) of choice for many contemporary authors, no matter their choice of genre. In *Becoming a Fly Fisher: From Brookie Days to the Tenth Level* (2002), John Randolph goes so far as to boast that the "best literature in the history of fly fishing has been written in the past three decades. Much of it has been written by American writers." Nationalism aside, when I drew up a preliminary list of candidates, the number of names, randomly jotted down, reached toward a hundred. Melville's lament in *Moby-Dick* that there is never enough time, strength, cash, and patience to go around applies here as well. Contacting close to a hundred writer-anglers, all of whose work in a variety of genres I had long admired and respected, loomed as large as the white whale itself. But I didn't go far down my brainstorming list before I had commitments on my dance card from enough respondents to make a volume a bit larger than *Afield*. (The estimable writers I never got around to contacting—some of whom are household names in the fly fishing community—could fill a couple more volumes of essays.)

I wasn't totally surprised by the sheer number of names on my original list, for I'd long understood the attraction of Izaak Walton's statement in his dedicatory preface to *The Compleat Angler*: ". . . I have made a recreation of a recreation. . . ." Which is to say that next to the fun we can have fishing, there's the fun of writing about it. The thing we love is research for the other thing we love. "Because you have to do the fishing first," John Cole writes in *Fishing Came First* (1989). "When you write about it, you get to do it over again. To my knowledge no one has come up with a better way to enjoy life." It's difficult to argue with Cole's judgment, though often it is hard to tell where the line between the two exists. Nick Lyons, to whom this book is dedicated, wondered aloud many years ago about this conundrum in his masterpiece, *Spring Creek,* when he asked whether "writing about fishing, which cannot occur without first fishing" had become "quite as important . . . as the act itself?"

Certainly we are "haunted by waters," as Norman Maclean wrote, but we are also equally haunted by words. For John Gierach, fishing and writing attract the same kind of detail-oriented people. Whether, as Mark Kingwell reveals in his dazzlingly intelligent *Catch and Release: Trout Fishing and the Meaning of Life* (2003), fly fishing and writing have the potential "to heal the breach between thought and deed, to bridge the world of imagination and the so-called 'real' one," or whether they are simply enjoyable activities we've devised to kill time, fishing and writing share intense processes and labors. "Fishing and writing," Kingwell continues, "are the only things I know where one can exert a concentration that almost annihilates the sense of self, so that the passage of hours is only registered after the fact. . . ." Not therapy exactly, but a kind of letting go into quietude and interiority is the aim.

This is not to say that one isn't easier than the other. "Compared to fishing, writing is like climbing Mount Everest locked in a straightjacket and shackles," novelist John Nichols admits in his Foreword to Taylor Streit's *Man vs Fish: A Fly Fisherman's Eternal Struggle* (2007). Degrees of difficulty notwithstanding, their tools and protocols, their physical and metaphysical similarities (and benefits) are numerous and, though their particulars and specifics, their linkages and analogies, vary from person to person, it's a grace note when these two ways of being in the world often align so well. It's what ESPN's talking heads call a win-win situation; it's what characterizes the essays in *Astream.*

In "Fishing in Books," a chapter in *Fisherman's Luck and Some Other Uncertain Things* (1927), Henry Van Dyke drew a hierarchical distinction in fly angling texts between "the literature of knowledge," which is primarily instructional, and "the literature of power," which concerns itself with the numerous "fascinations of the sport." Obviously, many of our most enduring books mix elements of both classes of discourse. (Think of Thaddeus Norris's *The American Angler's Book,* John Atherton's *The Fly and the Fish,* or

Datus Proper's *What the Trout Said*.) However, in nudging interest toward realms of personal reflection, Rev. Van Dyke highlighted a future trend in angling writing in which, as Gordon Wickstrom claims in *Notes from an Old Fly Book* (2001), it is often difficult to say whether the literature "describes" our angling or our angling is a "response" to the literature. But that is a happy dilemma I think we can all embrace.

Accounts of fishing—its memories, reenactments, rehearsals, stories, tales, yarns, or whatever—feed upon, are driven by, a basic narrative impulse that itself is nurtured by fictionalizing elements. This is not to say that all anglers are liars, as is popularly supposed, but, let's face it—to set pen to paper is almost always to enter the land of enhancement. We want to arrive at truth (or is it Truth?), but often find that the best way to do so is not by documentary objectivity or blueprint exactitude, but rather by indirection, expansion, elaboration, and tweaking, if not outright fibbing. It isn't that the facts aren't important—they are—but rather it is how those individual, discrete minutiae, details, events, and observations are transformed into a contextual narrative, a web of relatedness, a complex skein that delivers something akin to a life experience. The geography of water doesn't always translate seamlessly to the geography of words. Mind intervenes.

To write about fly fishing, even in its nonfictional first-person anecdotal form, as this collection demonstrates, is to engage in an imaginative dance with words. "To write nonfiction is to write imaginatively," *The River Why* author David James Duncan asserts in the brief manifesto "Nonfiction = Fiction" (1996). As the writers gathered here recognize, the river that "runs through it"—physical and material as it may be otherwise—is part memory, part language. The variations in style, tone, word choice, attitude, and vision displayed here all serve to enliven our collective conversation, enrich our sense of angling's possibilities, and keep threads of our common discussion and writerly discourse going. Stories are what we have; like our favorite bodies of fresh or salt water, these narratives draw our eyes and hearts at the same time they ask for our attentiveness, participation, and belief.

My request, then, to the poets, fiction writers, and essayists was simple: Turn in a literate, textured, memoir-style essay of at least 3,000 words, longer if necessary (as most of these proved to be), on some aspect of fly fishing life that directs our attention to its interior dimensions, those places best approached in language. Less of the "how to" and more of the "why to" was the target for which I hoped each author would aim. Caveats were few: avoid waxing mystical or pitching too much transcendental claptrap; and beware confusing fly fishing with organized religion, as that has gotten us into our current cultural predicament, as has the butt-kicking gonzo attitude of extreme fly fishing, which has popularized a dubious concept of lifestyle.

In other words, *keep it real.* No matter how much we wish otherwise, fly fishing won't solve the national debt crisis, deter proliferation of nuclear weapons, or make ours a more caring, equitable society. Yes, fly fishing has its own gear, vocabulary, bag of tricks, mindsets, technologies, economies, and playing fields, but seen with a long view, fly fishing isn't quantitatively different from other protocol-laced free market activities we engage in that have the potential to give us restorative pleasures and consolatory benefits. "Fly fishing," Frank Soos says in his lovely gem, *Bamboo Fly Rod Suite: Reflection on Fishing and the Geography of Grace* (1999), "takes a mulish patience, a recognition of limits, a willingness to put up with mistakes, take them in, learn from them." True enough, but to the dialed-in aficionado practitioner, playing tennis or golf, raising a perennial garden, or hunting upland birds with trained dogs requires the same resolve. They too deliver personal and even social benefits beyond the merely physical and quotidian.

To put it another way, fly fishing is like everything else, and unlike everything else. Defining what might (or might not) be "beyond" is the province of writers who understand fly fishing's Zen-like dualities and binaries: physical and aesthetic, aggressive and contemplative, cruel and gentle, business and pleasure, scientific and spiritual, commodified and sacrosanct (choose the pair or pairs that best applies)—often at the same time. Fly fishing is fun for us, but probably not for the fish (despite our best intentions they are mistreated more than we care to admit). But in attempting to define fly fishing, all streams lead to paradox, and paradox is the perplexing, challenging element that quickens fly fishing's appeal, value, caché, and especially its strenuous hold on our imaginations. Think John Keats, think negative capability: The capacity to be in "uncertainties, mysteries, doubts without any irritable reaching after fact and reason."

Or check out the two peering anglers in painter/writer Russell Chatham's lithograph, *Afternoon on Rock Creek*, which graces the dust jacket of this book. The two figures evoke—perhaps even embody—fishing's sense of mystery, anticipation, and unpredictability, and they signify angling's promise of something (good we hope, but not always) about to happen. We never know whether we will get what we want, never know whether we will fool, much less hook, the fish we desire. As anglers (and as writers) we are always in a state of anticipation, alive in the uncertainty of the "about-to-happen," so that the answer to our quest is almost always deferred. To my mind, the about-to-happen element keeps us all fishing (and writing) as though there's no tomorrow. I am pleased to say that, each in its own way, the essays gathered here demonstrate fly fishing's at-onceness, its quality of "fish and find out," as philosopher A. A. Luce memorably claims in *Fishing and Thinking* (1959).

4

As with its companion volume, *Afield*, this anthology features contributors who are, for the most part, exceptionally talented writers and artists first and sporting people second. And though some contributors have published books exclusively on fly fishing or related pursuits that many of the rest of us have read and reread, studied and memorized, then recommended to our friends, I doubt that any of them have TRTFSH, FISHON, RIPLIPS, or HDHNTER on their vehicle license plates.

Ted Hughes, the late Poet Laureate of England and a life-long angler, once told a biographer that the best place for him to write was nowhere near fishing because fishing is a perfect substitute activity that "short-circuits the need to write." Hughes has a point, and who among us has not indulged in guilty pleasure and sacrificed some pages for a few more casts? But even so, in nearly every instance, the accomplishments these *Astream* men and women have made in their sporting lives are tributaries to their mainstream work, which for the most part has been or is now fishing for words, angling for lines or sentences, hooking stanzas or paragraphs, and creating the nonfiction, poetry, short stories, novels, films, performances, and other texts that define their world view and help pay their bills.

The total number of books and films created by this gang is staggering; the artistic and literary prizes, awards, grants, and honors they have earned are enough, collectively, to fill a drift boat. If fly fishing aided and abetted that part of their expressive compositional lives, as I suspect it surely did, then more power to fly fishing. If we tell our stories often enough we become our stories. All the fly fishing we've ever done lives in us, and in writing about it, lives again. If, as Steve Raymond claims in *Rivers of the Heart* (1998), "words are the soul and substance of fly fishing," then from Barnes to Wrigley, and back again from Wetherell to Bennett, the contributors to *Astream* are of imagination, purpose, and effort all compact.

Why I Fish

Kim Barnes

It's not the first time I've been fishing, I'm sure, although I'm only four. It's 1962, and I live in the Clearwater National Forest of Idaho, along with my mother and father and younger brother, my uncles and aunts and cousins, in our one-room wooden trailers that are circled in a creek-threaded meadow we call Pole Camp—not as in fishing poles (it will be years before I hear them called "rods"), but as in the cedar poles the men fell and skid to earn their daily wage. They are gyppos, from the word gypsy, and like the Roma people, we are nomads, itinerant, our self-built eight-by-twenty shacks fitted with wheels and tires and a heavy tongue that allows them to be hitched from site to site. We circle our camps near springs and creeks and the North Fork of the Clearwater River—this our only running water. No electricity, but in the communal wash shed is a wood stove that, when kindled, heats a high-hung tankful, enough for a quick shower. I love standing with my mother beneath the warm spray, the miracle of it raining down.

But today I am in the company of my uncle, the youngest of the four Barnes brothers who left the impoverishment of sharecropping in Oklahoma for the impoverishment of cutting poles in Idaho, where they make up the crew of their uncle's family operation. "No man should go hungry here," their uncle has told them, remembering the Dust Bowl, the Great Depression, and it is true, just as it is true that hunger itself is relative. In another few weeks, we will fill our town lockers with huckleberries, and, in another locker, the

1

Photo by Robert Wrigley

Kim Barnes with cutthroat trout, Idaho.

venison we take each fall. The fish we catch the women will fry for breakfast, for lunch, for dinner, or they will slip them into milk cartons, and all through the winter I will study them there, caught in a frozen current of ice.

Today, my uncle and I stay close to home, fishing the narrow reaches of Deer Creek, which drains the meadow, parallels the narrow road. The day is hot, and we stop at a roadside spring to dip our hands in the water and drink. Sawbugs cut the quiet, their summer buzz a reminder that the woods are tinder-dry, that the men must rise in the dark and work with the dew lest the spark of their work set the forest aflame. "Hoot-owling," they call it, and it is why I have these afternoon hours with my uncle to fish.

But it is not the fishing itself that will remain with me—not the worm on the hook, the tug on the line—but how I work so hard to be silent, stay still, the feel of the sun on my shoulders, the powder-fine dust that sparkles the air, the smell of tarweed and pine. There is the fork of a willow branch strung with brookies, and I am proud that at least one of them is mine. None of them is more than eight inches, but we keep all but the smallest because pan-size are the sweetest, my uncle says, just right for the skillet. Some part of me must know that food on the table isn't a given, that you take what you can get, and that, today, the getting is good.

My uncle teaches me that what I catch, I clean, and so we squat low at the bank, and I learn the sharpness of a knife from vent to gill, how to thumb-strip the blood from the spine. I throw the guts to the orange-mottled crawdads that skitter from beneath the rocks. When I rinse the fish clean, they smell like the water, like mineral and silt. When we carry them back into camp, I am showered with praise—I have added to our family's bounty. Dusted in flour, fried in lard, the brookies come to the table salty and crisp, and this is another lesson I learn early on: how to peel the delicate skin, separate the meat from the tiniest bones. Fried spuds on the side, a peach cobbler in the oven, a pitcher of sweet tea—I am blessed in that circle of family as the larch and fir cast their shadows across the creek and fish dimple the surface for stonefly, caddis, mosquito, and midge. Maybe, even then, there was something in me rising with them.

The North Fork drains into the main Clearwater and weaves its way through the arid canyon to Lewiston, Idaho, where it meets the Snake and continues on to the Columbia. Rainbow and cutthroat run these waters. What salmon and steelhead remain beat their way past the dams to spawn, as do the last of the lamprey eels that once draped the Nez Perce drying racks, the oily meat one more stay against the deprivation of winter.

On this day, I am twenty-something, two years into my college degree, living on cases of Top Ramen and three-for-a-buck macaroni-and-cheese. I am in the first throes of what will become a life-long love: Bob, my new beau, fishes beside me. Since my family moved from the logging camps to Lewiston, I have chosen my boyfriends according to their affinity for hunting, fishing, and camping, judged them by their ability to rig a rod, pitch a tent, and build a campfire, attempting, perhaps, to reclaim some part of that childhood I have lost. I have fished the nearby creeks and rivers and lakes, wetting everything from night crawlers (pulled from the soaked lawn the night before) to Jolly Green Giant cans of corn (nothing but Niblets will do) to wedding-band spinners, Rooster Tails, Mr. Twisters, and Kastmasters the size of hubcaps (excellent for reaching the far current of a river as big as the Clearwater). I have learned that you know a fisherman by the tackle box he keeps (I am the only woman I know who keeps one), and I am housewife-proud of mine with its sharpened hooks and spinners shined with four-ought steel wool, just as I am proud of the steelhead eggs I have harvested and cured myself (an atomic red jar of Pautzke Balls o' Fire for backup). Somehow, all this gear—the care and preparation—makes me feel worthy of the fish I keep, as though my ablutions purify my intent.

Bob and I stand in the blistering heat, choosing our spots—mine at the mouth of a stream that feeds into the river. Over the years, I have learned to read water like I first learned to read books—instinctively, as though the ability were innate, part of my chromosomal map—and I know that the trout will be feeding there. Bob fishes thirty yards upstream. An Illinois flatlander by birth, a mountain-loving Westerner by choice, he came to the relationship still lugging his Plano of bass plugs, jigs, and poppers. He has his Eagle Claw, I have my Fenwick; this is our first time fishing together, and although we don't say so, we both know the challenge is on.

I wade out as far as I dare, the bald tread of my tennis shoes no help, and take up my cast. A few ten-inchers hit my Red Devil, and I drag them in, thread them on the stringer—that night's dinner. But I know there are bigger fish to fry. I pull out my largest Kastmaster, spit on my line for luck, wind up, and pitch like I am throwing for home. The filament shoots out, and I love the steady pull, how far the lure will take me. When it drops, I let it sink to a count of five, set my bail, and begin reeling in.

You know the saying, don't you? *Big water, big lure, big fish.* A rainbow the size of a steelhead hits hard, and I work hard to land it, the muscles of my arms aching until I can drag the fish ashore. My blood is singing in my ears and a fine sweat has broken out across my chest by the time Bob reaches me. I hold up the treble-hooked fish with both hands and wait for his praise.

"Nice fish," Bob says, and then, "Better throw it back."

"What?"

"Throw it back. He's too nice to keep."

I look down at my beautiful catch, his brilliant pattern of colors—the consummate keeper.

"He's three meals, at least," I say, but what I am thinking is, *You're just jealous.*

"He's good stock," Bob reasons. "He needs to stay in the gene pool."

I stare at Bob as though he has taken leave of his senses. To turn the fish loose would be like throwing a meaty T-bone to the dogs. Who knows when such food might be on the table again?

And here is the thing: I don't remember what I did with that fish, if I kept him and ate him or released him back into the waters I have known since birth. What I know for sure is that it wasn't the last time I would be hungry, but the hungry times would themselves grow leaner, become fewer and farther between.

When, two years later, Bob and I married, our honeymoon was a road trip to the Izaak Walton Inn in Essex, Montana. I remember how cold it was, even in July, and I remember bundling in my coat and crossing the road to the Middle Fork of the Flathead River, how I was mesmerized by its color—as though a turquoise glacier had bled its water down. I had my new husband there with me, we had our little pickup stuffed to the gills with everything we would need to camp and backpack our way across the state for a month, but the thought of dropping a Kastmaster into that crystalline water seemed suddenly profane. Still, the absence of the rod in my hands was like a phantom pain, as though I had lost my right arm. It was a different kind of hunger that I felt, then. It had nothing to do with food but with a desire to know that water, to feel its rush all around me, to see what secrets I might pull from its hold.

Another river, so close to my childhood home at Pole Camp that a crow could fly there in an hour. The dry dust of summer, the cold water at my knees—all of it familiar and where I always want to be.

I've traded my tackle box of Kastmasters and Pautzkes for a dank vest whose pockets are stuffed with more terrestrials than any one angler will need in a lifetime. Somehow, I'm sure that today's hatch will be the very pattern I don't have, and the thought brings with it a tremor of panic. Caddis in every possible stage, mayflies of every material, midges so small they defy tying, stimulators so large and flamboyant that they sail through the air like neon canaries—my eyes are bigger than my stomach, it seems, when it comes to these bits of feather and fur, my dead grandmother's sibylic words still echoing: *lean times just around the corner, sister—you can never have too much stock in the larder.*

Bob and I have been angling these waters for years now, dry-camping for weeks with nothing to do but eat, fish, eat, read our way through the heat of the day (Bob with his slender volumes of poetry or his go-to summer fare of James Lee Burke and Evelyn Waugh—go figure—while I critique a friend's new novel manuscript or maybe revisit, as I do each year—and this is true—*The Old Man and the Sea*), fish, eat, drink wine, and fish before falling asleep beneath the stars. I can't remember exactly when we put down our poles and took up our rods, but I know that, even after nearly two decades, we are still learning—learning how to present the fly, how to mend the line, how to roll-cast, back-cast, double-haul . . . how to shoot the line rather than lob the lure. In my worn waders and boots, I stumble and slide across the free-stone bed, curse wind knots and the tangled nest of line my cast becomes when I miss a strike and jerk the rod back as though I were setting the hook in stone.

Evening is coming on, and we're at the end of a long trek—hours of walking up the trail and fishing our way back down the river—and our take-out point is just around the bend. I'm tired, my lower back is aching, but I'm happy half-in, half-out of the water, where I somehow feel most whole. We've had a good day—net-fillers but nothing that we might brag about around our nightly fire. The river has gone to shadow, and the chill in the air is real. I shiver, remind myself to look up and around, to cast my eyes to the wooded flanks of the mountains, the patches of meadow that catch the alpenglow in an otherworldly light. I cross the shallows to better access the far bank, where an aged stump tips toward the water, its roots a catacomb of places a trout might rest.

If you are an angler, you know this feeling, you know that there, right *there*, a big fish resides. You believe that if you do everything just right—if you are smart enough, careful enough, patient enough, if you are true of spirit and pure of heart—the fish will rise.

I have learned enough to take my time, to study the wind, the water, the drag, the drift. Maybe I have been fishing a Humpy, or maybe a hopper pattern—but the shadows are deepening, the air gone cool, and I can feel that fish wanting something, feel him *hungry* for something that I might have. I rifle my pockets and patches, my magnetic tins and compartmentalized cases, but nothing seems right, not even the fairest Pale Evening Duns, the most minute of midges. I look to Bob, who fishes the river above me, his easy S-cast that I envy. In the past, I had tied my arm to the butt of my rod but to no avail—I have yet to break the habit of breaking my wrist. If this is my last cast of the day, I tell myself, I have to make it good.

I remember what a veteran angler once told me about fishing these waters. "What are you using?" I had asked after watching him net a fat cutthroat. "Nothing but Elk Hair Caddis," he said. "It's the only fly I carry." I had flushed with embarrassment at my own trove of tied treasures, no less burdensome than the twenty pounds of tackle I once lugged. Still, when I open my pocket, there it is: a #12 Elk Wing whose blonde hairs will make it easier to see in the greying light. I tie it on with great concentration, then position myself in the box of water below a large stone. Be patient, I tell myself and let my back-cast unfurl, the line haul out ten feet, then twenty.

And you know this story, too, or maybe this dream: the fly delicately dropping to the current just upstream of the stump, the drift dangerously close to the sun-silvered roots, and then the noise that isn't noise but the fish coming straight up out of the water like a Polaris missile (silly, I know, but these are the words that come to me). In my memory, it happens in a flash of golden light, the scarlet gill stripes and burnished sides, the thick body of him and the mouth—my god, I think, the size of that *mouth*—and then our two worlds are tethered.

Five/six rod, 4-pound test, that impossible barbless hook—how can I hope to hold on? Down the river he runs, my line zinging off the spool until I fear we'll be into the backing. And then the pause, the steady dead weight like a snagged log, the reconnoitering. *Keep your rod up*, I remind myself, but its supple spine is bent to the point of breaking. And then that almost imperceptible easing up, a second's give when I can take back an inch, and then another.

By now, Bob has looked up, is curious, is watching, but I can't take my eyes off that place where my line meets the water. When I move, the fish moves with me, then darts to the side and sounds, nosing in against stone. What can I do but hold on? When I work him around, urge him back into the swift current, he makes a streaking attempt to blow by me upstream . . . and so it goes, five minutes, then ten. Bob keeps his distance, afraid he'll spook the fish, but after another few minutes, the muscles of my arms begin to spasm. I want to call for him to help me, tell him that I can't get this fish in—not with this ludicrous rod, this fly with its insufficient hook. "It's me and you, fish," I say under my breath, but I am no Santiago, and this is no monstrous marlin but a Westslope cutthroat grown bigger than most. I begin to growl as I prop my elbows on my hips and arch back, reel in, arch back. My entire body is shaking from the adrenaline, the effort as though my very life depends on landing this fish—as though I might starve to death if I don't have him. But he is the one whose hunger has brought him to this place, who is fighting for his life, and by the time I draw him close, we are both exhausted.

I plow the net, using both hands to raise it, but I'm shaking so hard that I can't slip the hook. I tell him how beautiful he is, tell him to hang on, just a minute longer as I slog to the bank where I can lay down my rod and work him free. I cradle him in the current, move him to and fro, work his gills, croon to him because that is what comes to me to do. He's as long as my arm, from my shoulder to the tip of my longest finger—he would feed my entire family, I think as I rock him in my hands, feel him pulse once, then again. He flexes the muscle of his body, and then he is gone, lost to the river's shadows, taking some part of me with him, and I am glad.

I haven't forgotten what hunger feels like—not *that* kind of hunger— but I haven't felt it for a long time. I step from the river, replete. I know that Bob and I will return to our camp, take our tepid showers beneath the limb of a white pine—nothing more than a strung-up jug of warmed water, a hose, a nozzle—that we will make a fine dinner in our open-air kitchen and tell the story of this fish and then tell it again, the story itself my Horn of Plenty. All winter, as the snow deepens and the river's seams meld to ice, I will dream my larder full.

Black Quill

Walter Bennett

"[W]e have never found these mayflies to be a major hatch of concern to trout fishermen. . . ."

—Al Caucci and Bob Nastasi, *Hatches II* (2004)

Bridger Wilderness, Wind River Range, early July, 1983. Lake Victor and tributary streams. Camping and fishing trip. Beginner fisherman, *Piscator Ignarus, (Ignarus:* "untutored," "ignorant"), intently at work.

Four days of fishing in the short feeding season of the high country (10,000 feet) have yielded *Piscator Ignarus* a bounty of luck. Knocking them dead with five carefully selected fly patterns (his only fly patterns): Adams, caddis, grasshoppers, Royal Wulffs, and one mosquito, given to him as a joke. Hook size for any of them?—he has no idea.

Day five: wind-blown rain in the morning. Ignarus crouches under canopied branches of spruce at the far end of Lake Victor, where currents gather in deep holes and spill through boulders to the more open waters of North Fork Lake. Somewhere behind him, up the ridge, his wife is teaching poker to their kids in the tent, a skill she deems essential to childhood character development (math and physics major). Large drops of rain and small pellets of hail slash the slate-colored water. Ignarus opens a can of sardines, smears them with drive-through, plastic-pouch mustard, and eats them with saltine crackers. Blows on his fingers to keep them warm. Drops from the spruce boughs pop on his fold-up felt hat.

Photo by Robert DeMott

Walter Bennett (right) with Leon Sagaloff, Beaverhead River, Montana.

A bit after noon, the wind dies, skies begin to clear. Rain drops are sparser, form gentle rings on the lake's surface. Half an hour later, the rain stops altogether. Sun shines. The lake surface smooths to silver-blue in the sunlight, deep aqua-green in the shadows. Ignarus clips off yesterday's Adams, returns it to his fly box, and ties on a new one. He makes his first cast of the day. Then another. Then many more. Nothing. Very peculiar. Rings start to reappear across the lake's surface. Large, mysteriously dark insects emerge like magic from the water, flit about, and fall back to the surface—those that aren't lost in the spruces. Trout rise in a frenzy to take them.

This must be what they call a "hatch."

Ignarus tries to place his fly where the last trout has risen. But so many trout are rising, it's hard to make a choice. When he is able to place a fly in the ring of a rise, it is ignored while trout gobble the nature-made morsels around it. Ignarus pauses, watches his fly bob in the ripple from the last rise. What the hell is going on? Adams has worked every time before.

Ignarus changes fly to Royal Wulff, examines leader (nine feet, two days, and ten changes-of-flies ago—no tippit), and judges what's left to be long enough. Cast, cast, flip, flip—still, nothing. Ignarus tries a caddis. Nip, nip, nip go the trout around the fly. Bob, bob, bob goes the caddis in the intersecting circles of water. Half an hour passes. Ignarus takes a long look at the three Dave's Hoppers in his fly box. What the hell? He ties on a hopper. Nip go the trout. Float goes the hopper. Ignarus clips off the hopper, opens his fly box, and stares hard at the two bins of grey and brown Adams, hoping the stare alone will turn them black. In a brief "aha" moment, he remembers the black magic marker in his kids' paintbox up the hill. He packed it in; he can at least borrow it. Besides, tomorrow he'll have to pack it out. But, alas, on the label he remembers something like, "Water soluble; will not stain."

Ignarus sighs, ties on another Adams, gives it one last try. Same result. Ignarus throws down rod, stands with fists on hips, and watches the trout hit and hit and hit. He's heard that experienced fishermen often observe a stream for an hour or more to study how trout are feeding before selecting their fly and making the first cast. But he's observed for the last two hours and learned nothing except that fish are hitting every speck on the lake but his fly. Maybe, to make such a study, you have to sit down. Which he does. The rain is starting again.

Mayflies continue to swarm over the water, among the spruce boughs, and around his head. One lands on his knee, flits away. Another floats by his nose. He grabs it and examines. A big fly. Dark—almost black, especially the veins of the wings. This is nothing like any pattern he's seen in anyone's fly box or in the bewildering display bins in trout shops. Ignarus reopens his fly box. Mosquito! It's smaller than the mayfly in his hand, but it's mostly black—except for light grey wings and the tiny white stripes around the body—even blacker than the real item.

Ignarus has matched the hatch! He ties on mosquito, proceeds back to water's edge. The rain has turned to a pattering of hail, or is it sleet? He resumes casting with renewed determination. Trout continue to rise and take flies—real flies. One, in its rise, even nudges the mosquito. Then, nothing. Nothing, nothing, and nothing but endless rises all across the lake, all afternoon long. The rain/sleet/hail has stopped. Darkness seeps in. Circles on the lake continue as if they have become a permanent part of the ecology of the lake, indeed of nature itself. (Of which Ignarus, alas, is not a part). From up the hill behind him comes his wife's tentative call: "How many fish?" She's trying to decide how to apportion tin foil, lemon juice, dill, and butter.

Ignarus's last cast hangs in a spruce bow. He jerks the line, loses the fly, gives the rod a long, reproachful look, and leans it carefully against the spruce. Tramps up the hill to camp for a freeze-dried supper.

The next evening, having hiked out the eleven miles with my family, I'm back at the lodge, making up for last night's watery split pea soup and Mountain House lasagna with stove-cooked steak, potatoes, and chocolate pie. Across the table from me sits a guy I've seen around the lodge before: thin, with dark, cowlicked hair, waxed-tip mustache, quick smile, studied look. Strong wrists poke from the too-short, two-snap cuffs of his Western shirt. Wyatt Earp with a touch of Buffalo Bill. I've been told he's a regular at the lodge every summer, drives up from Florida to fish the upper lakes. Horse-packs in. Spends up to ten days at a time. He's headed up tomorrow with a group from California, earning part of his keep at the lodge by serving as an informal guide.

"So," he says, poking a piece of red meat beneath the bow of his mustache, "how's the fishing in the high country?"

"Fine," I say. "But yesterday at Lake Victor I got into some kind of hatch, and no matter what I tried, they wouldn't hit." I shovel in a mouthful of potatoes. "At least they wouldn't hit *me*."

"Hmmm. What did you try?"

"All of 'em—Adams, caddis . . . etc., etc."

"What was the hatch?"

"I don't know. Big and black."

Wyatt drops his fork to his plate. "Stay right here."

He rises from the table, strides in dusty cowboy boots from the dining room to the hall leading to the sleeping quarters, and returns with a small fly box. He takes his seat, scoots himself toward the table, and opens the box. It is filled with black mayflies. *Really* black with hints of brown around the thorax. Long tails swoop outward from the body like the part in Wyatt's mustache, with a smaller tail in the middle.

He picks one out by its hook, holds it at eye level between us, and says something like "Philadelphia Cupid."

"What?"

"*Leptophlebia cupida*. Your basic black mayfly."

"Oh, yeah," I say. "Should have recognized them."

"Well, there are other *Leptophlebia*, but we get *cupida* up here."

By now, in my mind, the hatch has taken on cosmic proportions—endless mayflies flitting about the sky, rising in great, black clouds toward the sun, with me bouncing on my tiptoes, trying to catch one.

"And where would I find that pattern?"

"Hard to find good ones in fly shops," he says. "I tie my own."

He twists the bend of the hook with his finger tips. The fly tick-tocks hypnotically back and forth.

"But, tell you what: I'll be tying some more this winter; I'll send you some."

He studies the fly a minute, glances about at the other diners to be sure no one is listening, and leans my way. "When you get into that hatch of black mayflies up there on Victor and you ain't got one of these, you just fucking the dog." (A term I recalled from my military days, meaning—I'm not sure what—but always used in situations of futility, fatigue, and disgust. It seemed to describe my afternoon of humiliation on Lake Victor to a tee.)

Somewhere around November of that year, I received in the mail a small package with six beautifully tied black mayflies—Black Quills—with a note enclosed: "Try these next summer. I nailed the hide to the wall with them after our talk. Caught over a hundred fish."

"Black mayfly" resonates with implications of dark, mystical power (Black Widow, Black Knight, Zorro, Darth Vader), but the fly itself rates near the bottom on experts' most-wanted lists. Its meager reputation has been gained primarily on Eastern and Midwestern streams. Caucci and Nastasi portray *Leptophlebiae* as the lazy brothers-in-law of the mayfly world: "Their environment is not synonymous with the swift-flowing mountain streams . . . that signify 'trout' for the fly fisherman. . . . [They] thrive instead on more sluggish, lowland, coastal waters. . . ." (One study was even conducted in swamp tributaries of the Cape Fear River in my decidedly non-Western home state, North Carolina.)

And—no surprise—they are not really black. This is an illusion produced by the contrast of their dark, chestnut bodies and slate-grey wings against sky and water. In other words, they're plain old dark-but-unsexy brown. They emerge early (April to mid–June) in the East/Midwest and typically in early afternoon. Duns linger on the water as if debating whether transmogrification to the next phase is worth the effort. Trout hit them hard. But Caucci and Nastasi confirm Ignarus's experience: They can be "extremely finicky to artificials on a mirror–like surface."

In *Western Mayfly Hatches from the Rockies to the Pacific* (2004), Rick Hafele and Dave Hughes echo Caucci and Nastasi's under-enthusiasm and agree that black mayflies are not a major Western hatch. They tell us, however, where to find them: ". . . shallow and nearly still water, where they inhabit slow pools and eddies along the banks of Western trout streams, and along the edges of ponds and lakes, especially where some wave action provides aerated water or a stream enters the stillwater." Exactly where Ignarus's confrontation with the species occurred.

I did not make it back to Lake Victor to try out my gift of Black Quills. That frustrating afternoon, casting my arm off with black mayflies all but flying up my nose and trout eating them on every side of my Adams/caddis/ Wulff/hopper/mosquito was my last trip to the Wind Rivers. I began to get myself educated. Read books on trout fishing. Bought a better rod and lots more flies. Began to pay attention to hatches and listened to advice from folks who knew how to fish. Started fishing the "big" rivers—Green, Snake, Madison, Big Hole, Gallatin, Yellowstone—and every time I looked in my fly box to pick out a fly, there in the corner bin was my trove of black mayflies. Years passed. The flies stayed in their fuzzy pile in the corner of the fly box as if in group hibernation, awaiting a Biblical seven-year emergence. There was a "hold-over" feeling about them, like a pair of penny loafers I'd bought in the fifties, gathering dust on the floor of my closet, and now it's the seventies, and everyone is wearing combat boots and sandals. "Oughta go on and throw them out," I thought at least a dozen times. "They must be peculiar to that part of the high country, and I don't fish there anymore." But there was that hibernating for *something* feeling. And in my fly box they stayed.

Yellowstone Lake, July, 1990: Four guys in two canoes headed south down the east side of the lake for three days of camping and fishing. Barrie

Gilbert, master outdoorsman and grizzly bear expert on the faculty at Utah State University, organizer of the trip, paddles stern in the lead canoe. Phil Urness, a colleague from the university, paddles with him, his straw cowboy hat dipping forward with every stroke. I am in the second canoe with Barrie's son, Doug, a natural outdoorsman like his father and smart as a whip, but who, due to some academic indiscretion, has in his wet bag the unopened textbook for a math course at Utah State he is required to take in summer school. Barrie is an expert paddler—strong shoulders; quick arms; deft, efficient strokes. He sets a cruiser-like pace down the twelve miles of lake to our first-night, designated campsite at the far end. Nevertheless, spirits are high when we pull ashore not far from a bull moose lounging belly deep in the shallows, watching us with water streaming from his muzzle and antlers and the long-stemmed aquatic plants hanging from both sides of his slowly working mouth.

It is during the unpacking of the canoes that our folly is exposed: We have left behind in the two vehicles (now a dozen miles back up the lake at the put-in) two of four spin rods; one of two tackle boxes of lures; one of three fly rods; four of five boxes of flies; fuel for the camp stove; one cooler with all breakfast food (except oatmeal); half the back-up supper food (in case the fishing was bad, a prospect we helped ensure through our self-depletion of gear); one bottle of single-malt scotch; and beer. I'm not sure how this happened, but I have an image of four car-weary, over-eager men, rushing around the Lake Butte put-in, grabbing satchels of gear from Barrie's ten-year-old Volvo and Phil's Nissan pick-up, and throwing them into canoes. It is also common practice, when one goes on an adventure with Barrie, that at least a few essential items be left behind—food, rain gear, extra paddles, etc. Otherwise, where's the challenge? The four of us look at one another and then back up the long stretch of lake we've just navigated. No way.

We cook over a wood fire the first night, eat lukewarm oatmeal for breakfast the next morning, and borrow fuel from a passing cabin cruiser on our way back up the lake to our next campsite. I loan my spin rod to Phil—didn't plan to use it anyway—and we begin to catch fish, beautiful Yellowstone cutthroats with a pink, salmon-like hue to the flesh because, according to Barrie, their diet is heavy in crustaceans.

So, enough for supper and a very tasty supper, too. And all in all, given the self-imposed handicaps, not bad fishing. Until midafternoon of the last day.

Shallow water—probably not more than a dozen feet deep 100 yards out. Six-inch waves lapping softly at the shore. Aerated but protected from lake winds by spits of forested land on either side of our small cove. Perfect.

Circles on the water, just a few at first, and then covering the entire cove in front of our campsite. Spinning lures haul in empty. My fly—Adams, BWO, PMD, whatever—is ignored. Puzzled looks. Much switching of lures. This time, I sit and watch the action. A suspicion grows in me. It is confirmed when Barrie holds a wet fingertip in front of my face with a dead spinner on it. "Ever seen one of these?"

Well, yes. And despite everything we did wrong on that first day at the put-in when we threw gear into the canoes from the vehicles, I had at least grabbed the right fly box. The black mayflies were right where they were supposed to be, hibernation over.

I couldn't miss.

"What are you fishing with?" says Phil.

I release my last catch, lift the fly between us so he can see it swinging at tippit's end.

"Black mayfly pattern."

I hand the rod to Barrie. Then the spin fishermen give the fly a try. Hits continue into the evening.

There's no more beautiful trout than a Yellowstone cutthroat (I don't care what the California Golden people say). When they hit, they really hit. The rod tip bends and jerks, the fight is side-to-side and down. (I've never had one run on me, and I've never had one shake the hook.) And sooner or later the writhing stops, the silvery-gold head and dark eyes emerge, the roseate gash gleams at the throat. Beautiful fish. That evening on Yellowstone Lake we released more of them in one hour than we'd caught the entire trip.

Victory and vindication. I had four well-used black mayflies left in my fly box by the time we quit. Packed them carefully for the next inevitable hatch on some yet unknown lake or river somewhere down the road.

Next morning, packing up to paddle out, light rain, fishing over. Doug Gilbert crouches under a spruce, math book resting unopened beside him on the damp needles, and stares at the pot bubbling on the cook stove. Barrie, old-school Canadian, dips a spoonful of oatmeal into a cup. "Porridge, Doug?"

"No thanks. I'll wait for the bacon and eggs in the restaurant at Fishing Bridge."

Phil scoops his last spoonful.

"What was that mayfly again?"

"*Leptophlebia cupida*," I say. "Black mayflies. The match is Black Quill. And if you ain't got that, you just fucking the dog."

Okay, the experts are right: not a major fly for Western waters. But when *Leptophlebiae cupidae* hatch (or the other Western *Leptophlebia* species: *gravestella, nebulosa, pacifica*), they are good, and when they are good, they are very, very good.

And, assuming a Black Quill is not a standard in your fly box, Hafele and Hughes suggest fishing an Adams with the bottom hackles clipped off. I've not tried this gambit, but had *Piscator Ignarus* known what a hackle was during his afternoon of agony on Lake Victor, perhaps he might have. . . . Nah!

A Set of Tides

Russell Chatham

I'm sitting in a cabin on the crest of a ridge high in the coastal mountains of Northern California's Mendocino County. The land is densely wooded with a fairyland mixture of oak, madrone, manzanita, redwood, pine, fir, and a practically impenetrable tangle of underbrush. It is essentially a wilderness—enormous, mostly trackless, and steep enough to defy all but the most obdurate and physically fit.

Eagles, vultures, and several kinds of hawks bank and float on the complex thermals, while beneath them surprising flocks of bandtail pigeons veer crazily into the treetops to feed on the abundant bright red madrone berries. Woodpeckers are ubiquitous, as are valley and the even rarer mountain quail. Jays squawk above them, while throughout the seasons an ever-changing cast of songbirds nest, zip, and flit through the impossible network of leaves and branches.

Far down in the bottom of the canyon, in a small tributary that eventually finds its way to the Russian River at Healdsburg, a few wild steelhead fight their way up to an impassable falls, spawn, and then flee these headwaters, leaving their progeny in the hands of fate. This happens in January or February, and the young, born in March or April, must somehow survive until the rains of December release them on their journey to the sea.

Some miles to the west of here, over several high ridges, lie the headwaters of the Gualala, perhaps the North Coast's most beautiful river. My

18

family fished it starting back in the 1920s, and I cast my first line in it when I was fourteen in 1954. As I write this, in the fall of 2010, my heart aches for the losses we have incurred through greed, stupidity, and ennui. The Gualala's great run of silver salmon was relegated to extinction by one of the most vicious episodes of irresponsible clear-cut logging on the Pacific coast. Its steelhead, too, were brought to their knees and saw a 90 percent loss in numbers.

The exquisite Gualala notwithstanding, the epicenter of my relationship with the natural world through the acts of angling for silver salmon and steelhead was Tomales Bay and the watershed that flows into the head of it, that of Papermill Creek. The Russian River was the most important river of my youth, but it lay sixty miles to the north of where I lived, a two-hour drive in the simple, old fashioned cars of the day on the narrow winding roads before freeways. From my father's driveway in San Anselmo, I could be parking my 1947 Plymouth at Papermill's estuary in just under twenty minutes.

Although today the silvers are virtually gone—and are unlikely to ever return due to unchecked piracy by factory ships throughout and inside the 200-mile limit off the entire coast of North America, rather than due to logging, as was the case up at the Gualala—in those bygone times, tens of thousands of them pushed up through Tomales Bay, finally crowding into the tidal part of the creek to await the first rains of the season that would send them thrashing upstream to the spawning beds.

This annual drama started around the end of October and, as a rule, by the middle of December they were gone from the tidewaters and had distributed themselves throughout the system in mainstem Papermill and its tributaries, from the junction of Nicasio Creek to the base of Carson Dam and throughout Lagunitas Creek from Shafter's Falls clear up to Woodacre. They populated the entirety of Olema Creek, as well. Prior to their departure, it was not unusual for me to have caught and let go many hundreds of silvers at a time when the admonition to "catch and release" would not be coined until at least two decades later.

The stage was now set for the arrival of the steelhead: curtains closed, footlights dimmed, the hall filled with the anticipatory scratchings of the orchestra tuning up. But once in a while there was a surprise, such as the one

**Young Russell Chatham with silver salmon,
estuary of Papermill Creek, California.**

I got on November 9, 1958. I know this date because I wrote it that evening on my rod—a converted six-foot spinning rod I had just made, for which I had also constructed a twenty-two-foot shooting head I thought would be a perfect tool for the Salmon Hole, and it was. Starting at dawn about halfway through the falling tide, lasting until dead low at about 11:00 AM, I caught seven silvers, none of which I killed.

It was a soft, bright, clear, windless day, and there were five other people fishing the hole. Three of these, including the game warden, Al Giddings, were bait fishing from the steep bank across from me, while the other two threw spoons with spinning outfits from the beach on my side. The tide had reached complete stillness and I prepared to head home. It was such a sublime, almost warm midday, however, that I decided to sit on the shore for a while soaking it in and listening to the idle if not goofy banter of the other fishermen. One of the spin guys had caught a nice eight-pound hen salmon, and throughout the tide, from across the creek, Al periodically reminded him that gentlemen shared their eggs. Soon the tide began its slow flow upstream, and within fifteen minutes was moving pretty well. I never fished the incoming tide, but decided to try just for the hell of it. I positioned myself at the extreme bottom end of the pool, not wanting to pick up the lines of the bait fishermen. I had perhaps a thirty-foot window to work through before I got to them, and did so slowly and methodically.

Just at the point where I dared not go any further, and where my fly was swinging through the low end of the tenderloin, the line tightened, and within seconds a bright, silver fish was high in the air, two, three, four times, taking line at will and picking up all three bait outfits on its spectacular trip upstream.

The bait guys were all polite, and two of their lines miraculously cleared while the third went for the rest of the ride. Finally, a chrome-bright thirteen-pound buck steelhead was nose to the gravel bar. I dispatched it with a stout piece of driftwood to the hurrahs of all present. My day had come to an unexpectedly dramatic conclusion, and I felt as though I floated back across the field to the car, the great fish's tail dragging in the grass.

Later that same season, the winter rains, which allowed all the salmon to reach the spawning grounds, subsided the third week of December, 1958, and Papermill dropped, turning crystal clear. It was a perfect time for rough counting and observing up close and in detail the salmon's yearly ritual, something I did for many years any time water height and clarity permitted.

A few days before Christmas, I checked all the known holes from the Highway 1 Bridge at Point Reyes Station down to White House Pool, through Giacomini's field to Railroad Point and Bivalve, where the creek becomes the bay, and I never saw a fish roll, nor did I get so much as a sniff. I was both surprised and disappointed.

Three days after Christmas, I was in my room at home above the garage tying some flies when I heard my mother call out that the phone was for me. It was Bill, a high school friend with whom I'd fished and duck hunted for the past few years. "Guess what?" he said. "I just caught a fourteen-pound steelhead on a Flatfish in the bay at the Steps." The Steps was our name for a popular fishing spot along the bay where we bait fished for stripers. Someone had taken the trouble years earlier to dig out steps in the steep sixty- or seventy-foot bank from the highway to the beach below. It passed through a tunnel in the windswept bay laurels. He said that as the tide dropped he saw a few other fish moving and hooked another but lost it. As far as I knew, no one had ever thought of fishing for steelhead in this place. But there had to be a reason why those steps were carved into the hillside. I figured it was striper-related and must have something to do with the configuration of the bottom. Naturally, I would be there the next day.

In late December and early January, this part of the coast experiences some of the most radical tides of the year. Highs can be 7.0 feet or even slightly higher, while the low can be as much as 1.6 feet, creating a drop of 8.5 feet, which was the cycle we were in. I checked the tide book and saw that low at the Golden Gate was at two-thirty in the afternoon. Adjusting for the delay north to the mouth of Tomales Bay of twenty minutes, and then to the head of the bay, of another hour and a half, that put the minus low at about 4:30 PM. At this time of year it was dark by six. I was there at 2:30.

Hanging in the area where Bill had caught his fish, I made a few desultory casts and scanned the water for any movement. The wind was blowing from the north at a very manageable fifteen knots, and this allowed me to see that the current was becoming confined to the channel directly in front of me, which was about sixty feet wide. Beyond it to the west looking at Inverness and stretching north toward Millerton Point, an increasing sheen told me the mud flats were about to become exposed.

Then, way off to the northwest, I saw something I couldn't identify at first, some sort of splashing commotion. As I watched, it kept up until, as it drew closer, its rhythmic, violent writhing became a fish zigging and zagging across the flat, its back out of water, a rooster tail of spray behind it. When it reached the channel, a mere 100 feet below me, it vanished from sight. Almost immediately, two more such apparitions appeared in the distance, which turned into two more fish desperately seeking the safety of the channel. Upon seeing that first fish, my mind instinctively said striper. As these next two approached, however, the water they were negotiating was only about four inches deep, and I could make out that they were unquestionably steelhead.

I didn't know precisely how deep the channel was, but based on what was then only several years' experience with the bay, I guessed between two and three feet at most. I was using an eight-foot fiberglass rod of dubious heritage, but what mattered was the line, a beautiful brown and black version of Sunset's "half and half," a woven combination of Dacron and nylon designed to sink slowly in estuarine environments. In today's terms, the outfit would probably be designated an 8-weight. With it I could work my fly around in a slow swing, presumably midway between the surface and the bottom. My wonderful friend Gene Thompson, founder and proprietor of the Western Sport Shop in San Rafael, had presented it to me a few months earlier. It was a most welcome gift as I had precious little tackle in those days—namely, one rod, one reel, and one line, altogether having cost just under $14. My regular straight Dacron line would have sunk far too fast to fish this water.

I started in with easy sixty-foot casts quartering downstream, the twenty-seven-foot head ideally suited to the task at hand. After only five or six casts and an equal number of steps downstream, there was a deliberate stop, and when I swept the rod horizontally back as was my custom, there was an instantaneous boil and subsequent thrashing that told me the channel was even shallower than I thought, two feet deep at the most. It was not a difficult fight, as there were neither depth nor snags to deal with. Still it was a spanking-fresh ten-pound steelhead, and while I was dealing with it, three or four more came wiggling desperately across the nearly dry flat, all of them reaching the channel.

I was using a simple no-name fly with a red chenille body and white hair wing over it, and I twisted it out of the left corner of that beautiful steelhead's mouth and turned the fish around so it could shimmy back into the bay. Collecting myself, I checked the leader for knots or nicks, and toward the now dry flat across from me, fired another cast. It had only swung about ten feet when it tightened and pointed right at a serious boil. This fish too had the expected resolve, and while I worked to get it in for a quick release, more fish could be seen fighting their way to the channel, farther downstream, as the flat nearby was dry. When the afternoon's episode was over, I had hooked fourteen fish and landed a dozen of them, and saw at least thirty others enter the channel. And who knew now that darkness had fallen what the night would bring?

The following day, I arrived again at 2:30, even though the tide was an hour later. I started blind casting over what was clearly a depression in the channel. Within five minutes, a fish was on and took yard after yard of line in long screeches from the reel, obliging me to jog down the shore after it.

The fish never jumped, and it took a good twenty minutes for me to nose it up to the beach. I didn't carry a scale or tape, but guessed it was twelve pounds. Unlike all the others, which were chrome, this hen had started to turn pink at the gills and along its lateral line, and this quality shone like mother of pearl in the afternoon sun.

I went back to casting, but nothing happened for the next two hours. Conditions were similar to those of the previous day: clear sky, north wind, and when the sheen over the flat began to appear, that's when I saw the first two fish pushing across it in the familiar zigzag pattern of yesterday, and a few hundred yards behind them were several more. They disappeared into the channel 100 feet below me as before, and I eased down to greet them.

Back then, I fished every single day without exception, but never had I been in a situation where I knew beyond any shadow of a doubt that the next cast, or at the most, two or three, would put me tight to a steelhead. It just took one cast and I was holding a living rod. During the ensuing struggle, more fish were finding the channel. I moved up the bank about thirty feet, thinking to show the fly to a fish in a calm resting mode who hadn't been spooked by the antics of its schoolmate. One cast did it again and the dance was repeated. To make a not very long story even shorter, I took the twelfth fish on my twelfth cast, and by the time it was dark I had landed nine of them.

I fumbled my way up to the car and found the Plymouth's battery dead, so I had to hitchhike home, not an unusual thing to do in those days. The next day I outlined my plan to my mother. She drove a 1950 Chevrolet, and what we would do, I said, would be to dress her up warmly then drive out to the bay with Dad's jumper cables. We'd get the Plymouth started and then I'd drive a few miles up and down the road to charge the battery. After that, I'd help her down the steps so she could witness the best steelhead fishing in the world.

My mother never once touched a piece of fishing tackle or a firearm, nor did she ever express the slightest interest in doing so. As a girl, she'd had polio, so one leg was shorter than the other. Her idea of a walk was going the twenty feet from the kitchen to the garage. But here we were, pulled up in front of the Plymouth, which started, and after the charging ritual I laboriously guided her bit by bit down the steps. She was bundled up in a coat of mine, and we found a place for her to sit back by the cliff. It was not a very nice day: Fog was spilling over Inverness Ridge, bringing with it a very cold wind right in our faces. Undaunted, I began casting even though the tide was still too high. But within fifteen minutes, I had one on and wrangled it to the beach. Looking over, I saw my mother huddled there like a little girl, a pained look on her face. I carried the fish over to show her.

"That's nice dear, but I really want to go home."

I ran back and turned the fish loose, then helped her labor up the steps. It took twenty minutes. She pulled out onto the road, and I stayed back to fish, keeping the jumper cables just in case.

Back down on the beach, conditions were deteriorating, and I was colder than my mother had thought she was. The tide, now yet another hour later than yesterday, had a ways to go before it fell off the flat. In my youth, it took a lot to daunt me, so I cast relentlessly into the teeth of what was now rather a gale. The optimism of youth was rewarded with several grabs that held.

I have always been fascinated by the phenomenon of fog spilling over a ridge, Inverness being my favorite of all, and I watched the beauty of it unfold. Then something inexplicable happened. Rays of light began flashing upward from the fog. The lights were very bright with a slight yellowish cast, and then the voices started. At the time I had never heard any of the great masses, such as Bach's *Mass in C Minor*, but now, having heard them all, it was like that, only deafeningly louder, like the wail of a thousand voices. I became terrified, dropped the rod, and ducked my head and held my arms around myself. It grew louder and louder until it seemed to be everywhere. The lights arched upward, too bright to look at. I suppose it lasted no more than five minutes before it began to subside and became once again just fog spilling over the ridge. I stood there for a while, trembling from more than the cold, wondering what had just happened. Fishing forgotten, I hurried up the steps to the car and sat there for a while, dumbfounded. When I finally calmed down, the car fortunately started.

What had happened that darkening afternoon? Maybe nothing; maybe I had only imagined it. But I had never so much as tasted a drop of liquor at that age, and drugs were unheard of. Some enormous force in the universe had addressed me; that seemed certain. Was it a warning, meant to frighten me off? That didn't seem right, as it had been an exhaltation, as if honoring heaven and earth. As Bach famously said, "Be content with your fate as it is the only road to happiness there is." Could that have been what was being revealed to me by the Supreme Spirit that gave us Bach, silver salmon, steelhead, and everything else, as well? Was it being foretold that, throughout my journey, I would sometimes minimize my calling, becoming distracted by the fool's gold temptations of society; that my unimpressive fishing stuff and fragile wooden sketch box, along with the pure love of using them, were the hand I had been dealt, and, in the most real and deepest sense, would be all I'd ever have? Fifty years later, I can still see that light and hear those voices. Some power beyond comprehension has protected me my whole life, and so long as I am still breathing, I will keep trying to reimburse the universe for that gift.

Clearly, the tide that had yielded such extraordinary fishing would now happen well after dark the next day. However, one of the characteristics of these big tides is that the interim one is much smaller. The next day, then, the high tide of perhaps five feet would be at 2:30 PM, and the low tide of two feet would occur at 8:30 in the morning.

I had to wonder where all those fish went. Physically, they could get to the Highway 1 Bridge and somewhat beyond it, putting them out of reach. But given the low water, were they in that much of a rush? I needed to find out.

At dawn, I was pulling off at Bivalve about a mile and a half upstream from the steps. The fog had somehow vanished, the sky was clear, the air dead calm. Here, the creek estuary became defined and turned sharply against the old railroad levee. An oysterman's house, long abandoned, stood there on stilts. From the first minute I saw it, right after my sixteenth birthday, I wanted it to be my home.

I was on familiar ground now, having plumbed every part of the creek in the off season from there to White House Pool in my eight-foot boat using a weight with a line attached to it. I knew right where the channel was and that on this mean low tide, it was four feet deep.

I started casting at the top of the hole. If the steelhead were lying there at all, they would be in a groove about 20 feet wide and 150 feet long. The current was almost imperceptible, but enough to keep them facing into it. I was pleased with my new line, which had a perfect sink rate, and after only a few casts I was trying to hold my own with a beautiful buck, which I returned to its element, confused but safe. About an hour and a half later, six others had a peculiar experience to consider, as well.

Knowing the tide would soon be coming in, I wanted to prolong the experiment, so I scrambled up the bank, jumped in the car, and raced around toward White House Pool. Approaching the Highway 1 Bridge, I slowed and glanced downstream, where I could see figures on the bank about 300 yards away. I knew the stretch they were fishing, a fairly deep straight slot near where Olema Creek emptied into the slough. Several hundred yards after making the turn, I pulled off. There had been dense willows on both sides of the creek there; a couple of the old timers from Point Reyes Station fished it using a rowboat, and the trout had been completely safe from any bank fisherman.

The summer before, though, all the trees were cleared, and now this great holding pool was naked for all to fish. The creek was only about thirty feet wide, and after walking to the edge I clearly recognized Giddings and two others from Inverness. I knew Al's penchant for using weightless roe, a deadly effective way to catch steelhead. The skeins of roe were preserved in Borax to toughen the outer skin. In bigger, moving water, the eggs were wrapped in netting to create "berries," but Al eschewed this, preferring instead to use a unique snell on an Eagle Claw bait hook to hold the roe in place. For quiet water this was just the thing. The previous winter in late February, right under the bridge, he had caught a spent fish that weighed eighteen pounds, which would have put it over twenty, had it been fresh.

"C'mon over," Al said. "There's plenty of room. There's a few in here, not many and they're not really biting, but maybe the fly could stir 'em up."

"No, I'm checking out a few spots, but so far nothing. I'm going down to White House, and if there's nothing there maybe I'll come back around." No sooner were the words out of my mouth and I thought, *You dumb shit, what if there's a pile of fish there? Then when you don't come back, Al and company will be on you like white on rice.*

Jumping the fence past the "No Trespassing" sign, I waded over to the east bank below the end of the pool, positioning myself just upstream from the lowest holding water, where the incoming tide would be stalled for at least an hour. Within ten minutes, a slow head-and-tail roll quickened my pulse, and to myself I uttered, "Saw you!" The line Gene had given me was so perfectly designed that the snap of my wrist straightened it out like a stretched string, the fly landing at the end of a fully extended leader, important in these close quarters where inches could spell the difference between a wild ride and a complete skunking. In those four-foot-deep waters, my standard count was to ten before starting the retrieve, but at the count of seven the line shot forward in a rare take on the sink, and I was involved in one of the most aerial ballets of my young life.

Fortunately, most of it took place fairly close to the steep bank by the road, where the few passing motorists could see it, and when one did go by, I released tension, pointing the rod straight at the fish, pretending to retrieve. Not wanting anyone to see what I was doing, when I thought the fish was ready I knelt down in about a foot of water and hand lined its head right up my thighs into the crotch of my Ballband waders, twisted the fly out, and turned it around.

Just as I was getting ready to resume casting, a car pulled off the road up near the culvert, and a guy got out and started slowly toward me. Even at some distance, I recognized Paul Mancini and could see him searching the water. Paul had graduated from Drake High two years ahead of me. The first time I ever hit the creek he was there. And after that he was always there. He had a light spinning outfit and never used anything but a red and white Dardevle. He never stopped casting and knew every single place where the silvers might hold. Paul was one of the greatest fish hawks I ever saw, but what he knew about steelhead I wasn't sure, though it figured he knew plenty. Throwing fish back was not part of his DNA, and, in fact, I was pretty sure that to him the three-fish limit was merely a suggestion. He rarely spoke, preferring the nod as a greeting, but we maintained an affable albeit distant relationship for many years.

I thought it wise to commence casting lest he think something was up. I cast perfectly because to do otherwise would have aroused his suspicion. However, I retrieved the fly right away so that it was only a couple of inches down where it would be impossible to get a take. Ten minutes passed and he stood still as a heron. It was a war of wills. The air was dead calm and there was little traffic. All I could think was, *Fish, don't roll, don't roll.*

He didn't say anything, but stood there in silence, then gave a cursory wave and started back. Right then there was another slow head, dorsal, tail roll, and I clearly saw the fish's eye. The action was soft and noiseless, and the minor disturbance was completely gone by the time Paul reached his car.

Soon after Paul's car was gone I hooked a fish, landed it, and about fifteen minutes later caught one more. By the time I freed it, the tide had turned and was slowly creeping upstream. That was it for the day, as the flood and high ebb were difficult for a couple of reasons. First of all, there was the disorientation factor, and that plus the sheer volume of water made the whole thing problematic. That's why I always had my paints in the car trunk, and I would spend the rest of the day in a different mode, rendering cows on hillsides and lovely sloughs reflecting the sky. A little salami and bread was a nice thing, too.

As always, next day the tide was an hour later, low water at Bivalve occurring about 9:30 AM, give or take. The barometer was holding steady, skies were clear, and the winds were going to be manageable. It was just getting to fishing light when I pulled into the turnout above the oysterman's house. I planned to make a pass through the slot, but my real target was Railroad Point, three quarters of a mile upstream. I half expected to see Paul's car and would have hidden mine, but there were no options in that regard. Besides, you couldn't hide at Bivalve; anyone could watch you from two high vantage points.

It was still two hours until dead low tide so the water had more movement than the day before. Starting at the top, I wondered if it was enough to prevent the half and half line from delivering the fly to the very point of the steelheads' noses. My answer came in the form of the most extraordinary take I'd ever experienced. As a rule, in this kind of fishing you get a stop and after you set the hook is when the mayhem starts. In this case, however, one minute I was slowly retrieving the fly, the next the line was snapped from between my fingers and was zinging through the guides until it hit the reel. It was like a wide receiver catching a pass on the fifty-yard line and then continuing on at top speed into the end zone.

I have never wanted a drag on a fly reel—still don't, believing if you can't manage to control things with your fingers, you deserve the backlash you're going to get. But I didn't want my fingers anywhere near that spool at this particular moment, and by this time the steelhead had out 200 feet of line and was down below the oysterman's shack making one of the highest, longest jumps I'd ever seen and breaking the leader. As a rule, broken leaders are the result of carelessness, but in this case I cut myself some slack.

It was still early, but I was concerned that Paul, or someone else for that matter, would arrive with the idea of checking out Railroad Point. Thinking that the atomic submarine I'd just hooked could have easily done a spook job on the groove, I decided to make just one pass through it. Right above the shack, I hooked and landed an eight-pound hen, and right below it hooked and lost another I never saw.

Reeling in quickly, I jogged over to the railroad levee, waded across the narrow gap where a short trestle had been, and walked to the hole, looking back every so often to see if another car may have parked on the bluff. None had. The sun was up, wind was calm, on an absolutely beautiful day. From the levee I could look into the ideal green water with visibility of about eighteen inches. Perfect.

This was one of the most interesting pools in the creek, and, along with the Salmon Hole in the middle of Giacomini's field, the deepest. The silvers loved it, and for there to be a thousand of them in it was routine. It basically had two holding areas in the shape of an "L." Coming out of the field, one channel went straight to the bay, but it was shallow and false. The real one turned sharply east, forming a deep-cut bank on its western edge. Then it ran straight into the railroad levee, creating a deep hole about 150 feet long, running north straight back toward the corner at Bivalve.

If there were steelhead holding here, they'd be in the larger, deeper, lower part. Faced with clear water, a nearly imperceptible current, no wind, and a bright sun overhead, I lengthened the leader to twelve feet and put on a very slim sparse #6 black fly.

One of the unpleasant difficulties of fishing this spot straight downstream was walking a sloping mud bank into which you sunk about twelve inches. There was a real danger of getting stuck and also of falling down, both of which I had experienced. In fact, the first time I ever fished there, I dubbed it "Goop's Pool." The trick I learned was to use a stout stick as a third leg. I had the perfect one stashed behind the levee where the tide couldn't reach it. It was half an old oyster stake, and as I slogged my way into position, I brought it along, planting it behind me when I reached my casting position right at the water's edge. I didn't want to have to move to land a fish, and whatever happened this morning in this hole was going to happen without my moving my feet until I was ready to leave. The bucket there was twenty feet wide and about eighty feet long, and at its deepest point was eight feet. There wasn't much variation in casting, so an arc from 11 to 1 o'clock was good enough. For the hell of it, I split the difference on the first cast and decided on a twenty-count retrieve.

As I began to move the fly, there was an odd sensation on the line, and

I knew what it was. It had brushed across a fish's back, and, feeling it, the fish had moved off. I kept stripping slowly until the line pulled tight and I had one. There were no histrionics, just a good solid tug of war. The sun was warm on my back and as it penetrated the water I could see the fish diving and thrusting. I had positioned myself appropriately for the landing and release.

On the next few casts the line rubbed fish every time, and on the fifth or sixth it came up tight, and the head shake told me it was fair, not foul, hooked. After that, even though the line was touching them every time, it took ten minutes to get another grab, which pulled out after ten or fifteen seconds. Being obliged to remain stationary is a bit of a tough situation because fish are so tuned to their environment. They may be fooled a few times, but they soon learn to fear and/or ignore all things suspicious.

For instance, you can be out on the Gulf Stream in a school of dolphin chumming them into a frenzy, then flipping them a fly. You'll hook three or four, and pretty soon they're still rushing at the phony but veering off at the last minute. Or on an Atlantic salmon river in Russia, where you know there are thirty or forty holding in a tailout, you'll catch two, maybe three, change flies, catch two more, and that's it. Same for a big pool on the Umpqua with dozens of visible steelhead in it. Up on Steamboat Creek one time, I sat watching a dense school of about 200 steelhead hanging in a crystal clear pool with little current, their fins scarcely moving. I flipped in a pebble and three fish rushed it, one of which ate it. A few minutes later I flipped in another, and only one fish broke ranks to grab it and immediately spit it out. After that pebble after pebble was completely ignored, other than a few aborted false rushes.

So that's where I was on that sublime early January day forty-one years ago at my favorite fishing place on earth. My deities the steelhead were grouped before me patiently awaiting a falling barometer and the subsequent deluge that would drive them to their spawning gravels, but for the time being they were killing time at the train station trying to ignore a panhandler. I caught one more fish—a buck of maybe ten pounds. No one was there to appreciate my grin, but the satisfaction was very sweet. Then the tide started rolling in and I was back to my paints.

The next day, the mean low was at about 10:00. Arriving at seven-thirty, I checked out the Steps. It was quiet as a tomb, with grebes and diving ducks going about their business, but not a fish in sight. No one would ever suspect the drama of fish and fog of only a few days ago. I looked up at the beautiful ridge that was now just a ridge. With the barometer still holding steady, my idea was to hit the Salmon Hole in the middle of Giacomini's field. A profound holding area for silvers, it was also a sanctuary for steelhead in low water conditions. I had a good place to hide my very recognizable car. It was a little road just west of Inverness Park.

The saga, if one may call it that, began at White House Pool a few years earlier. The popular fishing area ran from there upstream to the bridge on Highway 1. It was pretty much a story of people parking and fishing right by their cars, folding chairs being a common accoutrement. It was duffers and families mostly, drowning bait or else casting lures of one sort or another. I'd fished this reach of water with my dad and others since 1950, but not once with positive results. Then, days after my sixteenth birthday in 1956, I headed out there with better tackle and a new sense of curiosity and determination. Below White House Pool the creek veered away from the road, stretching off into a meadow. I'd heard the land belonged to Giacomini and that he didn't want people trespassing on it. I'd never seen a soul fishing down there, but overwhelmed by the youthful magnet of the unknown, and little fear of chastisement, I climbed the fence.

About three quarters of a mile into my investigation, the creek turned somewhat, revealing a beach on its west side, and on it a man was fly casting. I didn't want to crowd him but I had to get within about 100 feet to be in a nice hole boiling with salmon. I was using my Heddon nine foot, two-handed bamboo casting rod and Pflueger Supreme reel to throw a silver Flat-fish, and within ten minutes was tight to a fish that I landed and dispatched with a length of driftwood.

Reeling in, the man walked over to me, a large and confident presence. "That's a nice one," he said. "Al Giddings." And he offered his hand.

"Thanks, I'm Russ Chatham."

"It's a hen," he went on, "You gonna use the roe?"

"Probably not," I said. "I've bait and lure fished for years but I'm trying to learn fly fishing like you. It's just that I don't really have enough confidence yet."

"Can I have it then?"

The sinking sun glinted off his badge, and I realized he was the Game Warden. "I can't seem to get a hit today."

And he knelt down and with his pen knife opened the ten-pound fish and carefully removed the two large skeins of eggs.

"Steelhead'll be coming in pretty soon, so thanks. We keep the rumor going that Giacomini doesn't want anyone in here, even though he doesn't care, because we like to keep this hole for the locals, but it'll be okay if you want to park by the store over there and cross the field. It's a hell of a lot shorter."

In all the years I knew him, throughout hundreds of encounters, Al never asked to see my license. And when he did routinely check anglers at Papermill, if someone had forgotten to buy one, he never wrote a citation, but instead simply asked them to run into town and pick one up at the Palace Market.

About two weeks after meeting Al that first time, I was at the Salmon Hole again, only this time with my fly rod. Al was there along with one other man spin fishing. Neither Al nor I could get a bite. However, it seemed like the lure guy was hooked up constantly. He landed one, two, and three, whapped them and laid them up in the grass. He had his limit. But then he walked back to the water and kept fishing. Soon he hooked another, landed it, whapped it, and laid it up with the others. Al reeled in and walked over to me. In a low voice he said, "You saw what just happened?"

"Yes, I did."

"Well, there are 10,000, maybe 15,000, salmon holding between the bridge and Millerton Point. The lumber mill south of Olema closed this year, and this guy was one of many who were laid off. He has four kids and needs those fish to feed his family, so I'd appreciate it if you just pretend you didn't see anything."

In my view, Al was the truest of wardens, on the lookout for serious offenders like jack lighters, salmon giggers, or those who took ten times the limit of striped bass to sell on the black market.

Some cloud cover was developing and I sensed a change in the weather. But now it was calm. It's a straight shot from White House Pool to the Salmon Hole. Then, there comes a bend, and thus a groove on the far side five or six feet deep. The bend continues and then hits a steep mud bank and the depth increases to eight feet at low tide. Some ruddy ducks and mud hens were noodling around, but otherwise it was quiet. I worked through the hole without a touch, until I was at the low end where I'd caught that fluke steelhead on the incoming tide. Looking downstream perhaps 150 yards, I saw motion in the water. Often it's just a bird, but since there was nothing where I was, I climbed out and crossed the inside channel that made the Salmon Hole beach an island.

I sat down to watch for five or ten minutes, as there was a grebe working the hole and that could easily have been what I saw. The grebe wasn't too fond of me and paddled away downstream. I had become a bird watcher, not my dream as a fisherman, when right before my eyes there was a slow head, dorsal, tail roll about fifty feet below me. Without any need to move, or even stand up, I draped a cast over it and began the count, and then the retrieve. I guess I could have predicted the take, although I am rarely that confident. To land it I had to slide off the bank and would have gone in over my head were it not for a last minute handful of pickle-weed. The eight-pound hen dashed away healthily.

Climbing back up, I surveyed my domain. Minutes passed with nothing of any interest happening. Then I saw the wakes. The transition from where I was to the Salmon Hole was a flat about two feet deep. It had a hard bottom, which is where you crossed to fish the lower slot from the inside of the bend. I lost no time heading back upstream to the pool itself. As there was no one else there, I could position myself wherever I wanted, so I chose the heart of the hole right where Al Giddings would be standing if he were there. In the nearly imperceptible current I felt confident that the depths could be probed thoroughly and effectively. Three or four casts into it I was tight to a surging presence and ten minutes later released a hen back into the system.

Twenty feet upstream I saw a fish roll and I quickly walked above it and in one cast had it on. As I released it, another fish showed in the upper slot and I jogged up above it, too. It took two casts until I was fast to it. Working upstream I could see wakes deliberately heading for White House Pool. I worked back and forth through the hole but nothing else happened until the tide started in.

That night my father's barometer was falling, and some time after midnight the rain started. I got up anyway and headed out to try a nice little groove about 200 feet below the Highway 1 Bridge. It made sense in my mind. Somehow, I knew no one would be there, as it seemed the creek had vanished from most people's consciousness once the salmon were gone.

As I applied my beautiful half and half line over that precious water, I thought of Gene Thompson and how grateful I was for his gift. I would tell him about all this, of course, and he would puff on his cigar and not say much, probably figuring I'd made most of it up. Then, as the rain pounded down, dripping off my hood, I kept my composure and my ten count until the line came alive, and I was there in that most beautiful of places, my *querencia*, and I waltzed with my steelhead until it lay on the beach. I never kill without an apology, so when I slammed the driftwood over the hen's head, I was kneeling and asking for forgiveness. I would give the eggs to Al. By nightfall, all the steelhead would be safely miles upstream.

Remembering Woody

Guy de la Valdène

Woody Sexton and I sat next to each other in the stern of his wooden, sixteen-foot Nova Scotia skiff, waiting for the cloud that shaded the morning sun to pass. A soft grey mantle rested on the flat and there seemed little point in poling, so we waited—engine idling, the bow troubling the surface of the water—for the sun to escape and expose the flats surrounding Coupon Bight.

It was June 8, 1969.

We had been fishing for fifty-five days in a row and the skiff felt tight as a glove. The daily repetitions of launching and running, of poling and looking, had elevated the smallest, most idiotic hint of humor to the level of high comedy. I followed the last leg of a mosquito's journey from the mangrove shoreline of Big Pine Key to the skiff and watched it sink its stylet into Woody's neck.

"Goddamn bloodsucking son of a bitch," he said, jumping up. The skiff tipped to starboard. He took a shot with his hat, missed, and rambled on about malaria, dengue, yellow fever, encephalitis, and other insect-related diseases. Woody used words like *C.pipiens quinquefasciatus* for a house mosquito and *Lymphogranuloma inguinale* instead of VD. His forearms were knotted like a sailor's; his face, a reasonable façsimile of the Western landscapes he hunted each fall.

Endowed with a critical mind and a near-perfect memory, Woody Sexton (1922–1998) graduated in 1943 with a degree from Humboldt State

Photo by Guy de la Valdène

Woody Sexton at work.

University. With diploma in hand, he went into the U.S. Navy, and though he did not see action in World War II, he did witness the hubristic nature of his species at close quarters. Woody might have been a doctor, a lawyer, or an engineer, but instead, after being released from his duties, he made his way from San Diego to the redwood forests of the northwest and became a lumberman. For a decade he lived in a world defined by fulcrums and angles, exposed to the raw, often dangerous, physicality of his profession. Far from the confines of civilization, he burgeoned into a "master lumberman," skilled in the art of felling trees bearing the circumferences of school busses to an exact place in space, a designated piece of ground where other—less skilled—men could get to the wood quickly and dress it for sale. In his off hours Woody read books.

We had both celebrated birthdays in May. I had turned twenty-five, Woody, forty-seven, a fact that did not please him; I was too young to care. To retain a semblance of the physical strength he had developed during his years in the woods, Woody kept in shape by completing 200 push-ups and 200 sit-ups every morning. He would then twirl a forty-five-pound cement block tied to a rope around his body like a hammer thrower for fifteen minutes before we met for breakfast. One afternoon, after pushing his skiff for six hours, I watched him squat behind an unsuspecting guide who weighed upwards of 300 pounds. Woody wrapped his arms around the man's knees and picked him straight up off the ground. He grinned like Popeye the sailor.

When the tides were wrong or the fish elsewhere, we talked about river systems, ocean currents, books by Roderick Haig-Brown, migrations, bird hunting, and tools of all kinds, from bait-casting reels to Woody's navy-grey skiff. Quick and light over the water, she was a dream to pole, which more than made up for the fact that, because of her round chine, she was wet and tippy. The skiff had been built in Islamorada, Florida, from a cold-molded wood hull manufactured by the Chestnut Canoe Co. in Nova Scotia. From inside her confines we had jumped 150 tarpon since the beginning of the fishing season in April.

Outside the skiff, the water was syrupy and dark. Light fanned towards us in harmony with the cloud struggling from under the sun. The mosquito headed for shore. My guide, whose friendship I'd grow to cherish, shoved the fishing cap back on his short, white hair and sat down. All at once sunlight spilled over the flat and Woody relaxed his grip on the tiller. Hot, humid air enveloped us—a rallying call for tarpon to migrate from the comfort of deep, offshore water to the shallow flats that buttress the shorelines of the southern United States.

Woody allowed the skiff to lose momentum. We took turns sitting and standing, both of us watching from different angles for disturbances on the surface, for shapes inside shadows, for distortions in the slow, oily rhythm of the tide, motion of any kind: for rings, for daisy-tails, for the surge of water that shepherds the broad heads of shallow-swimming pelagic fish.

Woody raised the forty-horsepower engine manually, unleashed the push pole from under the bungee cords that bound it to the chocks, and moved to the bow. He maneuvered us into the sandier, shallower water of the northeast end of the bight, where on full-moon tides schools of smaller tarpon painted coin-colored shadows on its white sandy bottom. The big fish favored the deeper water to the southwest, where they slept like fat old men inches above the turtle grass. I pulled fly line off the reel. The skiff rose and fell with each stroke of the pole.

Woody poled with the same focus he devoted to bird hunting. "I miss the smell of mountains," he had said two weeks earlier, meaning that

Photo by Gil Drake

Guy de la Valdène with Pacific sailfish, Costa Rica, 1968.

his season in Florida was coming to an end. He was now dreaming of ana-
dromous fish and mountain-climbing birds. In a week, maybe two at the
most, he'd fill the cab of the Ford pickup truck with his spartan possessions
and drive to Northern California. There, he would look for housing in a
small, out-of-the-way town with a good library. In the fall, he'd relocate to
Idaho and fish for steelhead on the Clearwater River. Later, when the aspen
brightened the foothills and the mountaintops displayed the first signs of
snow, he would carry a shotgun high under the clouds and chase elegantly
feathered birds, imported long ago from Europe and Asia.

Woody worked as a flats guide in the Florida Keys for five months a
year in order to spend the following seven in the wilds. His yearly income
in 1969 was $8,000.

"I watched the entire side of a mountain run uphill," he said one day as
he poled the face of Loggerhead. He was referring to an October morning in
1964 when he pushed 2,000 chukar partridge into flight off a mountaintop
south of Orofino, Idaho. Another time, he described a foggy morning on the
Bryan Pool of the Eel River and of landing five steelhead on a Polar Shrimp
fly, each fish weighing between twelve and eighteen pounds: bright, powerful
sea-run rainbows, accommodating hosts to the sea lice they ferried to shore.

Woody came to the Keys in 1959 from those rivers of California—
the Mad, the Eel, the Trinity, the Klamath, the Smith—where he and other
young men of his generation braved cold, chest-deep water for the chance to
hook silver colored fish fresh out of the ocean. Men who hurled 600-grain
lead-core shooting-heads into deep, heavy water from dawn to dusk. Men
who were seen by other anglers as monoliths, fixtures in the rivers they fished.

Warm weather, shallow water, and the reports of tarpon by the thousands drew Woody and his peers south, much as gold had drawn their forefa-
thers west. Once these river anglers adapted to the wind and the converging
vectors of fish and boat, the mechanics of casting a fly while standing on top
of the water—as opposed to in it—became second nature.

"In those days, during a spring tide, we expected to see two, three, maybe four hundred fish in Coupon Bight," Woody said. "Now, with the boat
traffic and the commercial real estate development, we're lucky to see thirty."

He cupped the palm of his right hand around his sunglasses and scanned
the water from under the bill of his hat. "That first year my partner, Jim
Adams, and I used Fisher blanks and Jimmy Green fly rods." He added, "Our
reels were made by Young and Hardy. At night we hung from bridges and

floated flies on tides that flowed like rivers. A twelve-foot aluminum boat powered by a seven-horsepower engine drove us to the flats. We poled with a borrowed curtain rod. All we knew about tarpon was that they ate flies. We applied ourselves to that premise and cast at their faces. It made for good adventure."

As someone who spent the better part of his life on the edges of civilization, Woody took issue with those he viewed as degrading the natural world. "Politicians and lawyers are ticks," he'd finalize.

My sporting life before meeting him had been European in attitude, an ethos that translates loosely into, "Kill everything that moves." My new fishing friend and mentor was more interested in the health of his surroundings than in the ambitions of men. In time, he taught me to respect the playgrounds we played in.

Since his first trip to the Florida Keys in 1959, Woody had met all the great and not so great anglers, boat builders, and rod and reel makers of the era. Apte, Brooks, McNally, Wolf, Hommel, Captain Mac, and dozens more befriended Woody, whose acumen was appreciably more developed than theirs. Later, when a younger generation of men, such as Drake and Huff, moved to the Keys to fish, they too delighted in his company. Steve Huff, who carries the mantle of best "pound for pound" guide ever, scattered Woody's ashes over the waters of Loggerhead Key a few years ago—a good and fitting resting place for a special man.

"Fish!" Woody pointed to a disturbance 100 yards down light. He wedged the pole against his hip and spun the stern of the skiff toward the commotion. In the distance, the water chortled as if pressed over boulders. Moments later, early light fell on the chiseled heads of fish the color of bronze.

"Ten, maybe fifteen tarpon. Coming at us!"

The orange and yellow fly, tied to be fished in dark water, was wet in my hand, slick as a worm. One by one the tarpon surfaced—some with purpose, others playful—all causing the sea to part, each roll imposing levels of apprehension on the rest of the school. I rocked my right wrist back and forth, back and forth, forcing the belly of the line to roll and pull against the fly.

The closer the fish swam into range, the more the notion of time faded. I heard the rub of Woody's hands against the push pole and felt the skiff yaw to the left, inviting my back cast. The fly landed a leader's length ahead of the lead fish. A mouth rose, cavernous, out of the water and closed. I raised the rod, ran out of striking room, and watched the fly sail gracefully through the air. It fell in a melancholic tangle on the surface of the water next to the engine.

"Shit! Shit and shit," I yelled as I watched huge puckers of creamy water rise from the floor of the flat.

"Shit" I said again. Woody smiled and said nothing.

I poled and Woody fished. His regular fee was sixty bucks a day. He charged me thirty, we shared the fishing, I brought the lunch. That was our deal.

Some days we trailered the skiff and chased bonefish and permit below Key West. But Big Pine Key, Summerland, Cudjoe, the Seven Mile Bridge (during the palolo worm hatch), Monster Point, and the Eccentrics, where tarpon would swim out of the deep channels, looking like thick black eels, were the settings Woody was most comfortable fishing.

Every morning, with a notion of sunlight angling off the blacktop into the windshield, I would drive from Key West to Summerland Key and meet him at the Chat and Chew Restaurant. After breakfast, which often consisted of a foot-long hotdog, I'd follow him up to Big Pine Key where he kept his skiff.

In the afternoons the drive was tougher, the sun brighter, my eyes tired from probing through layers of seawater, overloaded from the incongruity of watching big fish fly across the sky.

Willie Mae, my wife's housekeeper, would greet me with a drink on the doorstep of the conch house on Duval Street we rented each spring. The children ran up from the street and hugged my legs. Willie Mae was a large and reassuring woman with shiny black skin. She wore a permanent smile and had a gift for making memorable chicken sandwiches. If I wanted sympathy regarding the hardships of my sporting life, it was to her I would turn.

Woody had the high casting motion of a deep-river wader. On the back cast, his right hand hugged his ear before rising straight up to the sky. His double-haul was concise and powerful. He was at his best when he saw fish late and made the throw purely from instinct; his forté, the short cast. A long string of rolling tarpon noodling up to the boat from a distance created an intellectual conundrum, much like a shooter questioning how far to lead a duck crossing the backdrop of a bluebird sky. Woody liked to snap his casts just like I liked to shoot a gun—quickly.

I poled the north side of Coupon Bight, the sun warm on my shoulders. The turtle grass seven feet below the hull chased the tide. Shallow coral heads scattered under the bow, adding to the difficulty of poling. For the sake of silence—the clang of a pole's hardwood foot hitting rock shatters the nerves of large, sleeping fish—I could not drive the pole with the speed I would have liked. Instead, I had to catch it before it reached the bottom and ease it the rest of the way into the grass. My hands hydroplaned on a permanent film of water. The power strokes ended at my knees.

Two tarpon swam parallel to the boat, a foot under the surface. Woody made a quick half-moon cast behind his right shoulder and drove the rod toward the fish. The fly turned over a few feet ahead of the closest tarpon, a fat eighty-pound female, followed by a smaller, leaner male. Both fish rose to the fly in a confusion of bodies. A large round scale spun luminous to the bottom. The smaller of the two fish knifed cleanly out of water close to the boat.

"I never struck him," Woody exclaimed.

A third fish, deep and more difficult to see, inched towards us on the bottom of the bight, sixty feet from the skiff. Woody retrieved the fly and made the cast. This time, when he stripped, something slow and confident rose from the grass, settled behind the fly, opened its mouth, and ate it.

The size of the fish in relation to the fly and the boat didn't fit the proportions of the tarpon we were accustomed to; the largess of its mass and purpose of motion was unsettling. The fish turned from the boat and Woody's white Shakespeare fly rod bowed. Moments later, the ocean came alive as a tarpon as broad as the wing of a plane cartwheeled through the surface and into the sky—a silverfish with golden eyes rising, shedding light, bending the scales of our imagination. At the apex of its jump, pinned by gravity, the tarpon seemed to hesitate for an instant before tumbling like an anvil back to the sea. Yards of white water rose into the air.

The fly rod in Woody's hand looked small, ludicrous. He turned, his eyes round under his sunglasses. He asked, "What do you think, 200 pounds?" His lips were stretched tight against his teeth. I dropped the engine and pulled the ripcord.

"Yes!"

We motored after the tarpon, guided by the tip of Woody's rod, as again and again this dancer of a fish sailed through the warm humid air dripping with light and power. Except for a handful of blue and black marlin, some sharks, a whale once, I had never seen a fish of that size before.

And so it went: eleven times the tarpon hurdled through the glasslike surface of Coupon Bight, eleven jumps into a foreign medium, eleven backbreaking falls. The fish dragged us to the entrance of the bight and stopped. Woody reeled. Sweat stained the middle of his back. To keep the slack out of the line, I worked at outguessing the fish's moves. Woody reeled the backing onto the reel. The angle of the fly line steepened. Beads of water fell in long thin strands into the bight. The giant rolled and jumped partially out of water one final time. It shook its gill plates in exhausted fashion and when it fell, it fell slowly and laid on its side like a timbered log, benumbed, the tips of its fins quivering.

We instinctively knew that our only chance to land the tarpon was to get a gaff into it quickly, that if the fish regained its senses, the twelve-pound-test leader would almost certainly lose the ensuing fight. I idled the skiff as close as I dared and, unwilling to disturb the fish's stupor, cut the engine. Woody reeled the tarpon closer to the skiff. It looked twelve feet long. I reached for the gaff we kept tethered to the gunnels. It wasn't there.

"Woody! We left the damn thing at the dock!"

We had both killed tarpon before, mostly for other anglers, and hadn't liked it. We had agreed a few weeks earlier never to kill another one. A tarpon is too much like a St. Bernard, a generous fish with a huge heart and a gift for jumping, a fish with a past, a fish with a soul, and who, except for a fool, would deliberately kill a soul?

But the truth was that neither of us had ever imagined that a trophy, fifty pounds heavier than the world record, would one day lay within arm's reach of our boat. I rummaged in the bow and found the lip gaff.

"When I get it in its mouth, we'll pull him in," I said reaching over the side. The tarpon dropped out of sight as did the tip of Woody's rod. Slowly, carefully, he raised it out of the water. The fish moved. The odds were against us. Even with a gaff hold in its mouth, the tarpon would turn the skiff over when we tried to pull it in. However, we would try, not for the killing, maybe not even for the glory, but because it was an integral part of the game we were playing.

I leaned over, my right arm completely underwater. The gaff glanced off the bony side of the tarpon's head. A broad, dark rimmed tail swiped at my arm and kicked the fish back to the bottom. Woody cajoled it slowly to the surface. This time, though, the tarpon—perhaps waking from a dream—sensed an unholy presence and resisted. Woody applied a little more pressure and the rod weathervaned in his hands.

The fish was off.

The big tarpon canted this way and that on its way to the bottom, righting itself just above the turtle grass. We watched its broad dark back melt into the shadow and dreamily, majestically swim out of our lives. On one hand, I despaired at how close my friend had come to angling immortality. On the other, I felt an odd sense of relief.

Twenty years later, Woody told me that he still dreamed about the fish that somersaulted across Coupon Bight, that he could still feel its power and majesty in his hands. I now know that the feeling of relief I felt that morning was spawned by envy.

There was nothing to say and nothing left of the day. We sat in silence, reliving the moment that had shaped the longest and shortest ten minutes of our fishing lives.

The wings of a cormorant ticked the surface of the water. A Navy jet howled across the sky, and the wake of a distant streamer passed under the hull of Woody's skiff. In the distance I could hear the manic voice of a flats guide berating his client.

A school of tarpon rolled into range. We did not stand up.

Deserve's Got Nothing to Do with It

Robert DeMott

Herman Melville, a writer who knew well how things can go wrong on the water, said it best in his Mississippi River novel, *The Confidence Man:* "Life is a pic-nic *en costume*; one must take a part, assume a character, stand ready in a sensible way to play the fool." Melville wasn't talking about fishermen, but he may as well have been. What are we fly fishers anyway, dressed head to foot in elaborate designer costumes by Orvis, Simms, L.L. Bean, and Patagonia, but actors in a cosmic drama of trouthood? Man versus fish, man versus nature—these ancient antagonisms, juicy as they might seem to the frontier mentality, more often than not falsely ennoble us puny humans. Let's not forget that nature goes on naturing, water goes on watering, flatly indifferent to our schemings and pumped-up aspirations. In the Big Picture, that's a good thing.

Possessing all that expensive signature gear, all that specialized angling information, and all those righteous piscatorial skills makes our collective fly fishing ventures appear to be bulletproof, beyond assault, impregnable to triviality, low-mindedness, and comic pratfall. Arrayed to the teeth in our cutting-edge gear, what could possibly go wrong? But the grandiose view and mythic portrayal of fly fishing, purveyed endlessly in various print and electronic media, are disservices to human frailty, which is the truest stock-in-trade for most of us day in and day out. "Limits," poet Charles Olson

Photo by Kate Fox

**Robert DeMott looking for answers,
Madison River, Montana.**

once said, "are what we are all inside of." The fish probably know that, but fortunately say nothing to bruise our egos any more than they already are.

Take falling in. Beginner or expert, elitist or extremist, traditionalist or fanatic, we've all done it. Let's face it: Falling in is one of fishing's ugly little secrets, a failure that can hardly stand public scrutiny. "Of all the maddening things" one could count among a fisherman's curses, "the worst is falling into the water," Henry Plunket Greene confessed in his genteel 1924 classic, *Where the Bright Waters Meet.* Rare enough for a proper Irish gentleman to admit, but also not quite the whole story. Like the most recent two-faced politician or pastor who has strayed from the straight and narrow but doesn't want his or her constituency to see who he or she really is, we mostly keep our dunkings in the dark and hope that by our cunning and silence they will go away. *Deny, deny, deny* seems to be our habitual response to these subaqueous slipups.

I'm not talking about the casual dousing, the wet sleeve or the dampened fly box or water-sprayed hat. Nor am I talking about drowning, because, what the hell, after that mishap you'd have nothing left to contemplate anyway. I mean the colossal dunking, the full, head-to-toe immersion involving extreme bodily contortions, imminent physical danger or injury, and possible lasting psychic damage (which might be the most enduring effect of all). These are the spills that ought to intrigue us most because such mishaps puncture the well-constructed image of ourselves as utterly competent, physically adept outdoor persons.

Print and online fly fishing magazines, books, DVDs, television shows, web sites, blogs, podcasts, tackle shops, and equipment and gear catalogs all conspire to keep that elevated image of ourselves sacrosanct and inviolable. There we are, true blue American sportsmen, on nearly every page or frame or byte—not just skillful, savvy, and knowledgeable, but also confident, even cocky, and flush with attitude, as though we deserve every ounce of our collective spit and polish. Leaf through any issue of *The Drake,* for example, and you'll see that edgy, cock-of-the-walk attitude on full display: We're here in the wateriest reaches of this whirling earth ball to rip lips, kick ass, and take names.

Enough entitlement already! Enough Paul McLean! Enough Tred Barta!

Call it a new dispensation: a way of aiding and abetting a new age of angling honesty and piscatorial transparency. For every iconic image of angling prowess gracing the covers of this or that month's fly fishing publication—the smiling face and slightly bowed head, the outsized *salmo* cradled in suitably wet hands (and, according to current protocol, about to be released)—there is another, less distinct, photograph, a kind of visual simulacrum, an image behind the image, that exists in a parallel world. This shadowy photo is a phantom snapshot of an angler going down in water, flailing helplessly, unmoored from his brand-name world, drifting in the fish's cloudy element, completely soaked, sucking for air, and looking or acting—sensibly or not—like a complete fool. To put it another way: For every bucolic angling painting by Ogden Pleissner or Arthur Shilstone there's a hyper-real self-portrait by Francis Bacon or Lucian Freud to counter the Edenic illusion.

Late one August afternoon a few years ago, wading thirty or forty feet out from the west bank of a relatively new-to-me section of the upper Madison River (which, as fortune would have it, I had almost entirely to myself), I was bringing up one nice trout after another on one of Craig Mathews's indispensable epeorus patterns. After a couple of days of humbling fishing, this was one of those perfect moments that happen too rarely; just the right conjunction of time, season, weather, water clarity, and temperature, hatch action, feeding fish, etc. You know the scene: The banquet is set, the platters are piled high with food, the rolls have come hot from the oven, and you're the only diner in the room. At times like this—potential for gluttony aside—you believe in a benign, loving God. All the celestial bodies align, and vanity of vanities, you are thinking rather highly of your skill as an angler.

A nifty curve cast put the fly on a left-hand seam of water, and a brown trout about nineteen inches long grabbed it. I got tight to the fish right away as it ran upstream to my left, looped around, and charged back down on my right-hand side, where it dropped into a deep, fast trough. At the edge of the drop off, gaining line, rod pulsing in hand, I leaned over to net the fish, a handsome butter-colored male with a kype, the fly inserted perfectly in the corner of his jaw. I noticed all this in one of those moments of intense clarity as I hoisted his head up and slid him to the edge of my net. *Nice fish! Good job!* echoed smugly in the dim regions of my hunter-gatherer consciousness.

It was not a place of slick boulders or moss-covered, ankle-turning rocks, but a place of easy transport on a sand and gravel deposit. Nonetheless, I can't remember slipping, stumbling, or tripping, but in the next instant I was in the drink, face down, running like a maniac under a long chute of fast water so my feet could catch up with the rest of my body and I could regain my balance and stand upright again. According to experts at Boy Scouts of America, the Red Cross, and National Outdoor Leadership School, it is best for a man in my woeful situation to flip over on his back, point feet downstream, and ride the dunking out, but things happened so fast that going by the book was impossible. It never occurred to me that I might drown (I didn't) or that this was a near-death experience (it wasn't), but the emptiness in the pit of my stomach seemed endless, as though I were free falling into an abyss. While I was in the Big Wet, I had the uncanny sense that I was away somewhere, not exactly on holiday or on a pleasure jaunt, but just away somewhere with enough carefreeness to realize that mail was piling up on the sideboard at home, though I had no qualms about not opening it nor any compelling desire to read it. I was not frightened myself, but was haunted most of all by the nagging premonition that while I was absent, beyond communication, someone dear to me would die and I would not know it until too late. I could not say who that person was or might have been, but the sense of absence, sadness, and even dread that attends a momentous loss filled every nook and cranny of my head. Shadows passed behind my eyes; time slowed to a tick.

In fifty years of fishing I'd fallen in plenty of times, but had always managed to pop right up and hang on to my rod without even getting overly wet. This time, when I regained my feet a few seconds later, the rod—a brand new 5-weight Sage ZXL with a Lamson Konic reel (an incentive gift from Trout Unlimited for having become a life member a few weeks earlier)—was gone, still attached to the rampaging trout, which immediately began putting on pounds and inches, at least in my imagination. My gut response was not just anger, but a kind of undirected fury that I had been tricked by a nameless, malicious, cozening god. If that's the case, then the instrument of my undoing had better be nothing less than the Boss Fish of the Madison, Moby Brown himself. Better to be undone by a colossal adversary rather than a dink. *I deserve at least that much*, I told myself. Meantime, like the Incredible Hulk, my primordial brother, I wanted to tear something limb from limb just for the unreasonably adolescent satisfaction of exacting revenge on something, anything. So much for the mystique of the "quiet sport."

A few minutes later, out of the drink and a bit steadier on my feet, and having gagged up enough river water to float a fish, I hobbled down the bank as fast as I could, looking for my runaway outfit, then waded across and came back up the other side. I was hoping to see the rod tip sticking out of the water, or the fly line, an eye-catching yellow, snagged around a tree branch or some other obstruction, but there wasn't a sign of either the errant graphite or demonic fish, both of which had no doubt plowed downstream past Three Dollar Bridge by then.

At dusk, hatless and rodless and starting to chill in the cool evening air, I skulked like a beaten dog back to my truck; shed my soaked vest, waders, and clothes; put on a dry shirt; and began to sort out water-logged aluminum fly boxes, a couple of which had been dented by my fall, though I have no recollection of having fallen *that* hard. The ring I wore on my left hand (a seal-the-deal gift from Kate, my fly gal partner) was gone, though again I haven't a clue why or how. No broken bones, no lacerations, but my left wrist was bunged up, and I felt shooting pain in my shoulder, but immediately I gave thanks that it wasn't my casting arm that had been winged. I was plug lucky and knew that my injuries and dunking could have been much worse (a tightly cinched belt around my waist kept my waders from filling with water), and of course I realized that if I had cracked my skull on a rock, that would have ended my adventure for good. Having that stretch of river to myself suddenly looked like a mixed blessing: No one else around to share the fishing also meant no one else around to help in direst straits. But even at that sobering thought, the voice of my most frivolous, superficial devil advised me to look on the bright side—never mind that I wasn't badly injured; more importantly, there were no witnesses to compound the shame, so the blow to my ego was mine and mine alone. For better or worse, I'd live to fish another day.

It would be pretty to say that my dunking had far-reaching repercussions. That symbolically I died, and, having seen God's foot on the treadle of the loom, I had been reborn a new man. Henceforth, I'd be kind to all widows and children, give alms to the poor, and worship punctually on the Sabbath. Those old sports, Izaak Walton and Harry Plunket Greene, I know, would have found that spiritual leap a distinct possibility. But because I am not half the man either of them was, I've found it more difficult to make sense of what happened.

That night trying to explain the fall to Kate, who was understandably concerned back in Ohio, I was still a bit rocky, and I hemmed and hawed and downplayed the whole affair when she pressed me for details, then gradually confessed that I didn't exactly know what to make of the event—it was all so random and quantum in the way it played out. I assured her that I didn't think I fainted, though when we agreed that I might have blacked out, that brought another level of discernible concern into her voice. If I blacked out it would have been the first time that a "sinking episode" (as I heard one metaphor-slinging doctor call such events) had ever happened to me. "Who knows?" is the best I could come up with over the phone.

Even as a lapsed Catholic, I know confession is good for the soul. Truth is, as the evening wore on, although my anger subsided, I was still upset at how blindly furious the fall made me. This episode felt like regression of the first order, and I realized the Waltonian goal of being a "well governed Angler" eluded me. In a nanosecond, blindsided by an unexpected slip of the foot, I had morphed into a spoiled child, acting out of base egotism and vanity, holding my breath for spite until my face turned blue, because I was not consulted beforehand, was not given a choice in the matter. Embarrassed and unsettled by my irrational reaction, I'd become a stranger to myself. Perhaps Melville was right: We all just have to stand ready to play the fool when our time comes, and leave the ruminations and second guessings for much later, after the waitress at the Grizzly Bar and Grille has announced last call.

Never before, never since. That's what was so unnerving about The Event: The cause of falling in—still undetermined and by now forever unrecoverable—was such an anomaly that I have had no neat compartment in which to place it. Even now I find myself stymied, not so much by the fact that I dumped, but by my inability to resolve the nagging allied questions raised by screwing up. Am I getting too old, too jaded, too stupid, or, worse yet, too unlucky to be on the river alone? It seems like a classic paradox: The closer I get to solving their implications, the further they recede from my grasp. Though my mishap paranoia grows each day, I am patently unwilling to concede that, in my late sixties, I might be getting too old to keep fishing. After all, I'm still playing ice hockey once a week from October to April, which is way more physically demanding than fishing. So even if I might be too old to be "much of a fisherman," as Norman Maclean's narrator says at the conclusion of *A River Runs Through It,* a fisherman—self-delusion or not—I still claim to be.

By which I mean, no longer flashy, extreme, or loose-limbed and jaunty as a fisherman, but more measured, balletic, and almost comfortable with the steady incremental dance of days. Like my friend Roger Ornduff, who has a decade on me and who plies the Madison religiously with nymphs day after day for two or three hours each outing, and is totally content in wind, rain, or sun with whatever that great river gives him. Or like that aged, white-haired gent I encountered one evening a few years ago on Pennsylvania's Yellow Breeches. He appeared to be well into his eighties (maybe even older). Not at all athletic, he was trundling on anyway, "making haste slowly," to use Eugene Connett's memorable phrase about fishing deliberately. I watched him work up the river toward me, moving so methodically and painstakingly as he laid out each cast that he might have been a heron in another life. When he reached me, he laid his cane rod on the berm then got down on his hands and knees at stream's edge and crawled up the bank to the Allenberry Inn's lawn. Then, straightened up to the best of his ability, he ambled off toward the parking lot and was gone. I did not speak to him and don't know if he caught any fish, though his deliberate method had much to recommend it. *That's pluck and luck at work,* I thought. *That's looking the death trout square in the eye; that's a way I'd like to be if I don't croak first.*

I'm not much of a believer in glad-hand panaceas, so I'm skeptical about claims of reaching "closure," that ridiculous buzz word of pharmaceutical companies, pop psychologists, and self-help gurus. I doubt anyone ever closes the door completely on past events, and I believe, as William Faulkner once said, "The past isn't dead, it isn't even past." Instead, the best I can do is to follow the fantasy route and wish for a couple of things.

First, I wish that I had a photo of the moment of going ass-over-teakettle into the drink, an eight-by-ten glossy snapshot that caught the utter surprise and incomprehension on my face. That would be a photo I'd most want to have, a trophy of the moment when the world turned upside-down and I'm on the wrong side looking out. ("Deserve's got nothin' to do with it," William Munny says to the dying Little Bill Daggett in *The Unforgiven*.) That photo would stand as a reality check, the thing about our human foibles, angling mishaps, and tenuous felt-soled hold on existence we should never forget and can neglect only at our own peril. But as falling in is one of angling's most frequently suppressed secrets, that photo would never make it into any glossy, well-scrubbed fly fishing magazine, so I'd paste it on the cover of my annual fishing journal, or tack it up next to the fish porn and family photos on the cork board above my desk.

Second, because what goes around sometimes comes around, I wish like hell that some fortunate soul found that runaway fly rod and reel before it got trashed by the elements. I hope it would be a young person, new to our sport, who could benefit from an instant upgrade in equipment. When he or she picked it up, I'd give anything to know if a hefty, lively brown trout was still tethered to the rig, still hauling freight to Ennis. Surprise of surprises, I continue to fantasize—that would be the best story of all to hear, a story something like redemption, something like a second life rising from a river of doubt, though of course that story might or might not be my own.

Brainwashing

Chris Dombrowski

Kierkegaard was right: You have to descend into the netherworld to rescue the beloved. But frankly, the beloved is usually yourself.

On my nightly descent that late winter, I would drive through the Deadstream, a flat, fishless reach of the Platte that meanders through jack pines and cedar swamps. The water was often milkish in the moonlight, the reflected moon staring singularly back, blank as a cooked trout's eye. Once I saw a porcupine crossing the road, its quills gossamer in the headlights, and often there were pairs of eyes, waist-high and mammalian, set like jewels in the textureless band of grey along the road's shoulder. But mostly it was just the high beams carving out the night, the aged folk icon–turned–blues troubadour crooning: *Spirit on the water, darkness on the face of the deep.*

I would stop the old Subaru at the bridge to look for steelhead fresh from the lake—or more precisely, for the streetlight-cast shadows of steelhead, which were easier to locate on the pearl-colored gravel. Some nights the redds were vacant, but other nights I would spot a lanky buck shivering as it brushed against a snubnosed hen to milt eggs.

A day or two prior, these fish would likely have sat moored in the bay, waiting for some ideal combination of air and water temperature known only to them, waiting for the proper angle and accumulation of daylight, before they made for this precise location twelve miles from the mouth, aiming themselves against the liquid, equally determined specie: the river. They had threaded the thread of it—negotiating plunge pools and wing dams and the

Photo by Alex Lafkas

Chris Dombrowski and son Luca with steelhead, Little Manistee River, Michigan.

spill of an inland lake, atop which ice clung and bellowed, cleaving beneath the first warm rains—to get here, where the female set to fanning the gravel and the latecomer male dawdled in a deep hole downstream.

The catch-minded angler might have swung a small streamer in front of the buck's kype and antagonized the fish until it flared on the fly, charged what it believed to be an egg-thieving minnow. But the fish wouldn't have been eating, merely moving instinctually against some man-crafted annoyance.

Downriver where the steelhead moved through the threshold between lake and river, they were still hungry and hadn't yet begun to neglect sustenance for procreation. I was headed there.

I think it's fair to say now, with the perspective several years affords, that I was, at best, clinically depressed. At worst I was suicidal. I didn't, however, want my body—which could make love with my wife, go sledding with my son, sip cold vodka from a double-walled glass, stand in a river—to be obliterated, only my mind, which had become so consumed with guilt and indecision that it had turned nearly cancerous, fatiguing me with dread.

I don't want to turn this into a sappy country song, but thanks to some of my patented financial wizardry, we were broke, chest-deep in debt, employed for a mere two more months, and living paycheck to modest paycheck in a Cold War Russia-esque apartment that was provided to us through my job as a one-semester writer-in-residence at a prestigious art school. We had quit our jobs and sold our house in our beloved Montana to chase another teaching gig that hadn't panned out, and we were mired in a limbo where the unfailingly grey sky dumped moisture by the foot and the sun appeared only to flirt before vanishing for weeks on end.

That I had become overly fond of watching YouTube clips of Muhammed Ali knocking out Joe Frazier while picturing myself as Frazier, or that I often envisioned the river as a keen silver blade eviscerating the most rancid portions of my brain, should have been sure signs that I needed professional help. My psychologist father could have referred me to any number of well-qualified colleagues. But out of some strange instinct or allegiance, I trusted only the river's treatments: standing late at night in the actual river while imagining that another river coursed between the skull's banks, its current worrying at my ill thoughts until they slipped downstream like the decayed flesh of a spawned-out fish.

I remembered vaguely, or perhaps had invented, an apocryphal story in which doctors in ancient India tied the mentally ill to trees beside the river. Sequestered near the sound of shallow water running over rocks, the mad were often cured. Driving to the river each night, feeling as if the marrow had been siphoned from my bones, I was hoping to fill just such a prescription.

One night, after a balmy day of rains, after I'd stood a while in my waders at the lakeshore waiting for a substantial moon to crest the dune, the first fish appeared to me in the window of a wave: just a small jack turned sidelong momentarily before it righted itself and rode the crest into the river, but a fish just the same.

To listen to the waves fall into the sand, their tinny slap against the rivermouth's resistance; to let the eyes adjust gradually to the lack of light; to put to use so many unused nocturnal faculties was like being awake while dreaming. And the steelhead, several of them now, their backs jade-colored in the shallows, seemed like fleeting dreams themselves as they disappeared past my feet and into a hole upstream.

I couldn't see the rod, and barely the reel whose drag I'd silenced, and as I pulled line from the large arbor it seemed as if I were pulling a vein from my forearm and flinging it out behind my shoulder then onto the river's surface, where the floating line glided unseen and the leader slowly sank. I had tied the grey soft-hackle with a few wraps of lead near the hook's eye so that, when drifting against the tippet's tug, the hook would keel upward and avoid being dulled by the stones. The beat of the hook against the bottom was the pulse of the river as it died into the lake, and I connected to it via synthetic line strung through serpentine aluminum guides thread-fastened to a nine-foot graphite rod with a cork handle I'd sanded precariously thin, so as to increase the rod's sensitivity.

I had cast upstream, mended down, let the line belly, and felt the fly tap the cobbles so many times that when *tap* was replaced by a *thump* and the line launched tight, tearing through the surface of the water, I was so late to set the hook I didn't even bother. The line slackened but tightened again, and I knew the mint fish had broken water and fallen back. Presently my stomach felt a late kick of nerves as I bent the reel seat toward the fish, playing the graphite against muscle, tissue, fins, and superior instinct, certain the line would break or the hook's purchase give out before the rod would snap.

A grey moon-cast skein lay across the river's surface, and when the rod would buck, the surface would come to a boil. But I never saw the fish in the water. It made one more dig-your-heels-into-the-sand run, leapt, and the line went limp. Or did it? I stripped my line back and felt a dead tension.

"He hung me," I said aloud, marveling at the strangeness of my own voice merging with the silence and water sounds.

I twisted my headlamp on (illegal to have lit while in the act of fishing and detrimental to night vision) and followed the filament across thirty-some feet of current to the other shore: The feisty buck had beached itself and lay coated in shining sand grains, gasping. I started across, hoping to unhook the fish, but it sensed the slack in the line and made one last awkward, spine-twisting flop onto its head before rolling back into its preferred environs.

There existed a few futile moments during which I tried to gather slack line, before the surface erupted in silver tatters and the buck was free. Then I let the fly-less line quarter downstream with the current, gave it a little tug when it came taut. It dangled there like viscera.

By the time I got back into town, the bank's digital clock read *36°*, then *2:47*, then LET US CON, then SOLIDATE, then YOUR LOANS!

I slept a heavy, dreamless sleep before heading in to teach at 9:00 AM, sunglasses covering up the bags under my eyes. Before my class, the chair of the Creative Writing Department popped into my office to ask if I had a problem she needed to know about.

I looked at her: *A problem?*

A drinking problem?

"Lots of problems, yes, but not that type of problem. I've been fishing all night, and it's hard to keep my eyes open without sunglasses on."

Okay then, she said, *get some sleep,* and shut the door behind her.

Fishing all night had proved a temporary nostrum against my angst, but the state of grace to which I had connected disappeared instantly after this departmental exchange. Within a few minutes, the financial and familial worries I had outrun for several hours began to consume me from the inside again like flames. *Maybe I'll teach some cheery Neruda this afternoon,* I thought: "Day, dead of a stroke," etc. I walked back to our apartment, lay down on the futon, unfolded a map of the Lake Michigan coastline, sank my face in the bay, and tried to nap.

A few years later, when I learned that Doc Ellis pitched a no-hitter for the Pittsburgh Pirates in 1970 while tripping on LSD, I began to question why I so dutifully tended my daily worries, but such levity was unavailable to me that winter. What is the brain that it requires the occasional cleansing? It comprises only two percent of the body's weight, but the person swallowed up in the everyday madness of a depression often feels as if he is carrying an anchor around in his head. In many cases deliverance is quite near but impalpable.

Most nights I drove alone to the bay, but occasionally the colleague-turned-friend who had tipped me off to the fresh night-run fish—I'll call him Ralph—would accompany me on the trip, not so much to fish, as Ralph had caught scads of steelhead in his life, but to trip up the monotony of his fifty-eighth northwoods winter.

"You gotta be crazy to enjoy living in northern Michigan in the winter," Ralph said one night as we drove through the Deadstream. "Hell, half of Traverse City is clinically insane. You're crazy, Dombrowski, you know that? Good crazy."

Ralph's favorite word was "crazy"; if he liked you, he called you crazy, and made his eyes go all beady, smiled a feral smile. If he didn't like you, he called you crazy, too, but with a blank look of utter disinterest.

"This night fishing is crazy, isn't it? Standing in the water you can barely see, fishing by feel alone. It's like McGuane said: Upon occasion a man has to manufacture his own particular brand of hellfire."

Ralph was a poet, an admired writer, had authored several books, and

I often interrupted his reveries to grill him for advice on publishing, etc. I asked some ridiculously banal question like, *Who do you think was more influential to your era of poets, Wallace Stevens or William Carlos Williams?*

"You're too ambitious. You know, you ought to find a rock on the lake shore tonight, just pick one that feels right in your hand and put it in your pocket. That's how much ambition you should have—as much as that rock. Shit, just keep going fishing—the returns are better."

"Do you ever wonder," I asked, "why it is so many writers like to fish?"

"No, I don't wonder about it at all. Fishing is pointless and intuitive, to crib from McGuane again. And a real fisherman, a real writer"—he took a sip of his gas station coffee—"he's crazy, crazy as a shithouse rat."

Standing at the shoreline on a clear night later that month, I watched slither through the currents beyond my feet a lamprey eel, serpentine, otherworldly. A few weeks ago such a strange creature might have startled me, but I accepted its appearance as a matter of course. I wondered if the deer and the raccoons combing the dunes had begun to similarly accept the nocturnal two-legged creature that appeared nearly every night and waved a long stick around in the air, quiet except for when the stick doubled over and the two-legged creature whooped loudly while running along the beach in chase. Shortly, two fish shaped like armadillos passed over the gravel— not steelies, but long-nosed suckers. Ralph had warned me that when the spawning suckers began to slip into the river, the steelhead run was almost over. High above the horizon line, above the softly churning lake, hung a sizeable moon, waxing gibbous. I figured I had a good four hours before the glowing rock set and disappeared between the distant lights of Chicago and Milwaukee. *If this is going to be my last dance with these mercurial fish*, I thought, *I am going to fish till dawn.*

The north-flowing river bent sharply west just above the mouth, and the incomers rested here, in the tailout, after passing through a roiling current tongue. They would gather themselves for a few moments before pressing upstream another twenty yards to a waist-deep hole against the far bank, a run I had named The Well. Sometimes the fish would venture out from The Well onto the gravel, but even at night they were easily spooked from the shallows, and I preferred not to cast to them there. I had to remind myself that, as fine-tuned as my nocturnal senses had become, they were far inferior to my quarry's. A botched cast or a boot-knocked stone could turn the glassy flat into a cacophonous mess of fleeing steelhead—the water and the fish, not to mention the heart, taking quite some time to settle back into rhythm.

I stood peering into the run for a good while before two stout steelhead and their shadows appeared against the bottom, where they wavered, flame-like, before vanishing upstream. Making my way cautiously up the shore about fifty paces, I peeled off some line then rolled out a few down-and-across casts that quartered and swung the number 8 Amherst Pheasant soft-hackle through upper half of The Well: no grabs.

The fish in The Well generally took on the first or second pass if they were going to take at all, so I moved downstream a few steps to cover the lower half of the hole.

I said in whisper: "I know you're in there." Then: "Maybe they want something less gaudy." Here was true sanity: a man speaking alternately to himself and to a fish he intended to hook with sharp forged steel and drag ashore. Mechanically, I rolled another cast out and sensed the textureless drift of the line across the water, then the weight of the line as it began to bow and drag, then the line-stretching, electric tug—it is electric, the entire body from brain to feet, and all its connections, suddenly charged with a new energy—of a steelhead take.

The fish bolted up river in three angry pulses, held firm, then gave to the downstream pressure I applied and came barreling across the surface straight at me. I stripped slack line as quickly as I could but the hook was already thrown. A wake pushed against my shins.

Two rod lengths away, in a foot or two of water, the fish sat righting itself. I know plenty of anglers assert that steelhead don't "eat" while in the river, but I flicked out a backhand cast and let the fly swing a foot in front of the fish I had just hooked—it hammered the fly again with utter vehemence. A few minutes later I beached him, a seven-pound buck, and had to use forceps to loosen the fly from the back of his throat.

Over the next few hours, I landed several more fish—how many exactly I can't remember, but enough so that I began to feel a tinge gluttonous. What can I say? I happened to be there when the bread came fresh from the oven. Among the fish I released: a few welterweight jacks that fought well beyond their weight-class; another large male whose toothy kype gashed my left index finger; at least a couple pissy mid-sized females; and the largest and last steelhead I caught that season.

There are those fish you gauge your life by. On virtually the same cast I had made countless times that night, a thirty-foot flip down-and-across into The Well, I hooked one such steelhead, a hen of about fourteen pounds. She bored straight upstream without a jump, felt the heavy resistance of the rod and turned, as so many fish do, toward the pressure. She came at me so fast I had to turn and run away from the shore with my rod held high to keep even a modicum of tension on the line, the felt soles of my wading boots squeaking as they slipped in the sand. I doubled the rod over with side-pressure and tightened the drag a click or two. Then she decided to run: upstream again with an unparalleled surge, then at me, then away again until I could hear the line-to-backing knot clicking through the rod's guides.

After a few minutes of dominant, ardent flight, she suddenly caved and angled towards shore, sashaying through the thin water, her wide back breaking the surface and gleaming momentarily like polished pewter. I moved to tail her, but too soon; seeing me, she engaged her final gear and raged into the backing again, this time headed downstream and into the lake itself.

I had to ford the river just above the confluence, cross a modest spit of sand, and hurry south down the coast, reeling frantically all the while, before I finally beached her; she looked like a wide plank washed ashore. The moon was low now, its glow faint on the fish and my fingers as I worked the hook from the center of her upper jaw—I could have used the extra light, but to turn my headlamp on seemed indecent. After a few minutes she kicked free of the grip I had on her tail, and I let my hands linger a while in the wave churn, in the cold water.

As the orangish moon set, extinguishing itself on the horizon without a trace of residue, I let out a wild yelp of gratitude—to whom I wasn't exactly certain, but now I believe it was to the gentle hands of the water that pulled a beleaguered man out of himself and set him back on the earth. Behind me, the sky in the east was bluing and I turned to walk toward it.

A Lovely Simplicity

Ron Ellis

"*Lepomis macrochirus*—it belies the lovely simplicity of the bluegill
to drape it in Latin; pumpkinseed, *Lepomis gibbosus*, of the bright
orange belly, with shimmering green-blue sides and that prickly
dorsal you must smooth and lock back with a thrust of your
palm; low on the pecking order, high in hearts."

—Nick Lyons, from "Homage á Bluegills—
and Pumpkinseeds Too"

From the very first tug and the erratic dance of a red-and-white bobber,
I have been enchanted by the simple pleasures found in fishing for bluegills.
It was my Great-Uncle George, during the all-too-brief summer vacations I
spent with my grandmother near Maysville, Kentucky, who first introduced
me to these fish and then fed my passion for the mystery that still pulls at me
from the deep end of a tight line, which, by now, is always attached to a fly
rod. Fishing for sunfish was certainly my initiation into the "Brotherhood of
the Angle," and as such, in the spirit of Izaak Walton's The Compleat Angler,
I have come to think of Uncle George as my Piscator.

In the beginning, I fished with a simple cane pole, which measured
about nine feet long, fitted with a length of braided fishing line roughly
a couple of feet longer than the pole, a red-and-white plastic float, and a

Ron Ellis at Elkmont, Tennessee.

piece of split-shot mashed onto the line above a long-shanked hook. The bait of choice varied, but most often we fished with the red worms we dug out of my uncle's garden the night before and stored in a red coffee can, which we peppered with coffee grounds and topped with a plug of wet moss. We caught stringers of bluegills from the network of ponds Uncle George maintained throughout the countryside, and then we cleaned and hauled them home to my grandmother, who passed the tiny filets through an egg-wash, dredged them in cornmeal, and then fried them to a crispy golden-brown.

Later, the man who would become my step-granddad also took me fishing when he was "courting" my grandmother. After dinners on summer evenings, he took us out for ice cream and then on long drives into the country to fish his favorite creek, where he introduced me to pumpkinseeds, the bluegill's brightly painted brethren. We always went to the same pool—a deep hole where the roots of a large sycamore, looking very much like a human hand, appeared to have crawled out from beneath a badly eroded bank. I sat on those gnarled knuckles and lowered my bait (again, we used mostly red worms) into the water. From that perch, I could look down on any pumpkinseed that might snatch the bait, sending the float skittering across the creek, and see that first exciting flash of electric turquoise and orange shimmering in the creek beneath my dangling feet.

After they married, Granddad moved my grandmother across the Ohio River into a house he had built especially for her. In the carport closet of that house, he stored both his lawnmower and his fishing equipment, composed primarily of a couple of spin-cast outfits, a bait-casting rod and reel (a Pflueger "Trump" loaded with heavy black line, which now sits on a bookshelf in the room where I write), a battered minnow bucket, and a green metal tackle box. The box was loaded with a bait-fisherman's selection of hooks and sinkers, a wide variety of floats and bobbers, and two surface plugs: a classic frog-pattern Jitterbug and a black Hula-Popper. Back then that closet smelled like what I thought fishing should smell like—dried grass clippings mixed with the scent of dried minnows and red worms and a splash of 3-IN-ONE oil.

The last fishing trip I took with Granddad was on an incredibly hot and humid August evening. After supper, we went out onto the carport and pulled the gear out of the closet, loaded it into his new Chevrolet, and drove up into the hills with the windows rolled down and the Cincinnati Reds on the radio. We parked at a gravel pull-off along the two-lane, close to where Ellis Run joins Big Three Mile Creek, which eventually empties into the Ohio downstream from Fishing Gut Creek, the place where my ancestors first set foot in what was then the Northwest Territory and would soon become Ohio.

With those thoughts occupying some space in my head, we baited our hooks and worked our way up Big Three Mile, fishing red worms through the deep holes. At the tail of one long pool, we encountered an old man fishing night crawlers with a bamboo fly rod, which was the first time I can actually remember seeing anyone fishing with one. We introduced ourselves, and as we talked in whispers he hooked a fish on the far side of the pool—the long, soft rod bent and pulsed with the tugging of the fish, a chunky rock bass, or a red-eye, as he called it, which was quickly landed and placed on a chain stringer, along with a few sunfish, including a couple of pumpkinseeds, as I remember it. After a while, we continued on, working upstream and only beginning to fish again when we were well above the old man.

In time, we caught a couple of nice pumpkinseeds and a red-eye of our own. We came off the creek at nightfall, and as we walked the road back toward the Chevy, I could hear quick water tumbling over rocks, running swift and free toward its blending with the slow, dark Ohio

Photo by Ron Ellis

A fat, lovely bluegill.

down below. And while I remember thinking again about my ancestors and this country they helped to settle, mostly I thought about the old man and the pulsing of that bamboo fly rod.

Soon, I was hunting for a fly rod to call my own. My father–in–law told me one evening about his favorite fly rod and then he dug around in his basement until he found it—a long, brown, willowy affair fitted with an automatic fly reel, which he said was perfect for "coaxing them in," especially when he was after big bluegills. His said his bait of choice was a single night crawler threaded onto a light wire hook with no more weight than a single split–shot. "It works real well," he said, smiling. "You should try it."

And so I vowed that I would.

First, I began to read about the charms of fly fishing and how the "long rod" imparted magic to the entire fishing experience. The fly rod converts were evangelistic about its benefits. There were hundreds of stories about fly fishing for trout, largemouth bass, and smallmouths, or "green trout," as Dr. Henshall calls them in his celebrated Book of the Black Bass, which I was also devouring at the time, but I feel certain the first story I read about fly fishing for bluegills and pumpkinseeds was written by Nick Lyons, probably in his celebrated column, "The Seasonable Angler," in Fly Fisherman magazine, and first collected in his Confessions of a Fly Fishing Addict (1989).

Since I more or less lived in a "trout-less land," there were not many places to buy a fly fishing outfit at that time, especially if your budget was well south of $200. In time, I found an outfit I could afford: a 7-weight (a bit heavy for panfish, of course), eight-and-a-half-foot fiberglass rod by Garcia and a Pflueger "Medalist" reel spooled with twenty-pound backing and a peach-colored, weight-forward floating line, which was described as a "bass-bug taper." I flailed about with that outfit for a few years, occasionally reverting back to fishing with a black plastic worm on my semi-retired bait-casting outfit, but in time, I came to prefer fly fishing above all other forms of fishing, especially when on a perfect summer evening the cork popper I twitched through a weed-bed suddenly disappeared down a swirl and then reappeared in the mouth of a thick, bright, pumpkinseed.

That first fly rod was eventually replaced by an eight-and-a-half-foot wand of slick, green graphite, a 5-weight, which I felt was better suited for bluegill fishing (and the occasional bass), and I began favoring a black, bead-head Wooly Bugger over a popper, with some gold tinsel threaded through its feathers to add more flash to its sex appeal.

My uncle, grandfather, and father-in-law are all gone now, and I no longer fish the ponds and creeks near Maysville, but my passion for bluegills and pumpkinseeds has not diminished. Even now, after all these years, I still feel the same incredible thrill when a big bluegill snatches the fly and resists my attempts to drag it out of its watery world with the long rod.

I attempted to pass along my simple love of fishing for bluegills and pumpkinseeds to my son when he was five years old. It was on a warm summer evening, at a pond close to home, where he learned to cast his new Snoopy spin-cast outfit (I planned to introduce the fly rod when he was older and I was certain he was hooked on bluegill fishing). I can see him now, dressed in khaki shorts, a striped T-shirt, a blue ball cap, and a pair of bright red canvas sneakers. That evening he caught and released twenty-three bluegills using a red-and-white plastic bobber, under which we threaded red worms on a gold hook, but it wasn't the fishing or the number of fish he caught that made the evening so memorable. Rather, it was the way he continuously laughed and giggled as he reeled each fish into the shallow water, almost winding them up to the toes of his red sneakers, before shouting, "Free him, Dad!" And free them we did.

He's twenty-six now, and he doesn't care about fishing, at least not that I am aware of, but I'm still hopeful that someday, maybe on a warm summer evening, he'll remember his first outing and call and say, "Hey, Dad, let's go fishing. I think I'd like to learn how to fly fish for bluegills now."

While I wait on that day, I mostly fish alone, although my wife has just started to fly fish for trout in the Smokies—she's already learned a great deal and is quite a good caster, not to mention how great she looks in her new waders and how her hair smells like the sun when I stand close as she makes a difficult cast—and, of course, having her in this part of my life pleases me immeasurably. In the mountains, we have both fallen in love with the clear, cold streams and their wild trout—especially the native brookies, or "specs," as they call them down there. Stealth and a near-perfect presentation in the gin-clear water are required to catch these trout, which are often no more than nervous, fleeting shadows on a cobbled stream bottom. Slender fly rods and light lines work best for the trout in the Southern mountains, and they are, coincidentally, a perfect match for bluegills and pumpkinseeds.

So, when we're not at our cabin in the mountains, I mostly fish alone, in a friend's lake near home, a pleasant place where the bluegills are often large and usually hungry. I prefer to fish in late evening, beginning almost at dusk, with the ever-present crows fussing in the distance and the night creatures serenading the fading light. I park my truck where my friends can see it from the house and then I go through the ritual of sitting on the tailgate and getting into what Tom McGuane calls the "voodoo of rigging up." I usually fish a 4-weight with a black, bead-head Wooly Bugger. The last time I fished at this lake it was dead still and dreadfully humid, with the water flat and calm, and so naturally I heard that little voice saying, "It'll be like fishing in bath water. You better use a popper." I ignored the voice and stayed with the bugger, thinking that the really big bluegills would be holding down deep.

And so I crept down the bank to a mowed path along the water's edge, knelt, and made a short cast, which produced a hard strike on the very first strip. I lifted the rod and stood up to find a thick slab of a bluegill shoveling water with its broad sides and bucking hard against the rod, putting up as much of a fight, if not more so, than the average largemouth bass I had caught here. I steered the bluegill back into the shallows, where it tilted to one side, showed the purple-smear on its flanks, and then made a last run before surrendering. When it seemed calm, I stooped and slipped the fly from its lip. The bluegill disappeared into deep water, headed, or so I imagined, for a cool spring, down where the heat could not go.

I groomed the fly and checked the knot, before casting again. While stripping in the slack, a dragonfly appeared and hovered above the taut line. The little fellow seemed damp from all the humidity, with its clear wings appearing to wobble rather than whirr, but he jumped up and buzzed away when I raised the rod tip to make another cast.

By dark I had caught and released thirteen bluegills, and despite the superstition associated with that number, it had been a surprisingly lucky evening. The fly was a bit ragged by then, so I wondered if I should tie on a new one and fish my way back toward the truck, or just call it a night. As I considered my choices, three mallards came in over the pines and glided in, their wings set and feet dangling in the dusky air, and as they landed a single, soft swishing sound rose and then faded away just as quickly as the wake. I took this as a good sign and decided to fish on.

With the moon beginning to show itself, I tied on another Wooly Bugger, with more bright strands of metallic gold threaded through its feathered blackness. A big bluegill ate the fly on the first cast, nearly jerking the pole out of my hand. I steered the fish into the shallows, swung it onto a flattened patch of yellowed grass, and squatted down to remove the hook, holding a small flashlight in my teeth to aid in the effort.

Next to brook trout, I thought, bluegills were the handsomest of fish. This one glistened in the light, a wash of iridescent purple on its flanks, its gills edged in bright blue. I placed the fish on its left side in the palm of my hand, with its mouth touching the tip of my index finger and its tail extending midway into my watchband. Later, I measured that distance and found it was just shy of nine inches.

You've got yourself a fat one, I thought to myself, and then gently sandwiched the fish between my hands and turned it so that it rested in the palm of my opposite hand, and I discovered it had a dime-sized eye of solid, wet gold, without so much as a trace of the usual dark pupil. Another gift, I thought, as I held the fish against the sky and admired its silhouette, and then I knelt at the water's edge and released it. The bluegill darted away from the bank and swam to the edge of the moon-bright shallows and vanished into the deep water through a dark seam.

I told myself I would make just one more cast, and then head for the truck.

The slender 4-weight passed back and forth and then, like a metronome gone quiet, the line settled onto the pond. As I stripped the line in short jerks, making the fly dance in the dark water, I wondered if the gold tinsel produced metallic smears in the fly's wake, like jagged flashes of lightning etched into the dark water. And I wondered, too, what the fly might look like to that bluegill with the golden eye.

With no takers, I reeled in the line and then, close to where the willow weeps into the lake, I began to cast again. Just one more, I thought, and then the line was unfolding, stretching into the darkness behind me and whispering past on the forward cast, the fly entering the dark water with a soft plop. As I stripped line, I glanced at the moon and thought about how all of this began with those glorious summers spent fishing for bluegills and pumpkinseeds with my great-uncle and step-granddad and that encounter with the old man and the bamboo fly rod. But mostly I thought about my son's laughter as he slid those bluegills to the toes of his bright red sneakers and about the great gift of stillness I experience when fly fishing for the magic that has always been present in the bright, liquid colors of sunfish.

Let's Do It Again
Next Year

Jim Fergus

It is 2010, the fortieth anniversary of the first Boys' Annual Fishing Trip, and we have reconvened in Saratoga, Wyoming, to float the North Platte River, a blue-ribbon trout stream. Four old friends since college, we are, of course, no longer boys, but suddenly, astonishingly, late-middle-aged men. (Although as we frequently point out to one another, as none of us is likely to live to be 120 years old, possibly even middle age is behind us.) Nor, truthfully, has the Annual Fishing Trip been held continuously each year; over the past decade in particular, we have frequently let the trip lapse, unable to find a long weekend in the summertime mutually agreeable to all parties. Indeed, as each summer approaches, we squabble over dates like grumpy old men, until everyone is so irritated with the others' self-important inflexibility that we call the trip off altogether. "Fine then," we say in frustration, after a dozen or so potential dates are eliminated by one or more of our schedules. "Fine, we won't do it this year. . . . Maybe next year we won't be so busy." How is that we had so much time for such things in our youth, we wonder?

But this year, in honor of the occasion, we have actually managed to organize the trip, and as we often did in the past, we have invited two guests along, also old pals. Presently, we're following another tradition, which is to dine our first night in town at the venerable Hotel Wolf. As in previous years, over cocktails in the bar before dinner, we shoot pool and notice an old, time-faded *Denver Post* review of the hotel framed on the wall, dated 1982, and with my byline on it. That's how long we've been coming here, and then some.

Photo by Stephen Collector

Jim Fergus and friends on North Platte River, Wyoming.

In the restaurant we order the "Wolf Cut" prime rib, gigantic slabs of beef, each of which could feed an entire Third World family for a month. As only old friends can, we catch up instantly, the years seeming to fall away in the spirit of the event; we may look older to one another, but we quickly regress to the most immature behavior of our college days. We tell vulgar stories in overly loud voices; we drink too much and laugh riotously.

Sitting at a table next to us, an elderly ranch couple dines in stunning silence, presumably having exhausted over the past half-century their full marital repertoire of conversational topics. With nothing to distract them at their own table, they naturally can't help but overhear ours.

One of us now poses the question to the others, "When was the last time you made love to your wife?" And someone else answers eagerly, "I can tell you, because I remember it so vividly. Yes, it was my birthday, June 13 . . . 1996." And everyone howls.

Finally, the neighboring rancher has had enough of our childish shenanigans. He stands and turns his chair around so that it faces our table and sits down again, crossing his arms and fixing us with the iciest of stares. He is older than we are, it is true, but we recognize that he could probably take all of us . . . all of us at once. The laughter dies in our throats; we suddenly feel like schoolboys caught in a circle jerk by the headmaster. "Please excuse us, sir," one of us offers. "I'm afraid we got a little carried away." This apology seems to satisfy the rancher. Having protected the honor of his wife from the vulgarities issuing from our table of louts, he turns his chair back around to resume their silent dinner vigil. It occurs to us that if they had a little conversation of their own, they wouldn't have to eavesdrop on ours. We look at each other and begin sputtering like kids.

Colorado Springs, Colorado: June, 1970

We made the pact back in college—J. D., Johann, D. C., and I—four fresh-faced young men just preparing to go out into the real world. It went like this: No matter what happened in each of our adult lives, no matter where we all lived, what obligations and responsibilities we accrued in the coming years, come hell or high water, poverty or riches, we would make an annual fishing trip together once every summer. For the rest of our lives.

A sub-clause of the pact was that when one of us hit it big, made our first million, we would treat the others to a trip to New Zealand, Chile, or Argentina—exotic destinations that occupied in our youthful dreams the status of the promised lands of fly fishing. In the meantime, we had plenty of fine water to cover on our own continent.

Saratoga, Wyoming: Fortieth Reunion Trip

We are up before dawn this first morning, in order to be on the river by 7:00 AM. We have rented two of Stoney Creek Outfitters' "river cottages," steps from the North Platte and next door to the fly shop and headquarters—all owned and operated by Wyoming native Shilo Mathill, a lean, energetic young man in his middle thirties. This first day we will put-in at Bennett Peak campground in the foothills, a half-hour drive from Saratoga, and take-out twelve river miles downstream at Treasure Island in the lower ranch meadowlands.

Our guides—Shilo, Todd, and Rob—unload the three fourteen-foot drift boats at the ramp and then busy themselves rigging rods, hunched in their seats, intently tying on leaders and flies while bantering lightly among themselves, already in good-natured competition. We sports mill about on shore, possibly with mild cases of the cocktail flu, reminiscing about earlier trips, still somewhat unaccustomed to being pampered in this fashion. Over the many years of the Annual Fishing Trip we can count on less than one hand the number of times we've hired guides and outfitters. "Remember when we used to tie on our own flies?" someone remarks.

"Yeah, back when we could still see to do it."

Kamloops, British Columbia: July 1975

It's true that right from the beginning there were some years in which all four of us were unable to reach consensus on places and dates. Sometimes only three, or even two, made the trip, but that was enough to keep the tradition alive.

J. D. got married early, D. C. went off to be a sailing bum in the Caribbean for a couple of years, Johann and I moved to distant states—all of which created further logistical problems. But none of us had exactly traditional starter jobs for young men of that era, and we were still at the age where a nonstop cross-country drive in a tiny old sports car was not only quite feasible, but even fun.

This particular year, Johann and I were the sole attendees of the annual fishing trip, and we decided to drive from Colorado to Minnesota lake country in order to fish for bass and pike. From there we wandered north into Canada, hung a left on Highway 1 in Ontario, and drove nonstop through Manitoba, Saskatchewan, Alberta, and on into British Columbia, drinking beer and smoking cigarettes (behavior, by the way, that is not recommended to aspiring young sportsmen), taking turns at the wheel and laughing with sleep-deprived hilarity the entire way. Beyond the fishing, that's what we would remember most about those days—how much we laughed.

In British Columbia, we stayed at a fish camp outside Kamloops. On our first day, we rented a boat and went out on the lake, where we caught a couple of Kamloops rainbow trout. At the end of the day, as we were cleaning our catch at one of the fish tables by the dock, a little girl, maybe ten years old, approached, dragging an enormous trout longer than her arm. "How'd you fellas do?" she asked, peering up at the table where our two little twelve-inchers lay gutted.

"Oh, we caught a couple of real nice ones," Johann said, as we both tried to block the girl's view. "You know, for our first day out anyway . . ."

The little girl dropped her fish on the wood plank walkway; it made a sound like a side of beef hitting the floor. "Can I see 'em?" she asked, moving in for a closer look.

Reluctantly, we held up our trout. "Oh yeah, those are real beauties," said the little girl, politely stifling a laugh. "If you're finished cleaning 'em, could you help me lift mine up on the table?"

Saratoga, Wyoming: Fortieth Reunion Trip

It occurs to us as we are finally seated in our respective boats, one angler in the bow and one in the stern, and the guides push us off from the boat ramp as if we are conquering emperors, that we have been fishing this river together since before any of these young men were born. As the boats spread out on the river, the sounds of oars dipping into the water, line stripping from reels, happy men talking softly, morning birds singing, and the varied tones of the river itself drift out in symphony over the water. "Good lucks" are exchanged, plans made to meet downriver for lunch.

There is always that wonderful sense of promise on the first morning of a fishing trip, and nothing quite delivers on it like the sight of the first fish of the day, in this case a large brown feeding in a back-eddy, his dorsal fin and tail breaking the surface as he rolls lazily.

I am fishing with J. D. out of Shilo's boat today, and, lest there be any confusion on the matter, let me say right off that just because we've been fly fishing for most of our lives does not make any of us experts. This is, admittedly, an old person's observation, but we grew up in a simpler, less technological fly fishing era, an era when our fly boxes were stocked with a few Royal Coachmen in different sizes, a few grasshoppers, a few Adams, a few Light Cahills, and, oh yes, my personal favorite, a few Irresistibles. Sure, we had some of the classic wet flies and streamers in our boxes, as well, and of course, a few nymphs (particularly the perennial favorite Gold Ribbed Hare's Ears), but for the most part, unlike our young guides, we were rather low-tech generalists. Still today, when I pull out some of my old, now mostly vintage, gear at the beginning of the season—my ancient, stained, tattered vest, an old Hardy reel and the Orvis 99 bamboo rod my dad bought me when I was fifteen years old, I'm struck by the fact that it's all begun to re-semble a museum display of grandpa's stuff.

In any case, on this first fish of the day, neither J .D. nor I have quite limbered up our somewhat out-of-practice casting arms (at least that will be our excuse), and perhaps, too, there is the matter of a little first-fish jitters. The trout appears to be taking emerging insects just under the surface, but early on, one—or maybe both of us—lines it with a sloppy cast, putting it down. No matter. Shilo has plenty of experience with hackers and, with a perfect guide's equanimity, he rows us to next run.

North Park, Colorado: July 1978

Somewhere around the mid-seventies I purchased a red 1968 Volkswagen camper and pasted a jumping trout decal on the back. We would park the camper by a favorite creek, pop the top, set up the attachable tent, break out the Coleman stove, and presto: the official movable lodge of the Boys' Annual Fishing Trip. Who needed guides?

Somehow all four of us, and sometimes even additional guests, managed to sleep in the camper and attached tent. One year, camped up on the Michigan River in Colorado's North Park, Johann drew the straw to sleep in the little hammock-like cot that folded out in the poptop. At six feet tall and 180 pounds, he was not, even then, a small man, and the fact that he had drawn the cot had been cause for a good deal of amused chortling among the rest of us. Late the first night, Johann suddenly started howling in his sleep, and began frantically trying to climb down from his perch, the top-heavy camper rocking precariously like a ship in heavy seas.

"Wake up, Johann!" hollered J. D., as we both tried to extricate ourselves from our mummy bags before we capsized, or Johann crushed us in his descent. "You're having a nightmare!"

"Yeah, wake up!" I chimed in. "You're sleepwalking, Johann!"

"I am awake, you fucking morons!" Johann hollered back. "I'm not sleepwalking! I've got a leg cramp! Out of my way!"

Saratoga, Wyoming: Fortieth Reunion Trip

Our drift boats hopscotch down the river. With the water low and warm, the guides have to work particularly hard for fish, and by this point in mid-season Shilo, Todd, and Rob are all lean as whippets from day after day of rowing a bunch of porky sports who've been beefing up on the "Wolf Cut" prime rib.

They have two rods rigged up for each angler—a lighter weight to fish dry flies, a heavier weight for nymphs and streamers. And each rod is rigged with a lead fly and a "dropper"—depending on the line weight, some combination of dries, nymphs, or streamers, with weights and strike indicators where appropriate. In order to find out as quickly as possible where and on what the fish are feeding, generally one angler in the boat fishes one combination of flies, and the other another—thus covering all the bases.

This upper-canyon stretch of the river is studded with rocks and boulders, pocket water of fast riffles and runs, and deep pools on the bends. "See that seam between the fast water and the slower? Drop your fly right in there," Shilo instructs J. D. "Perfect. Now mend your line. Perfect. Okay, now give it the 'twitch of death.' Just as J. D. is executing "the twitch of death," which involves wiggling the rod tip to give the nymph action as it rises, a fat, beautiful, seventeen-inch rainbow nails his fly.

A mixed bag of browns and rainbows follows, caught on everything from tiny trico spinners to nymphs to streamers. If the fishing is not exactly "hot," it is, for this time of year at least, consistent. When things slow down, the guides change flies and add or subtract weights with nearly obsessive attention.

In the meantime, a spectacular array of wildlife greets us along the river—red-tail hawks and ospreys circle overhead, bald eagles roost in the cottonwoods, deer graze on the banks, woodchucks peer down from shallow caves in the canyon walls, beaver swim across the current, and, toward the end of the day, an enormous great horned owl squats on a gravel bar along the river, watching us impassively as we float past.

Saratoga, Wyoming: August 1982

It was the first year we'd ever floated the North Platte, and feeling unusually flush, we decided to break precedent and hire an outfitter for that year's Annual Fishing Trip. Of course, Shilo was only in the third grade at the time and was thus unavailable. Our guide went by the name Big Ed, a stolid blowhard sort of fellow whom we quickly discovered knew little more about fishing this river than we did. Not that the poor fishing was entirely Big Ed's fault; we had come during the dog days of August when the North Platte had gone low and slack and hot. The fish were holed up in the bottom of the deepest pools, and we did not yet understand the river well enough to know how to reach them. Nor did Big Ed appear to have the slightest clue, other than suggesting that we tie on large metallic zonkers and "fish the foam"—the foam being the sudsy stuff that looks like washing machine effluent and forms in the back-eddies of some of the deep pools. It's true that hatching insects get caught in the foam, and that trout frequently feed beneath it, thus safely hidden from avian predators. However, on this particular trip, on the rare occasions when a fish was actually spotted working the foam, Big Ed would holler, "Fish the foam!" Then, being careful not to maneuver us within fly casting range, he would drop the oars, whip out his spin casting rig, kept handily by his side, and plunk a panther martin lure directly on top of the rise, immediately putting the fish down. "Damn, shoulda hooked that one," Big Ed would say, proud of his deadly accuracy with the spin cast rod. "Hit the son-of-a-bitch right on the head, didn't I?"

Saratoga, Wyoming: Fortieth Reunion Trip

After nearly twelve hours on the river this first day, we unlimber our creaky legs at the take-out. One of us complains about tennis elbow from casting all day, another of a sore shoulder. Let's face it: We are not in tiptop fishing condition. Plus, of course, we're older now, and we watch somewhat enviously as the young guides, who have done the real work all day rowing our fat asses down the river, scamper about, securing gear and loading the boats on trailers as if they have energy yet to burn. On the drive back to town in a pair of venerable old Suburbans, plans are made for the next day's fishing.

After showers back at the river cottage, we sit on the deck, having cocktails and trading tales of fish caught and lost during the day. As always happens in the retelling, fifteen-inchers become eighteen-inchers, eighteen-inchers stretch to more than twenty. We tell stories of our own and our boatmates' less-than-stellar casting performances, of impenetrable leader snarls that would have taken us hours to straighten out, but which the guides untangled like magicians. And we laugh.

Saratoga, Wyoming: July 1986

Despite the poor fishing and dicey outfitting that first year on the North Platte, we would come back here regularly over the following years. By the mid-eighties, we began to hold the Annual Fishing Trip at a regular spot—a huge private ranch that sold, by today's standards, ridiculously inexpensive permits to fish better than twenty miles of the river. North of Saratoga, this stretch of the North Platte was an hour's drive off the highway, through a High Plains desert landscape and over a long, tooth-rattling dirt two-track that crossed the Oregon Trail. We pitched camp in a grove of cottonwood trees on the river, gathered firewood, and, if there was still enough light, fished the evening hatch, convening back at camp at dusk for the time-honored tradition of trading fish tales over cocktails while building a fire and prepping and cooking dinner.

Among the prolific wildlife on this lower stretch of the river was a healthy population of rattlesnakes, and no trip went by without at least one close encounter. One morning at dawn while lighting the propane burner to make coffee, D. C. discovered a large rattler curled up beneath the Coleman stove. Another year, Johann left a tent flap open and a rattler made itself at home on his pillow. And once, while standing in the river fighting a fish, the water within an inch of the tops of my waders, I noticed out of the corner of my eye a rattler floating lazily toward me on a direct collision course. I froze in position, solid as a statue, as the snake spotted me just in time to scoot out of my path, arching his head like a snake charmer's pet as he passed, not eighteen inches away, looking me right in the eye, tongue flicking. Far more than tales of individual fish caught or lost, statistics quickly forgotten from one year to the next, these would be the events that would enter the collective lore of the Boys' Annual Fishing Trip.

Saratoga, Wyoming: Fortieth Reunion Trip

On this second day, we are fishing the middle stretch of the river, from Treasure Island, where we took out the day before, to town, a stretch in which the North Platte flows through irrigated hay meadows and private ranchlands. Everyone switches boats and fishing partners this morning, so that in the three days on the river, each of us will fish with all three guides, each of whom have subtly different though no less effective techniques and styles. This prompts D. C., who has over the years always been somewhat more interested in the bird life than he has been in the fishing, to reflect, "You know, I've been fly fishing since I was about fifteen years old and now that I'm over sixty, I think it's about time I learned how to do it right."

North Park, Colorado: September 1996

By the mid-nineties we had settled into our middle forties, and remarkably the Boys' Annual Fishing Trip was still more or less intact. But in that inexplicable phenomenon by which free time in general, and summers in particular, seem to get shorter with each passing year, some years the trip got pushed back into the fall and morphed into the Annual Cast and Blast, or sometimes even well past the fishing season altogether so that it became the Annual Bird Hunting Trip. The old VW camper had been long since retired, and I had upgraded to a 1971 Airstream trailer, which often served as base camp and kitchen commissary for our outings.

The year in question was a "Cast and Blast" trip; in the cool fall mornings we hunted sage grouse in the high desert flats of northern Colorado, or jump-shot snipe along a meandering willow-lined creek. In the afternoons, we fished the tail end of the season in the old streams and ranch ponds of my own home country, where we had been casting our lines now for two decades, and upon which we had always fallen back when we had neither time nor resources for trips further afield.

Though only mid-September, there was already a distinct wintry chill in the air, and in the evenings we lit a fire in the cookstove of my old log cabin. We grilled the day's bag of snipe and/or sage grouse over coals outside and panfried brook trout on the cookstove, while puttering around the kitchen, drinking wine, and squabbling over dinner preparations like little old ladies. And, as always, we laughed.

Saratoga, Wyoming: Fortieth Reunion Trip

From the beginning, eating and drinking well has always been an important element of the Boys' Annual Fishing Trip, and for this reunion we have outdone ourselves: Besides a full assortment of fine beverages, we have brought French cheeses and Italian salamis, home-smoked trout, choice ribeyes, racks of lamb, farm chickens, and home-grown garden vegetables supplied by one of our guests, Steve, who has attended enough of these trips over the years to have become a full charter member.

We settle into our roles as only old friends or old married couples can: I obsessively prep and issue commands, largely ignored, while Johann relaxes on the deck with a glass of scotch and a cigar, and D. C., too, a notorious shirker, drinks a beer, his head buried in a map of the river. J. D., the Grill Maestro, fires up the grill, while our other guest Robo lays out an elegant cheese tray. No Annual Fishing Trip is complete without at least one cooking argument, and this time I (a.k.a. the Grill Nazi) engage the Grill Maestro in an argument ongoing for some forty years now about the correct cooking of the meat. J. D. likes his medium well; I like mine rare.

However, all is quickly forgiven, dinner delicious despite the fact that under my relentless insistence, half the meat is raw. The wine flows and a loud, lively discussion ensues, though tonight we are free of other diners to disturb. And we laugh.

1999 to 2010

By the late 1990s and on into the new millennium, our old pact began to unravel. More moves, divorce, family illness, the death of loved ones, sundry professional and personal obligations, and financial responsibilities: Everyone seemed to be running harder as they entered their fifties, and not getting any further ahead, either. And somewhere along the line, a sea change occurred. Just as it had been assumed for nearly thirty years that the Boys' Annual Fishing Trip would take place, now it gradually gained the status of a relic of our past, something to be remembered in old photo albums. There came a point when we didn't even try to organize it any more, didn't even make the initial phone calls. But then this year, well past the watershed date of July Fourth, long past the time when it might reasonably be expected that four old friends with a collective mountain of life's detritus between them might be able to come to agreement on dates, a phone call was made. "What do you think about trying to put together a last-minute Fortieth Reunion Boys' Annual Fishing Trip?" J. D. asked.

"What's it been," I answered, "four, five years now? I've lost track."

"Something like that."

"Okay, you call D. C., I'll call Johann."

Saratoga, Wyoming: Fortieth Reunion Trip

It is our last day on the river, and we are floating north of town through arid sage flats, past sandy ridges and high buttes towering above the river. It is the beauty of the North Platte that, in three days of fishing, we have floated through three entirely different ecosystems, from the rocky pocket water of the upper foothills to the meadowlands to this high desert stretch. And despite the fact that we are here in August, the fishing has been surprisingly steady. We have all caught (and lost) our share of browns, rainbows, and a few hybrid "cutbows," everything from six to twenty inches long.

This last day in the lower desert stretches will be the slowest of all. But so what? We have already deemed this one of the best ever Boys' Annual Fishing Trips, a combination of fish caught, knowledgeable and companionable guides, beautiful landscapes, incredible wildlife, great food and wine, and, as always, plenty of laughter.

Over dinner our last night we toast the trip, renewing our forty-year-old pact and promising not to let it lapse this time, although, of course, it surely will. "Hey, but when are we going to New Zealand, Argentina, or Chile?" someone asks.

"Yeah, who's going to make that first million bucks so that they can take everyone else?"

We chuckle and shake our heads, remembering the youthful dream that seems as far away now as it did then . . . farther, in fact. We have, all of us, made rather modest middle class livings all these years. But that, too, is okay.

There is, finally, the matter of the Boys' Annual Fishing Trip Official Theme Song, the first stanza of which was composed as a goof many, many years ago around a campfire on this very river . . . yes, possibly alcohol was involved. The plan was that each year on the last night of the trip we would compose a new stanza, until eventually we had an entire song. But despite half-hearted attempts over the years, we never got past that first idiotically lame verse. Now suddenly J. D. breaks into song:

"Pack up the rods, fellas.

Sure has been swell, fellas."

And the rest of us join in: "Let's do it agaaaain nexxxxt yeeeaaar . . ."

And we laugh.

Life Among the Anglish

Kate Fox

I caught my very first trout on a dry fly. Despite my partner's whoop and ear-to-ear grin as he scooped the little ignoramus from the spangled shallows of the Elk River in West Virginia with his 48-inch Brodin ghost net, then held the stunned, speckled youngster in front of me for a shot of what he calls "fish porn," I couldn't for the life of me see what all the fuss was about. And I still can't.

Even after almost five years of wading or floating along beside Bob on the Madison, the Yellow Breeches, the Gallatin, the Au Sable, the Big Hole, the Paradise Valley spring creeks, and the aforementioned (and my favorite) Elk—as such terms as "rise," "epeorus," "water column," "emergers," "headwaters," and the exotic names of dry and wet flies drift around me like cottonwood fluff—I have never felt the electric charge that devoted fly fishermen describe when they hook that elusive adversary. And I doubt I ever will. Having read way too much poetry in my lifetime, I find there's something a little too symbolic and close to home about being caught by your own hunger.

Having said that, though, there are few things that please me more than fly fishing, and for two reasons: It allows me to re-enter the male realm, where I spent much of my childhood, and the rhythm of casting is as inspiring and comforting to me as guitar chords or Shakespeare's "That time of year thou mayst in me behold/when yellow leaves or none or few do hang
. . ." Norman Maclean, in his autumnal novella, *A River Runs Through It,*

Photo by Robert DeMott

Kate Fox releasing a brown trout, Elk River, West Virginia.

begins his tale with "In our family, there was no clean line between religion and fly fishing." In my current family, there appears to be no clean line between metaphor and fly fishing.

When it comes to fishing, I'm no Cathy Beck or April Vokey, but I can make a fair cast. In fact, I must have been born for fly casting, because I remember my father taking my brother and me reel fishing, and casting the line was about the only tolerable thing about the whole endeavor. I had too much empathy for both the worm and the fish to ever rig the line, my Scottish skin blistered almost immediately under the reflection of hot sun on the water, and the algae scumming the edges of the ponds or lakes where we fished was both gelatinous and rank. It was altogether a test of endurance for us all, my father especially, who had no patience with children in the first place and had probably been saddled with us on a Saturday so that my mother could have a well-deserved moment to herself. The day would typically end with my father accusing me of "whacking the water and scaring the fish" because I so loved the sound of the line whizzing off the reel. Half of the time, he would also be digging a barbed hook out of the crown of my brother's head and swearing never to take us anywhere with him again. Ever.

He never made good on that threat, though, and I have him and my brother to thank for making me welcome and privy to the male world and its attractions. My father was a mechanic and junk dealer by day, a musician who played bass and Piedmont blues-style guitar by night. From the time I could walk, I remember following him—once to my detriment, as I followed him down twenty-seven wooden steps in my metal walker because he had failed to latch the child gate across the doorway. He could tear down and reassemble an engine, and I still remember being called upon to retrieve the right socket (standard, not metric, in those days), and the lock-sound the ratchet made as it loosened the bolts. He took me with him when he went across the street to Delbert's Pool Hall and Barber Shop, where the smell of spruce-green cue chalk, Clubmen talc, and bay rum all commingled as the men talked about wheat futures, combine repair, and the pros and cons of the new sprinkler irrigation systems being sold by the Stratton Co-op. I was also taken to the dump, along with my brother, where we learned to shoot rats with a .410 so that we would later be equipped to hunt rabbits, pheasant, antelope, and whitetail deer—or defend ourselves against the occasional rattlesnake—that populated our part of northeastern Colorado.

As with the worm and the fish, I was too tender hearted to become a hunter. But because I was taken along, I became comfortable in the company of men—accustomed to their direct and practical way of assessing the world and their apparent ease with long pauses in the conversation—and they seemed to tolerate me because I didn't throw or run like a girl and didn't threaten to tell on them if they occasionally spit through their teeth or interjected "fuck" between every other syllable.

I first met Bob before fly fishing became the dominant expression of his natural gift for detail. When we became engaged in 1987, he had been fly fishing for three decades, but lately had gotten more heavily into upland bird and duck hunting—so much so that he loaded his own shotgun shells, spent a small fortune on his bird dog, and displayed an entire grouse tail, like a Geisha's fan, in a vase on the fireplace mantel. I joked to my friend Donna that our wedding colors would have to be grouse and teal. His priorities were apparent early on: One of our first dates included a run through the McDonald's drive-thru, where he ordered two Big Macs. *How thoughtful!* I marveled, until he promptly fed one of them to Rosie, the golden retriever in the back seat. I never spoke up, though, and that vignette became kind of a dance pattern for the collapse of our relationship. After three years, we called it quits; Bob moved on to his second wife, who gave him ample reason to pursue fly fishing much more intently, and after twelve years, I moved on to yet another Bob—writer and musician Bob Fox—bringing my total partners named "Bob" to three and establishing my reputation as a "serial Bob" kind of girl.

It would take twenty years for what our friend and fellow angler Craig Nova called "the most romantic story I ever heard" to evolve, proving both that Bob and I have the tenacity of wolverines when it comes to learning from our mistakes and that Craig has a pretty low standard for romance. I had been widowed in 2005 when Bob Fox died of lung cancer six short months after being diagnosed. The following year, a chance encounter with my "former" Bob at Ohio University's Spring Literary Festival led to our getting together and comparing notes on caring for a loved one with cancer, as his father had recently been diagnosed, and Bob was traveling to and from Connecticut to be with him.

After rattling around over a few casual dinners, Bob took the plunge and asked me to accompany him to a literary conference in Salinas, California, a really weird romantic destination unless you happen to hold a doctorate in American literature—which we both do. We had attended several conferences together our first go-round, but this time, there were some distinct differences. First of all, Bob was solicitous, tentative, considerate—not alien traits, by any means, but just noticeably more present and consistent than what I remembered from before. Second, instead of flying back to Ohio with me, Bob escorted me to the San Jose airport, carrying with him some of the most malformed and unwieldy baggage I'd ever seen. As we checked various green satchels and leaf-blower-shaped cases, he explained that he was flying to Bozeman for his annual month of fly fishing. I'd see him again in September.

Thus began a life attuned to the piscatorial calendar. The next year, I would accompany Bob to Montana, but not before we made several trips over to the Elk River near Monterville, West Virginia, where we could walk straight down to the river from Elk Springs Resort, or we could make the greater commitment of driving and then walking over the abandoned railway trestle to the more remote waters of the Slaty Fork. It was there that Bob patiently schooled me in fly casting, explaining that Maclean's father's dictum—"It is an art that is performed on a four-count rhythm between ten and two o'clock"—wasn't quite reliable, because rhythms vary with the caster and releasing at nearer to one o'clock can sometimes shoot the line with greater velocity when that option is needed. He taught me the line would go wherever the tip of the rod pointed, which for me was often right in front of me because, happy-hour person that I am, I would wait until four or five o'clock to halt the rod.

A certified casting instructor, Bob took these lessons seriously, as did I, but having been with me all those years ago, he also knew I didn't like being told what to do—that an impatient "No, you're doing it all wrong," would most likely result in "You are not the boss of me" and an expensive fly rod being launched like a javelin toward his head. We had an unspoken compact: Never once did he raise his voice, or complain about untangling snarled leader and tippet, or balk when I refused to wear a vest that he had so lovingly and carefully outfitted because it made me look like a frontier peddler. In turn, I would not complain of sunburn, mosquito bites, or a hundred other onslaughts wrought by nature on the delicate Templeton skin; or try to climb up his waders when a water snake floated by; or whine about my shoulder after the 142nd cast ended up snarled like a sixties hairdo on a downed log. In that way, side by side in the middle of a fast-running stream, we found our footing and learned to live together. Bob would choose the weight of the rod, rig it up with flies carefully and ditheringly selected from a plethora of metal boxes with tiny hinged compartments—all organized according to stream location and marked with the names of flies. (I remember coming up on Bob at his desk one morning, with boxes, flies, and sticky labels strewn all around him. "This is when you know you have too much time on your hands," he announced solemnly.)

I would then take the rod and cast and cast and cast until the stars finally aligned perfectly, and I would almost feel the line shoot straight out from my shoulder; the fly would land with a light peck on a seam running straight under the undercut bank where a suspicious shadow repositioned itself for a better glimpse at whatever it sees from below. Too often I mended too energetically and scared the fish, or I jerked the rod back with such exhilaration that the trout didn't even have a chance at the hook. And that was fine. I wasn't there to catch fish.

In "Why Fifty Million People Fish," from *Fishing Widows* (1974), Nick Lyons writes:

> There is a curious rumor that fishing is idyllic and pastoral, that it rejuvenates the spirit and excites the blood to high adventure, that it requires high intelligence. Here in the city I often dream of idyllic days, when mayflies, tan against a sinking sun, crowd off

the water, flutter in clouds down the alley of a stream, and the fish make the surface pocked and choppy with their feeding.

But then I remember: my experience has been otherwise.

No one has a more honest and clear-sighted love of fly fishing than Nick; it is to his books I turn to help me understand the peculiar mindset and perspective of an avid fly fisherman, and I have him to thank for reading my first fly fishing article, making editorial improvements, and then recommending possible places to submit. Once in a starry-eyed moment, I mentioned wanting to write an article about the correlation between writing and fly fishing—that a majority of good anglers also appeared to be excellent writers. The founder of Lyons Press and editor of countless books on fly fishing and other outdoor pursuits looked askance at me and replied, "Oh, you might think otherwise if you had read the number of manuscripts that I have." And I have no doubt that the polish and perfection I see demonstrated by some of those writer-anglers I respect might indeed be due to Nick's behind-the-scenes editing.

Though I've never fished with Nick, Bob and I have visited Nick and Mari, his partner in art and life, in New York City and in Woodstock, where Nick's study is practically a fine museum and where Mari has let us wander through the paintings in her studio. In fact, Bob and I celebrated our "recommitment" in 2007 by acquiring four of her paintings for our new house. Nick quipped as we wrapped and packed the stretched and rolled canvases into the car, "You now hold the largest collection of Mari's paintings in the world—except, of course, for us." Had I known sooner that Bob would lead me to Nick and Mari Lyons, I might have been tempted to skip the other Bobs altogether.

For better or worse, we both write poetry. For our friends, it means having to put up with drafts of poems in their email, Christmas poem overkill—one from each of us—in December, gifts of our favorite books of poetry (yawn), and beloved lines quoted when memory and the situation permit ("Suddenly I realize/That if I stepped out of my body I would break/Into blossom . . ."; ". . . like the action of a *wave*, which is *not* water, strictly speaking, but a force that water welcomes and displays. . . ."; "The art of losing isn't hard to master. . . ."). So it's no wonder that a pastime based solely on the length of a line enamors us so: the weight of the line, the resistance, the roll, the viscosity, the sink rate, the taper, the drag, the tension, the strength. Bob fiddles with reels and leaders and tippets, and I watch as he casts, amazed at the perfectly looped line, at the deft way his gaze, his shoulder, his un-broken wrist, and the rod tip all go in the same direction with the same single-minded purpose. The fly hits exactly where he intends; he mends upstream a bit and then begins to gather line in an accordion motion until . . . WHOCK! a trout hits, then almost folds in half in its attempt to wrench away: a perfect description, perhaps, of desire and its aftermath.

I didn't wrench away. The line he used was the strongest I'd ever en-countered: "I promised myself that if you gave me a second chance, I would do anything to keep you." It reminded me of the line my dad used when my mother said she didn't think she loved him enough to marry him. "I'll love you enough for both of us," he said. And the hook was set.

But here, the metaphor begins to unravel. It's here that the definition of the word "angling" becomes slippery, and it's impossible to determine who caught whom. I just know that a line brought us together, and another line, "Till death do us part," foretells how it will end.

Bob is patient, but not delusional. He can tell that I don't share his ob-session with fly fishing, but, dedicated professor that he is, he thinks better instruction is the key. To that end, he has enrolled me in a weekend drift boat workshop in Wyoming and in a crack Orvis fly casting clinic at the Homestead Resort in Virginia . . . both with marginal results. The drift boat workshop was an unmitigated disaster, recounted in "Confessions of a Drift Boat School Dropout." This is what I learned in drift boat school: If you never learn to row, then the only thing left to do in a drift boat is to fish. It was a lesson well worth the registration fee Bob paid to the fine women at Reel Women Fly Fishing Adventures, and to underscore it, I also kept the payment from *Gray's Sporting Journal* for the article.

And though I can't say my skills improved considerably with the fly fishing clinic at the Homestead, I can in no way fault the Orvis-trained guides or the incredible setting. The instructor-student ratio was one-on-

one, I was given my own copy of Tom Rosenbauer's *Orvis Vest Pocket Guide to Leaders, Knots, and Tippets*, I was provided with a crash course in angler entomology, and best of all—since the Cascades Stream had been blown out by three days of hard rain and the Homestead grounds and roads were all flooding—we were allowed to practice our cast in the Homestead's grand ballroom. You have not lived until you have had to untangle your line from a chandelier. Best of all, we were given a discount to stay in one of the most luxurious rooms I have ever seen—and I am including Versailles and the Biltmore Estate in that comparison. I have found that Bob and I look much more presentable when set against such an opulent background. But in spite of my "schooling," I have reconciled myself to being better at casting aspersions and casting about for excuses than at casting for fish.

Recently, I came across Kirk Deeter's *Field & Stream* blog entry entitled "Fly Fishing Should Be Less Manly," in which Deeter states, "I am absolutely convinced that women are born better natural fly fishers than men," and then goes on to mull over the reasons that fly fishing is still such a male-dominated sport—the main one, for him, being the lack of gear designed especially for women. It's true that fly fishing can vie with cigar-smoking or peeing from the back of the boat as the most male-identified pastime, but I seriously doubt that "gear" is holding women back from the sport. A better hypothesis might be the one that Nick Lyons describes in *The Seasonable Angler* (1970) in a hilariously astute essay entitled "Family Interludes," in which Nick, the harried family man, having "engineered my wife into saying, 'A few solid hours of fly-fishing for Dad—poor Dad, who never gets out on the streams anymore because he loves his family so much,'" takes off on a Father's Day family fishing trip that is met with every obstacle imaginable. Resistant wife, bad weather, four unrelenting kids, and inappropriate recreational attire all come together to create a perfect storm of a fishing expedition, about which Nick concludes, "I consider it a holy miracle of the first water that I survived that day."

This is my theory of why there are fewer women anglers: We are more practical than men and we have a lot less money and free time. Provide child care and housecleaning services to women interested in fly fishing, and the

ranks will swell accordingly (Nick captures perfectly the multilevel challenge of fishing with children in tow). Pay women a truly equal wage, and
the pricy gear will naturally follow. I can say this from personal experience
because I have a partner who shoulders all of the cooking in our house and
does at least half of the housecleaning, including all of the yard work. I know
how exceedingly rare this is, and the fact of it is what allows me to pursue an
interest in fly fishing, as well as other interests. It also allows me to give him
over to fly fishing and hunting trips with others without resentment, worry,
or jealousy. Lucky me, though; even after almost five years, he still actually
likes to take me with him.

Despite what Nick says, I still believe that there is some inexplicable link
between writing and fly fishing, some way of perceiving and ordering the
world that lends itself to both pursuits. Maybe the patience of searching for
exactly the right word is analogous to matching the hatch; maybe the natural
reclusiveness and ease with being alone required of writing also lends itself
to remote streams and hours of solitary casting and leaving adequate space
between anglers; even a natural tendency to depression—sometimes self-
medicated with excessive drinking—shows up in both writers and anglers.
I know that part of the reason Bob and I have made such a go of this second
round at a relationship is that we recognize a certain congruence in our per-
sonalities that allows us to accept each other with as much understanding as
we accept ourselves—which on some days is more, some days, less.

I see some of these congruences, too, in Bob's friends and fishing bud-
dies—many of them people in this book with whom we've fished, thanks
to their welcoming a nymph-level angler into their ranks. I have gone back
and read or reread their work and found that their respect for their chosen
craft and absolute precision with the language parallels the same respect and
precision they demonstrate in fly fishing.

Nick may be right; there are probably as many bad angling writers as
bad writing anglers. But in my narrow experience, those people patient and
disciplined enough to become expert anglers almost always have a way with
words. And perhaps no better example is Nick himself, who writes both
pragmatically and metaphorically in *The Seasonable Angler*'s "The Rich Diversity of Spring":

Most often in those early springs of fly fishing, since no one taught me, I learned by necessity. I learned to roll cast one long afternoon on the bushy Amawalk when there were trout rising and no room for a back cast. I learned how to drift a nymph—and appreciate the nymph—one almost frustrating evening near the Beaverkill campsite when the bulges were tails, not lips. I learned to release trout when I saw that taking them indiscriminately would deplete fisting for all time thenceforth. I learned to approximate a hatch when I saw that there is a time for the Hendrickson, the Quill Gordon, the Cahill, the March Brown—that it is not a random but a lawful business.

The eye and mind—and the fish—are ennobled by fly fishing.

Every time I read it, this passage reminds me of Mark Twain's classic essay about two ways of seeing a river, which begins, "Now when I had mastered the language of this water and had come to know every trifling feature that bordered the great river as familiarly as I knew the letters of the alphabet, I had made a valuable acquisition. But I had lost something, too."

Nick, too, often writes about knowledge and experience, about what is gained, what is lost, about nature and its lessons. And the one lesson—on this natural plane, at least—is that it is not a random but a lawful business. And we are ennobled by that knowledge.

My couch potato friend Donna can't fathom what I see in a weekend spent on the Elk River, even though she lives in Beckley, near the New River Gorge, one of the most beautiful places in West Virginia—or the entire United States, for that matter. Like Mari in Nick's essay, she frets about the bugs, the heat, and what she calls the "general ickiness" of the outdoors. Her idea of getting out into nature is to switch from HBO to the Discovery Channel. And I mostly concur with her assessment. But when I think of a late spring afternoon on the Elk, with the sun spangling the water, and Bob standing close behind me with his hand over mine, showing me once again how to "stop" and "stop," while the line whizzes out perfectly to the spot where I intended it to go, I could care less about hooking a fish. I just want this moment, with us together in the middle of this river, to go on forever.

Rivers Owned in the Mind

Charles Gaines

My friend Hughie McDowell and I took a break from fishing around noon and sat on the bank for a sandwich and a few pulls of Glenfiddich from the silver hip flask his wife Knuckles had given him. I couldn't remember ever in my life being happier.

This was in April of 1986. It was my second month-long trip to the trouting moveable feast that is New Zealand and my first visit to the Ngaruroro River, a thirty-minute helicopter flight from Turangi back into the sublime backcountry of the Kaimanawa Mountains of the North Island. I had just cast a #14 Adams to an eight-pound-plus rainbow, who ate the fly and promptly broke me off behind a rock. The Ngaruroro (pronounced "nigh-ru-roara," a sound like waves on a beach) seemed to be a necklace of emeralds separated by diamonds—a thing of ineffable worth that literally filled you with a buoyant and radiant well being while you were on it. I had fallen in love with almost every river I had met thus far in New Zealand, but I adored this one. I said so to Hughie, and he smiled. Hughie was then a *non pareil* trout angler, guide, and fly-tier with a trenchant Irish wit and a poet's soul. On that April day he and I were both drifting a stretch of quiet water in our lives, but just around the corner were some howling Class VI rapids that would spit us out separately a few years later, still afloat but in serious need of the kind of solace Hughie spoke of then after the smile. He tapped his temple and said, "You know, I own this river in my mind. And whenever

Charles Gaines salmon fishing on Grimsa
River, Iceland.

I'm in, say, a bus station in Los Angeles, all I have to do is say its name and
everything is fine."

Both before and after that day with Hughie, I have had occasion to fall
in love with other rivers. Some—like the Test in Hampshire, the Jardine
in northern Australia, the Nolichucky in the Smoky Mountains, the Eg in
Mongolia, the Hatiguanico in Cuba, the Grimsa in Iceland—were unforget-
table one-night stands. With Argentina's Traful and Quebec's Bonaventure,
Bruce's Spring Creek on the South Island, the Zolotaya on the Kola Peninsula, and others, there have been long affairs. And then there are a few, along
with the Ngaruroro, that have gone from my heart into my mind and live
there, summonable to rustling life whenever I call them up.

Though there are countless lakes and flats, shorelines and oceans that I
am devoted to, none of them inhabits me the way these rivers do. Wondering
at this moment why that is, it seems to me to be because it is in the flow of
rivers that fishing most fully becomes the act of self-emptying, giving it its
most meaningful and durable resonance. If intruding yourself into the eating

habits of pea-brained creatures with fins is—as my wife, for one, suspects—a pastime for dull-normals, it is also one easily flogged into a sort of sublime obsession by the saintly eagerness to unite yourself with something only blind belief can assure you exists. What is called patience in fishing is really just the ongoing belief that the next entreaty you cast into the void (or the one after that, or the next) will connect you to the 2,000-pound black marlin, the five-foot Atlantic salmon, the ten-pound farm pond bass of your dreams. That is why, for many of us, the nut of the thing is that moment when the fly stops, before the line begins to rise—the moment (perhaps not unlike our last) of being tight to something unmanifest, but imminently about to be.

I would aver that those moments are what keep coots like myself stringing up rods year after year in out-of-the-way places long after the urgings of blood-lust, competition, and hang-it-on-the-wall frenzy have subsided. In fact, it is the very absence of those demands, in the "poof!" disappearance of one's self, that best defines such moments and that can make one's angling in them seem sacerdotal. For me, this flushing out of the stridencies of self-awareness, and the subliminal, soul-feeding connections that flushing out engenders, happens most often amid the phantasmagoria of rivers. And on a few of those, it has happened so fully and vividly for me that, like Hughie McDowell, I can conjure myself out of any old Los Angeles bus station I find myself in simply by speaking their names.

My sons Latham and Shelby, then twelve and seven, and I are in my green canoe, "The Recruitment," named for a magazine short story that paid for it. It is a late summer afternoon thirty-four years ago. We have put in the Blackwater River below Webster, New Hampshire, and are floating to the bridge by the Pope's house in Hopkinton. In the bow, Latham is using my father's old Abercrombie & Fitch glass fly rod to drop a big yellow popper up close to the bushy bank and into the fishy-looking pockets made by branches of trees that have fallen into the river. Shelby sits on the carrying thwart, flipping a Rapala, and I paddle in the stern, easing the canoe around the slow, snaking meanders of the exquisite little river. Its banks are only thirty feet apart in places, its water the color of espresso, and each turn opens a new, small tableau—turtles on a log, a pair of wood ducks exploding off the water—and a new picture-perfect smallmouth hole.

There may be, somewhere, a lovelier woodland smallmouth river than the Blackwater, but I have not met it. It is a petite, raven-haired vamp of bottomless eyes and few words, who can sulk one day when a three-hour float might produce four or five fish on the top (where we always fish), and stand your hair on end the next—on a day like today.

Shelby is fighting a three-pound smallmouth up to the gunwale, the ultra-light spinning rod bowed almost into a full circle. As I lean over to lip the fish, I see a bigger one porpoise and crash Latham's popper, its thick furrowing back black and bronze. We will release a dozen and keep two for supper before the bridge in Hopkinton, and we will never, in five years of floating the river, see another person fishing it.

The river I hope runs through it for me on the other side will look something like the two-and-a-half-mile stretch of the Ruby near Alder, Montana, that belonged to my friends Craig and Martha Woodson: dainty and purling, its banks a manicured comeliness of cottonwoods, its amber water dimpled with brown trout rises. And those browns are some of the feistiest and most agreeable anywhere: beautifully colored, acrobatic, quick-to-take fish that are found exactly where they are supposed to be, in the river's textbook runs, seams, and pools.

The Ruby is a river to make you feel like Izaak Walton—a wet-wading and bank-fishing river that invites long, meditative breaks for reverie, a pipe, good conversation. It is also a river that can toss out epiphanies like flowers from a basket.

My young friends Ethan and Jason have their first day of trout fishing just under their belts. Yesterday they floated a hot stretch of the Madison, lobbing nymphs under indicators into runs beside the boat and letting them float there until their guide told them to strike. They caught lots of fish that way and decided they were naturals at the trout fishing game. Today we are on the Woodson's Ruby—a different kettle of fish. I walk the banks with them, looking for rises, then they take turns blowing the fish. They can't reach it or line it, they drag over it, they hook willows and each other. But the Ruby is, as ever, open-hearted and generous, and maybe even a little smitten with my boys. First one then the other finally gets everything right, releases his first dry-fly trout, and looks up at me from knee-deep in the Ruby with a fresh, thrilled, lifetime scar of comprehension on his face.

Midway through our second morning at Jack Cooper's Minipi Camp in Labrador, our guide, Rol Burry, ran Perry Munro and me all the way down the lake to a little river running between Minipi and Anne Marie Lakes and named for the latter. It was late August. Rol thought the spawners might be well up the river, and no one had been there for more than a year. It might be good, he said. If it was not, all we would have wasted would be an afternoon, and he believed Perry and I would like the river.

We ate lunch at the outlet pool of the Anne Marie, then started rock-hopping upstream under a hot sun. The river was ice-clear, cold and fast, with needle-nosed spruces crowding its banks. We saw wolf tracks and fresh moose droppings, and the utter wildness of the place felt like testing the blade of a sharp knife against your thumb. In every pool were brook trout in their metaphysically beautiful rust, cream, and olive spawning colors. Perry and I leapfrogged each other from pool to pool, casting big, barbless Muddlers. After only two or three pools, we began to wonder out loud, among all the laughter and shouting, if this would ruin us for any fishing ever, anywhere again.

We didn't leave the Anne Marie until nine that night for the hour-and-a-half moonlit run back to camp, and leaving then was a wrench for me that bordered on panic. We had fished maybe three or four miles up the river, about half of its length. In my notebook, I had recorded what we caught, knowing it was a catch I would not want to be inexact about: sixty to seventy-five fish of a pound and under; fourteen between one and three pounds; and eleven glorious brookies over three—including two over seven, and five more over five.

On our hurried scramble back downstream to the boat, Rol said that, as far as he knew, no one had ever fished all the way up to Anne Marie Lake, and he let that thought hang in the darkening air.

We called it *la vie de truite*—jumping into the freezing, muscular current and letting it carry us downstream to whatever sandbar we had pulled into to camp for the night. Jerome and "Spinnerbait" Carlson and I would participate in this trout's life every evening after we had built a fire we could run back to, submerging ourselves in the glacial blue Mulchatna and facing upstream while we were whipped downriver. We almost lost Spinnerbait like that one night—and had to go retrieve him in one of the four rafts in which the eight of us were presumptuously floating that grizzly-wild, killer-beauty of a river—but the ritual seemed to make more comprehensible the outsized, preternaturally fit rainbows we were catching all day.

It was supposed to be a guided trip, but wasn't. The wine, the ribeyes, the lobster tails had gone missing, along with more basic items such as bread and lettuce. But we had about forty pounds of moose jerky and the fish we caught. We had maybe the only six straight days of clear, warm, windless weather in Alaskan history, exhilarating company, *la vie de truite,* and the experience of the river itself, which was pushed from being just attention-worthy into riveting by the outfitter having forgotten the maps along with the mayo, and by our having only a vague idea of where we would have to meet the float planes that would carry us out.

I have never concentrated on a river so hard for so long. Right now, in a writing shack in Nova Scotia, I can see the Mulchatna's bodybuilder curves; its giant, pale rainbows; the grizzly tracks in the sand at one of our campsites; the eagles feeding on rotten sockeyes. And I can see to this day, as if I had been caught there and later released, the chill, blue, hazardous rush of its current over my open eyes.

Now as much home water to me as the Blackwater once was, Nova Scotia's Margaree is a river that escapes the forest to flow through widening, sunlit pasturelands and meadows on its way to the sea. And I believe I love the river as passionately as I do partially because I feel associated with it in that escape—sunnier, more exposed, and closer to the sea myself than I was on the Blackwater.

I also love it because it was my dues-paying river in salmon fishing. No form of fly fishing is more difficult to do well or looks easier than that for

Atlantic Salmon—the things the real experts do differently than you being hidden, or at least hard to identify, until you are one of them. My cherry day at it was on the Margaree almost thirty years ago. I bought a few flies at a convenience store, waded into that flirting little hussy, and expected my first salmon within ten casts.

In fact, my first salmon from the Margaree came well over 10,000 casts and almost a decade later. Over that time, the river gave me the gate in every way imaginable. But it always did so like Katharine Hepburn turning down Spencer Tracy for a date early into one of their movies—firmly, but leaving the door open for later with a wink. Like Spencer, I kept coming back, and the first time I finally scored on the Margaree, with a bright henfish of about eight pounds, is one of the river moments I summon most often.

Since that moment I have had flings with more than a seemly number of salmon rivers here and there, but it is the Margaree I always come home to. She is more beautiful to me than ever now, with her gay, skirt-gathering pace, her meadow pools, the way she stretches like a cat just before the sea. She is far more generous to me, too, these days. And yet every fish I catch there is one I'd like to tell Hughie McDowell about, sitting together on the bank of the Ngaruroro or some other river owned in the mind.

A Line in Still-Cold Water

Bruce Guernsey

It's the last day of November, and all month at my desk I've been casting for steelhead on a coastal creek in southern Oregon. Tomorrow, I'll flip the page of my Trout Unlimited 2010 calendar and, just like that, I'll be nymphing for browns on DePuy Spring Creek. Time and place, place and time: These two great coordinates of human life are particularly profound for a fly fisher. TU's calendar is my proof: Each month is a place, and each place, the rush of white water, the dark of a pool.

But if we could keep time in a bottle, or a flask, perhaps, maybe we could find a way to slow it down, as I inadvertently did a few years ago in a season of endless springs . . .

I'm standing waist-deep in a limestone stream in county Sutherland, Scotland, outside Durness, the most northwesterly village on the British mainland. Five miles from here, forever growling at the cliffs that hold these highlands up, is the frigid north Atlantic. Under my 3mm neoprene waders I have on some polypro long johns, and over them, a new pair of polar-tech sweats. Need I say more? "Hoot man!"—it's cold outside. It's also the fifteenth of June.

A few days before, I was double-hauling against an endless wind on brackish Loch Stenness, one of the many Precambrian lakes laden with

**Bruce Guernsey as
Darth Wader, with
landlocked salmon,
Maine.**

browns on the Orkney Islands. To set the human clock back forever is but a short plane ride to Kirkwall, the capital of the island of "Mainland," as it's called—an oxymoron like the omnipresent past that's everywhere on the Orkneys, from the Ring of Brodgar to the lost village of Skara Brae, preserved for thousands of years under the drifting sands.

Treeless, the Orkneys have no salmon, either, a refreshing change from the legalistic hub-bub of private beats and "keep-out" posts that dot the Tweed and Spey. But the waters are thick with broad-bellied "finnock," though seldom were they interested in the contemporary patterns I'd brought along. Instead, through a continual drizzle, I was slowly stripping a tandem of Greenwell's Glory, Leadwing Coachman, and one very tattered Silver Doctor—soft-hackled wets I'd picked up locally that were first fished, I'm sure, by Sir Izaak himself.

From the briny bedrock under my feet, I could see a half-mile west to freshwater Harry, and on the promontory between that loch and this, rising wraith-like through the mist, stand the eternal Stones of Stenness, their mysterious circular pattern a Neolithic reminder of my mayfly of a life. How symbolic, this smaller version of Stonehenge, here between the salt and the fresh, between 5,000 years ago and now.

But "now"—what's that, I ask?

In May, just a month ago, I was wearing the same early-spring gear while matching the hatch in New Hampshire. The birches were then that lovely lime-green their leaves have when budding. Dandelions dotted the pasture I'd hiked across like flocks of migrating goldfinches. Swift in the Newfound River where they tumbled in from the lake at ice-out, the land-locked salmon hungered, flashing like mica. My fly? A March Brown, it was still that early.

Ahh, the Newfound, where as a boy of eight or nine, under a yellow "Fly Fishing Only" sign, I once snuck a worm on a hook and proudly brought home my first trout still flopping at the end of a string, its slime and gurgling sounds, very like a chub. The Newfound—where a man, my age now, still wades waist-deep in my memory, rolling a line across the watery pines, dark green, as I watch on the bank in wonder. The Newfound, born of that lake once known as Pasquaney, where centuries before the French explorer checked his traps and paddled toward Canada; where the last Pasquaney once knelt to the water and stared at the color of his skin.

But home for me *now* is East-Central Illinois, and April is its coolest month, the temperature perfect for getting outside to search for the first morels under a blush of redbuds. After a long winter's nap, the big-time farmers are just waking up, checking their seeds and herbicides. The little-time gardeners like me have peas and lettuce in the rich soil already. Smell the sweet air!—it's time to head to Missouri, its spring creeks ripe with rainbows.

"Go west, young man," and I go, across the Big Muddy from the Illinois plains, then into the Ozarks from Rolla to Dora, on single-lane roads like "PP" and "H." Not one has a name, as if they belong to a time before words, these ancestral footpaths nearly as old as the North Fork itself, fed by springs that keep it trout-cold all year: the Blue, the Hicks, the Double, each day pumping millions of gallons of pure Perrier into the river on its way to Arkansas and the Gulf. I tie on a Black Ghost, roll it across the current, the arc of my line the sweep of a swallow. Blessed be the big wild 'bow that hammers the dart of my streamer and takes it down.

A year of three Aprils this has been for me. A line in still-cold water, my talisman for time. I confess I didn't plan my year this way, but will my future ones, if I can. There comes the dreaded moment in our lives when the reflection in that windless pool on the bathroom wall shows a fringe of ice around the ears, a bit of snow in the beard that sends a chill.

But the search for eternity lies deeper than hair dye. By our symbols we are known and know ourselves. If the whack of bats and balls in Florida each March gives hope for baseball fans, why not a timeless year for fishermen, too? An endless series of springs. A forever of opening days.

Imagine Adam naked in the Garden naming the mayflies, if there were any. *Ephemera* would be as far from his lexicon as would its Greek origin, "day." Instead, searching for Eden in chest-high waders, we fly fishers have human names like Quill Gordon or Griffith's Gnat for the flies we use, the mortals who first tied them reborn each season. But to cast an Adams in April is to hear the tick of time, that thump at the wrist.

"What is nature," wondered Thoreau, "unless there is an eventful human life passing within her?" When we find ourselves scoffing at the brief diurnal life of a *stenacron interpunctatum*—better known for its human name, Light Cahill—shouldn't we be packing our gear instead, hurrying to catch the plane that wings us high and then spins us down to yet another spring, each twenty-four-hour year?

And just like that, where has the time gone here on DePuy Spring Creek? I look up and see that somehow tomorrow is December 21st, the shortest day of the year, with a full moon besides. And soon, perhaps, along with my new TU calendar, will come a January thaw, and a few pools and rapids later, I'll wake to hear the red-wings, singing, like the rest of us:

"From Rain"

Around Easter
when the woods are still pastel
and the air is damp with April,
I need to feel the river's pull
I haven't felt all winter,
this longing I have for water
that leads me here where cutbanks swell
with spring from every hill,
mysterious, maternal,
and into that fullness I enter,

myself no longer
but one with the shifting gravel,
and, like these mayflies hatching in swirls,
from rain I've come, will spinning fall
as once and ever,

both son and father,
eternal and ephemeral
while the current around me curls
and I lift my line in this ritual
of rod and river, of Adam and lover.

Older Fishing

Jim Harrison

Ultimately, I don't know exactly what happened in my angling life. I had gone fly fishing for thirty-three years in Montana and then we moved there, so now I'm up to forty-two. Mind you, this doesn't mean I'm good at it. Good and bad aren't part of my fishing lexicon. The good can be part of the quality of light that day, or the quality of bread, salami, or hot peppers at lunch. The bad can be weather under forty degrees, which I no longer care for. In the last nine years, having moved from Michigan to Montana to be closer to our daughters and grandchildren, I've upped my fishing to sixty to seventy days per season. I have reams of empty paper containing what I've forgotten. Certain good fish are only remembered when I pass the landscape on the river where I caught them. We can be as honest as we can be and still be hopelessly dishonest. Our private mythologies have a soft stranglehold on us. Fishing elicits tales and fables from us from another time. The first three minutes of hooking a 250-pound striped marlin on a fly rod is all grunts and howls, but then so is a two-pound brook trout in a beaver pond or a five-pound brown in a river.

Trout fishing as an obsession frequently begins in childhood. At five I was fishing for bluegills with worms, surviving all day on saltines and pickled baloney eaten with worm-dirty hands. Late in the season we'd catch big bluegills with hoppers and crickets. Starting at about seven, when I lost an eye in an accident, my dad would take me along trout fishing on weekends

Jim Harrison at the oars, with Dan Lahren and his French Brittany, Jacques. Big Hole River, Montana.

on the Pine or Pere Marquette. I had to fish a big hole on the Pine all day so I wouldn't get lost. I clearly remember the day sixty-five years ago that I caught five suckers and three brown trout. I threw the suckers back, but the brown trout, freshly caught and glistening, seemed the most beautiful creatures in the world: They were miracles and still are.

In the past year I've come upon an ancient Eastern text called "The Logic of Birds and Fishes," and this has come close to dominating my mind. I've lived actively with birds and fish all my life and know, once my mind has released them to live with me moment to moment, they treat us similarly and their behavior is equally evasive. You don't completely plan out fishing. It's something you do when you don't absolutely have to do something else. As a child in the summer, fishing or fishing-related activities, such as walking far enough to see where a stream comes from, filled up all available time. This is not good logic unless you think of trout fishing as the ultimate good, a position it has not attained in most places.

Fishing does what poet Tom Crawford said about bird watching: It removes the weight of what we're not. It's a little embarrassing to admit how much I fish to someone from Maryland who has saved his or her money for a week's trip and a guide. So I mildly blunder along in this obsession, obtusely serene about good and bad days. I've caught a number of large brown trout in recent years, but then I should by fishing that many days. I fish with a guide out of a drift boat because it's very hard to wade at age seventy-three, and my vision is so poor it's nearly impossible to tie on a fly, though I've been slow, indeed, to admit it. Since my mid-forties, on most occasions I've had to have a guide tie on a small fly. The primary thing that led me to guides and skiffs was that I started falling in my late forties if I looked straight down. After getting wet and sometimes very cold a couple of dozen times, I gave up. Another factor in those days was that I was in a bad way mentally from Hollywood film work, and if I didn't book a guide for three solid weeks on our Montana vacation, I might go sulk in a shed.

My faulty vision provides a good break for guides though, because they get to fish half the time. Since age five when we got our first wood rowboat, a lumbering five-seater, for thirty-five bucks, I've had a passion for rowing that comes close to fishing. I mean fishing is still primary, but if it's with a dry fly and the fly begins to disappear from the field of my vision, I'm eager to row for an hour or so before I resume. Plus I like watching a fine, accomplished angler at work.

And with rowing there's the added advantage of studying the landscape and current. Coming from an agricultural family I never lost my interest in farming and ranching practices. As a county ag agent my father judged cattle at county fairs, and, having accompanied him, I look at all cattle with a critical eye. I can say "long back, short neck, thin withers," then move on to varieties of birds. Rowing enables me to bird watch, and though I've been at it sixty-five years, since the second grade, I'm limited because of my poor vision. Last late May there were five different warblers on the Big Hole River, but though only twenty feet away they would appear and then disappear as if on a timer, the same as the leader in my fingers. *There it is. There it isn't.* One stormy day on the Big Hole we saw seventy-two colorful Western tanagers in a riverine thicket at migratory time. Another day there were thousands of swallows coursing above the stream, and I counted fifty common nighthawks—a wing brushed my face—plus we caught thirty-five brown trout, adding to the birding pleasures during a nearly two-hour-long hatch, an occasion a trout fisherman lives for. However, it hasn't happened again, so back to the logic of fishes and birds.

Fishing is a mental feast. I've written three dozen books and know that literature can be a truly nasty business. Now that I don't bird hunt much anymore, except for doves and a few quail along the Mexican border where we live in the winter, fishing is the activity that ensures my sanity. Simply thinking about fishing during a recent eighty-day plague of shingles was helpful. I early determined that my wobbly casting arm was okay by throwing the ball daily to Zil, my Scottish Labrador. I couldn't write because of the minute-by-minute painful spasms, but I could remember minutely.

Early in my career I did a goodly amount of sporting journalism, which now seems to have been problematical. At first it was wonderful because I was broke, and writing general sporting pieces for *Sports Illustrated* paid well, but then I branched out into magazines more of the trade variety—the hook and shot type where my possible novelist talents could be less well displayed. I have to be able to include the human community, possibly Native history, geology, geography, and the natural world. So I don't do it any more because such magazines don't exist. I recently read an article about an area I love on a back road between Vera Cruz and the capitol, Jalapa, in Mexico. There's a truly mighty river there, and orchids hanging from phone wires. This article mentioned nothing except Americans and their paddleboats and the imminence of drowning—not a bad idea—and nothing about the inhabitants, the jaguars, the monkey-eating eagles. What's the point? It would be okay if they were writing about old stuff, like baseball or football. We've been told quite enough about Wrigley Field, but kayaks in a remote place do not simply exist in the void of fast water. There might be something to be said about minimalist trout magazines that exist for trout obsessives, like stamp journals do for collectors.

Which is to say that I suppose I'm ultimately interested in not missing anything in the fishing experience. Sometimes it's a matter of taste. No one seems to know more about trout than Tom Rosenbauer of Orvis, whose book about nymph fishing is marvelous. However, I don't care for nymph fishing, and there's currently a shameful reliance on it by guides and their miserable casters who drag their nymphs and pink indicators from the back of drift boats. Of course the guides just want clients to catch fish, even though there's no negotiable difference between that method and perch and bluegill fishing with bobbers. Even my uncles knew that—they used to net grasshoppers and chum with a gallon of hoppers, which is more effective than nymphing.

In a new Everyman's Library anthology of fishing poems, *The Art of Angling* (2011), there is a snippet from Ted Leeson's *The Habit of Rivers* (1994) that seized my attention: "The craft of angling is the catching of fish, but the art of angling is receptiveness to those connections, the art of letting one thing lead to another until, if only locally and momentarily, you realized some small completeness."

This reminded me that what has urged on and freed my mind most for my fiction and poetry has been walking, solo driving trips, and fishing. We all know the openness and relief of launching a skiff or stepping in the shallows in our waders for a day of fishing. "Free at last, free at last, thank God almighty, I'm free at last." Your professional and personal problems drift away into the smell and sound of the river, into the peopleless landscape that neutralizes the poison. The connections that Leeson speaks of come together by themselves in this state of grace. This metaphor of wholeness enacts itself because you are being drawn into the patterns and rhythms of the natural world. As Octavio Paz said, "Beyond ourselves,/on the frontier of being and becoming,/a life more alive claims us."

On a more ordinary level, older fishing is gentler, far less aggressive and far less acquisitive. One day it was so gentle I fell asleep while rowing; sometimes a nap is needed. I'm not just there to willy-nilly jerk a fish out of the water. One day I got stuck trying to sleep on the floor wrapped around the seat in the bow of the boat. We take our time in May and June with long walks to find mushrooms for dinner. Another advantage for a guide is that I never want more than a five- or six-hour day, which enables my guide to fish again. When we're done for the day on the Big Hole he continues down to the Beaverhead for late afternoon or evening fishing.

In terms of competition and aggression I have a truly ugly memory. Back when I was working with Guy de la Valdène on his tarpon movie, we were shooting down at the marina in Key West when a flotilla of Miami anglers pulled up. They were a club and had caught hundreds of fish, which they slammed on protruding spikes on a huge board. I got out of there fast, in a state of nausea, so I don't know what they did with the fish. I have never seen anything so repellently at odds with the spirit of angling. Even catch and re-lease contests seem questionable to me, but there are those who are addicted to them. But then I've always been irked by fishing in a barrel. At one time I caught so many browns on consecutive casts of salmon flies that I was irritated that I didn't get to make a decent cast. I like the idea that you can catch a lot of small brook trout for breakfast, but it's hard to catch big ones. Once I caught a three pounder on a small Muddler Minnow after a two-hour walk into a beaver pond, but we didn't get out until 4:00 AM. We didn't have any alcohol along, which was unwise indeed. So is stepping into a runway in a beaver pond.

On the lighter side, when fishing there are my lunches. In the past I was also the food columnist for *Esquire,* and I have written a book about cuisine called *The Raw and the Cooked,* which is to say I'm peculiar and particular. You can't buy a good sandwich in Livingston early enough in the morning, though there's now an excellent wine and cheese store, the Gourmet Cellar. I'm lucky to have Mario Batali and his father Armandino as friends so that I'm never short on fine salamis. Some reasonably good bread and fine French, Italian, or Spanish cheeses and some Louisiana hot peppers and we're in good shape. I don't drink while fishing because of Type 2 diabetes and a consequent tendency to fall asleep. We're fortunate when we fish the Big Hole or Missouri because we can stop at Butte's Front Street Deli and get all the food we need for fishing in one stop. If the weather is coldish I take a good bottle of wine, always French, for the last hour. Good food while fishing is a morale factor. If you eat shit you feel shitty, to paraphrase Roderick Haig-Brown.

Anglers can be divided into many different groups depending on their interests, but each one believes it is completely right. I am relatively modest, being so often wrong. As a young man I was a very aggressive wader in the Manistee and the Pine in northern Michigan. After I went under five times I became more cautious, and then my dad's secretary's husband was swept under a logjam and drowned, and the caution stuck. The Manistee has some huge mayfly hatches on broad stretches of river, but that wasn't worth death when Marilyn Monroe was still alive.

When I started thinking about fishing as one grows older, I assumed that it wasn't that much different, but frankly it is, because you are a different human being. I no longer fish the Middle Branch of the Ontonagon from five in the morning until eleven at night. That was when I was home from a far away job and the odor of a trout stream was highest on my ethyl index. It still is.

Most of the changes in older fishing are toward simplification. I must own twenty-five trout rods but only use two. I think I know where they are. Of the thousands of flies I've owned I doubt if I ever use more than a half dozen a day. In short, I don't want to be best. If someone asked me to go bluegill fishing with worms I'd say yes. In the Yucatan I speculated on catching an anaconda with a fly but no one was eager. When you're on free time, limitations are not acceptable. Several times I've nearly drowned trying to get at an unapproachable trout that was wrapped on some underwater snag. You do this not out of wisdom. As you tumble down the rapids you wonder if you are getting your cigarettes wet, not if you're drowning.

Of course, every angler has his idiosyncrasies and prejudices. My current big "no" is to over-large fish. Years ago, a few miles north of Zihuatanejo, I caught a thirty-two-pound Pacific snook on a fly rod after a rainstorm had broken through a dune, draining a swamp and lagoon. I was utterly exhausted in the ninety-degree heat. An hour later I fought a fifty-five-pound Roosterfish for an hour, and the mate lost his leader grab; I had another full hour fighting the fish to a point of nausea. I would bet any amount that if a Rooster lived in a strong river current, no one would catch one over twenty pounds on a fly rod.

The worst experience I ever had with big fish was out of Anconcito, Ecuador, with Guy de la Valdène. We were there trying to imitate Lee Wulff and Woody Sexton catching striped marlin on a fly rod. In addition, Guy was trying to get the first underwater photos of fighting marlin. To my peril I fought the fish on a boat rod with a lot of effort, not wanting Guy to get speared in the process of my catching four striped marlin about 200 pounds each and a Pacific sail of about 180 pounds. I was so tired that evening I couldn't even go to the obligatory strip club, but had to sit around the hotel pool watching twenty Braniff stewardesses flit around like June bugs in their bikinis. Fortunately I fell asleep before I could do anything.

The first year in Zihuatanejo we killed several big fish through stress by using too-light size twelve tarpon rods, so that the next year Scott Rods built me a fifteen-weight, which was heavy enough to handle anything without killing fish. Much more fun was casting to schools of bonito, which resemble steelhead for power. There is also the question of at what point fishing should be punishment. One very hot morning in Key West, we jumped a half dozen tarpon and had to go back in because we had drunk up all our drinking water. Another time in Montana we got caught in a snowstorm a mile from takeout for more than an hour, and never has a launch site looked more attractive.

Frankly I don't think of myself as a particularly good angler. My path has been wide but not very distinguished. Once on the Yellowstone River I jerked a streamer fly away from a big brown because I thought it was an otter. My boat comrades hid their faces in shame. A continually exciting thing in the Yellowstone is the chance of catching a large brown; for me, it is my obsessive fish, though a permit is a close second. I must have cast to permit for fifteen years before I finally got one on with a woman guide, Linda Drake. I carelessly bulldogged the fish I was so desperate. A hot school came over a reef line, and a couple dozen fish competed for the fly, when in all the past years before that we didn't have a fly that worked. I have had this happen with tarpon when you see nothing for hours, then finally off Bow Channel near Loggerhead you see a school and every single fish goes for your fly. It is best described as a depth charge.

I suspect that a sense of humor is the most valuable thing an angler can own. Don't bother blowing your horn. A few years back I caught two browns and a rainbow that were all five pounds plus. I thought, *That's not bad,* but then it occurred to me that those successes occurred over a period of sixty-five days of fishing, so I refused to allow myself bragging rights. Just keep fishing and you'll have a nice life. Once I was so stunned seeing a whale surface fifty feet away in the Humboldt Current of South America I forgot to throw the fly at gamefish we were chasing. But you're better off fishing a bit on the goofy side. It isn't a tragedy to lose your footing and slide down the bank into the water and under the boat. My fishing partner, Dan Lahren, is small but massively strong and jerked me out pronto.

You must develop your own ethic and record book. I don't count the five-pound brook trout I caught on a Muddler on a small Canadian lake because I was asleep in the boat when it hooked itself. In early May we used to fish the mouths of creeks on Lake Michigan in Leelanau County where smelt had gathered. The smelt drew in steelhead and browns, but mostly lake trout, in quantity into only two or three feet of water. That was food fishing at its best, but sometimes if it wasn't frigid I'd use one of the Leon Martuch System 8 lines and a big blue-and-white streamer. One night on this outfit I caught a fifteen pounder, which I thought was an Atlantic salmon until a friend, who is an expert, said it was a brown trout with its color leached out by the waters of Lake Michigan. It was hard to tell the difference. To me it's still not a "real" brown, though he was a big boy and I was lucky I could beach him.

You can easily minimize a sport by coming at it with too sharp an angle in the manner of a technocrat. Fishing, however, is a slow grower. You start in your youth and slowly progress to the full meaning of what you experience. Day after day your memories accrete and the fish gather and seem to own their splendor. You are living in the background movie of their lives. Since they exist comfortably within their habitat, you return to the river and think how naturally the river is also your metaphor. Who is good at fishing and who not so good doesn't generate a proper metaphor.

I'm still at it. At my age I occasionally think I'll cack on the water, but then, it's a better place to go than anywhere else.

In the Company
of Men (Redux)

Pam Houston

When I look back on my life here at the half-century mark, I tally up five books, sixty-eight countries, a dozen excellent dogs, a handful of misbehaved horses, and a hell of a lot of men who fly fish. Which gives me pause. My father spent not one night of his life in a tent or a sleeping bag, didn't own a pair of jeans, would not have had the first idea how to make a campfire, and did not once take me fishing. Both of my grandfathers passed away before I was born, and I was an only child with no older brothers to teach me to hold a BB gun or cast a spinner. My mother caught a sailfish once off the coast of Florida, years before she had me, but it was a publicity stunt for an off-Broadway play she was in, and she barely stopped puking long enough to smile for the cameras next to the big shiny fish the crewman of the fishing boat had hauled up on the winch. Even Martha Washington, the babysitter/ nanny figure without whom God knows what would have happened to me; the one who taught me to read and say "please" and "thank you" and hold open doors for my elders; the one who took me to the boardwalk and let me go on anything I liked, the one who played Parcheesi with me for hours and hours and helped me make forts under the card tables with sheets—even Martha never took me fishing.

And yet, how many long late summer afternoons have I spent watching the sun glint off the surface of the upper Rio Grande, or the lower Frasier, or

Pam Houston

any number of the several Platte Rivers in the world, or creeks that are sometimes named Fish, and sometimes named Rock, and sometimes named Deer, while the man I love writes poetry in the air with his leader. There's a hatch of caddis flies around his baseball cap, and the whole afternoon seems to hold its breath in that moment of grace that is out of time and some kind of magic, when he casts his line forward and sets it down on the mercuried surface of the river like a kiss. A lot of afternoons, is the answer.

"You fish," Greg, the fly fisherman I've been hanging around with for the last five years, says now, reading this over my shoulder. And it is true, I do. On any of those afternoons you would have found me in the water, too, if you had gotten there early enough, before I got bored, or decided I wanted to take a picture of the late blooming Indian Paintbrush in the elongating light, or collect river stones in the shapes of animals, or read one of the three books I have in my backpack just in case Greg got into some monster rainbows and decided to stay in the river till dark.

I have dedicated a lot of my life to learning how to do the things I saw the men I loved doing, especially in the out of doors. I worked as a white water river guide back when only a few outfitters hired women. I worked as a Dall sheep hunting guide in Alaska, where women guides were even more scarce. I've trekked in the Himalayas solo and skied with the Air Force in Jackson Hole and ridden my bicycle alone from Maine to Vancouver and half way back, but if I were to call myself a fly fisherman, it would make me a flat out fraud. I go out on the river of an afternoon, not to catch fish, but for the pleasure of watching my man.

For what is more irresistible than to watch your man hard at what he loves? What is more loveable than a man who knows how to be quiet with the river? How beautiful a thing it is to watch big freckled hands tie tiny tiny knots of line around bits of fuzz and feathers. How hopeful to watch him land the fish, and how infinitely more so to watch the care with which he removes the hook and puts it back.

I have always loved poetic, outdoorsy, melancholy men, which, as you know, if you are holding this book in your hands, can often be found chest-wader deep in trout streams. And maybe it all goes back to my first time fly fishing and what happened after midnight in a frigid stream in northern Michigan. I wrote what follows here a long time ago—nearly twenty years—but I will never write an account of fly fishing that means more to me than this one, and I am pleased to see it surface in this book.

I can't remember the last time I envied a man, or, in fact, if I ever have. I have loved men, hated them, befriended them, taken care of them, and all too often compromised my sense of self for them, but I don't think I have ever looked at a man and actually coveted something his maleness gave him. And yet envy was at least one of the surprising things I felt last spring when I found myself standing armpit deep in a freshwater stream at 2:00 AM, near Interlochen, Michigan, fly casting for steelhead with a bunch of male poets.

Winters are long in northern Michigan, and dark and frozen. Spring is late and wet and full of spirit-breaking storms. The landscape is primarily forest and water and has not been tamed like most of the Midwest. Both the wildness and the hardship show on the faces of the people who choose to live there.

When a man named Jack Driscoll first calls and invites me to Interlochen, he tells me about the Academy, a place where talented high school students from forty-one states and fifteen countries are given a lot of time to develop their art. Although he makes it clear that I will be expected to read from my fiction and talk to the students about my craft, every other time we speak on the phone all he really wants to talk about is fishing.

For all the time I spend outdoors, I am not much of a fisherman. And fly fishing, like all religions, is something I respect but don't particularly understand. If Jack bothers to ask me if I want to go fishing, I will say yes. I have always said yes, and, as a result, the shape of my life has been a long series of man-inspired adventures, and I have gone tripping along behind those men, full of strength and will and only a half-baked kind of competence, my goal being not to excel, but to simply keep up with them, to not become a problem, to be a good sport. It is a childhood thing (I was my father's only son), and I laugh at all the places this particular insecurity has taken me: sheep hunting in Alaska, helicopter skiing in Montana, cliff diving in the Bahamas, ice climbing in the Yukon territory. Mostly I have outgrown the need to impress men in this fashion; in the adventures I take these days, I make the rules. But, as my trip to Michigan draws nearer, I feel a familiar and demented excitement to be back at the mercy of a bunch of lunatic outdoorsmen, a stubborn novice with something older than time to prove.

I fly up to Traverse City on what the woman at the United Express counter calls the "big" plane, a twin-engine that bumps between thunderstorms and patches of dense fog for an hour before skidding to a stop on a bleak and rainy runway surrounded by leafless April woods.

I am greeted by what looks like a small committee of fit and weathered middle-aged men. Their names are Jack Driscoll, Mike Delp, Nick Bozanic, and Doug Stanton. Their books are titled after the landscape that dominates their lives, collections of poetry called Under the Influence of Water, The Long Drive Home, and Over the Graves of Horses, and Jack's award-winning collection of stories, Wanting Only to Be Heard. They fight over my luggage, hand me snacks and sodas and beers, and all but carry me to the car on the wave of their enthusiasm.

"Weather's been good," Mike says, by way of a greeting. "The lake ice is breaking."

"It's a real late run for the steelhead," Doug says. "You're just in time."

"Any minute now, any minute now," Jack says, his mind full of the long dark bodies of fish in the river, and then, "You've got a reading in forty-five minutes, then a dinner that should be over by ten, the president of the local community college wants to meet you. At midnight, we fish."

By 12:25 am I am dressed in my long underwear, Jack's camouflage sweat clothes, Mike's neoprene liners, Doug's waders, and Nick's hat. I look like the Michelin tire man, the waders so big and stiff I can barely put one foot in front of the other. We pile into Mike's Montero, rods and reels jangling in the back. Jack and Mike and Doug and I. Nick, each man has told me (privately, in a quiet, apprehensive voice), is recovering from bursitis and a divorce, and for one or another of those reasons, he will not fish this year.

No one asks me if I'm tired, nor do I ask them. These men have had nine months of winter to catch up on their sleep, cabin fever reflecting in their eyes like exclamations. The steelhead will start running soon, maybe tonight, and there is no question about where they should be.

It takes almost an hour to get to the river with what I quickly understand is an obligatory stop at the Sunoco in the tiny town of Honor for day-old doughnuts and Coca Cola and banter with the cashier. Along the way we listen to what Mike and Jack say is their latest road tape, three Greg Brown songs recorded over and over to fill a ninety-minute drive. "Gonna meet you after midnight," say the lyrics repeatedly, "at the Dream Café."

The rotating sign on the Honor State Bank says 1:51 am and twenty-two degrees. The men have bet on what the temperature will be. They have also bet on how many cars we will pass on the two-lane highway, how many deer we will see in the woods between Mike's house and the bridge, if it will snow or rain, and, if so, how hard (hardness gauged by comparison with other nights' fishing). Doug wins the temperature bet, closest without going over, at twenty-one degrees.

The betting is all part of a long conversational rap among them, a rap that moves from Mike's last fish to Jack's latest fiction to concern for Nick and his lost house to the girl at the Sunoco to an in-unison sing-along to their favorite Greg Brown lyrics. The whole conversation is less like speaking, really, and more like singing a song they've spent years and years of these cold spring nights together learning, nights anybody anywhere else in the world would call winter, nights filled with an expectation that can only be called boyish and shadowed by too much of the grown-up knowledge that can ultimately defeat men.

Sometimes they remember I am there; sometimes they forget I am a woman. I feel, in those moments, like I've gone undercover, like I've been granted security clearance to a rare and private work of art. And though I have always believed that women bond faster, tighter, deeper than men could ever dream of, there is something simple and pure between these men, a connection so thick and dense and timeless that I am fascinated, and jealous, and humbled, all at the same time.

"Shit," Jack says, "Look at 'em all." We have come finally out of the woods and to a bridge no longer than the width of the two-lane roadway. As impossible as it is for me to believe, at 2:00 am the gravel areas on both sides of the bridge are lined with pickups, a counterculture of night stalkers, two and three trucks deep. I can see by the posture of the men who line the bridge and look gloomily over the edge that they do not teach poetry at

Interlochen Arts Academy. One of them staggers toward the truck, reeling drunk. A boy of nine or ten, dressed all in camouflage, tries to steady him from behind.

"They ain't here yet," the old man says, an edge in his voice like desperation. "It may be they just ain't coming."

"They'll be here," Jack says, easing himself out of the Montero and steering the man away from the broken piece of bridge railing. "It's been a long winter for everybody," Jack says, almost cooing, and the old man drunkenly, solemnly nods. Mike pulls me out of the truck and hands me a flashlight. We creep to the edge of the bridge and peer over. "Just on for a second and off," he whispers. Even to me it is unmistakable; the flashlight illuminates a long, dark shape already half under the pylon. "Don't say anything," Mike mouths to me soundlessly. Jack leaves the oldtimer to sleep in his car and joins us. Mike holds up one finger and Jack nods. "We'll go downstream," Jack says after some consideration. "Nobody's gonna do any good here."

We drive downriver while Mike points out all the sights as if we can see them—a place called the Toilet Hole, where Doug and Nick got lucky, the place Mike got his car stuck so bad that four-wheel drive couldn't help him, the place Jack caught last year's biggest fish. We can see the headlights of people who are smelt-dipping out where the river empties into the lake, and a red and white channel marker lit up and looming in the darkness, its base still caked with lake ice and snow.

We drop Doug off at his favorite hole near the mouth of the river, drive back upstream a few hundred yards, park the Montero, and step out into the night. "It's a little bit of a walk from here," Mike says, "And the mud's pretty deep." It is impossible for me to imagine how I will move my stiff and padded legs through deep mud, how, at twenty-two degrees, I will step into that swift and icy river, much less stand in it for a couple of hours. I can't imagine how, with all these clothes and pitch dark around me, I'll be able to cast my fly with anything resembling grace. Two steps away from the truck and already I feel the suction. The mud we are walking in ranges from mid-calf to mid-thigh deep. I'm following Jack like a puppy, trying to walk where he walks, step where he steps. I get warm with the effort, and a little careless, and suddenly there's nothing beneath me and I'm in watery mud up to my waist. Mike and Jack, each on one arm, pull me out so fast it seems like part of the choreography.

"Let's try to cross the river," says Jack, and before I can even brace for the cold, we are in it, thigh . . . hip . . . waist deep, and I feel the rush of the current tug me toward Lake Michigan. "One foot in front of the other," Jack says. "The hole's right in front of you; when you're ready, go ahead and cast."

I lift the rod uneasily into the night, close my eyes, and try to remember how they did it in *A River Runs Through It*, and then bring it down too fast and too hard with an ungraceful splat. "Let out a little more line," Jack says, so gently it's like he's talking to himself. A few more splats, a little more line, and I am making casts that aren't embarrassing. Jack moves without speaking to help Mike with a snarl in his line. "This is your night, Delp," Jack says, his shadowy form floating away from me, a dark and legless ghost.

What in the world are you doing here? a voice giggles up from inside me, and the answers sweep past me, too fast to catch: because I can't turn down a challenge, because my father wanted a boy, because touching this wildness is the best way I know to undermine sadness, because of the thin shimmery line I am seeing between the dark river and the even darker sky.

Soon I stop thinking about being washed to Lake Michigan. I marvel at how warm I am in the waders, so warm and buoyant that I forget myself from time to time and dip some unprotected part of me, my hand or my elbow, into the icy water. A deer crackles sticks in the forest across the river; an angry beaver slaps his tail. In whispers we take turns identifying the constellations—Ursa Major, Draco, Cassiopeia, Mars, and Jupiter—and murmur at the infrequent but lovely falling stars. When we are quiet, I can hear a faint crashing—constant, reverberant—sounding in the dark for all the world like the heartbeat of the Earth. "Lake Michigan coming over the breakwater," Jack says to my unasked question. "There must be a big wind on the other side."

My fishing is steadily improving: every fifth or seventh cast hangs a long time in the air and falls lightly, almost without sound.

"You know," Jack says, "there aren't too many people who could come out here like this and not hook themselves or me or the shoreline . . . isn't that right Delp?" Mike murmurs in agreement, and my head swells with ridiculously disproportionate pride. The constellations disappear, and a light snow begins falling.

"God, I love the weather," Mike says, his voice a mixture of sarcasm and sincerity, and for a while there is only the whisper of the line and the flies.

"Fish!" Jack shouts suddenly. "Fish on the line!" I am startled almost out of my footing, as if I've forgotten what we've come here for, as if the silence of the night and the rhythm of the flies hitting the water have become reason enough. We reel in our lines and watch Jack land his fish. It is long and thin and its speckled belly gleams silver as it thrashes in the tiny beam of the flashlight. Jack looks at us helplessly, delighted by his luck and yet wishing, simultaneously, that it had been me who caught the fish, wishing even harder, I can see, that it had been Mike.

We fish a little longer, but now there's no need to stay. The spell has been broken; the first steelhead has been caught in its journey up the Platte.

"Let's wade down river a little," Jack says, when we've reeled in our lines, "to try to avoid the mud." I take short rapid breaths as we move through the water. "This part is deep," Jack says. "Take it slow."

The water creeps up my chest and into my armpits; I'm walking, weightless, through a dark and watery dream. For a moment there is nothing but my forward momentum and the lift of water under the soles of my boots that keep me from going under. Then I feel the bank rise suddenly beneath my feet.

"No problem," I say, just before my foot slips and I do go under, head and all into the icy current. I thrash my arms toward shore, and Jack grabs me. "Better get you home," he says, as the cold I've ignored for hours moves through my body with logarithmic speed. "You've gotta meet students in a couple of hours." Back at the truck Doug is curled under a blanket like a dog.

The next day Jack sleeps while Mike makes sure I meet my classes. The students are bright, skeptical, interested. My head buzzes with the heat of the all-nighter, a darkness, like the river dark, threatening to close in. Mike and I drink bad machine coffee in one of the tunnels that connects the English Department to the other school buildings, tunnels to keep the students from getting lost in the storms that bring the blowing snow.

"It's hard to explain how much I love these guys," Mike says suddenly, as if I've asked him. "I don't know what I'd do without what we have."

The cement walls of this poor excuse for a lounge move in on us like the weather, and this poet who more resembles a wrestler looks for a moment as if he might cry. It is late in the evening. I have met three classes, talked to at least thirty students, given another reading, signed books in Traverse City, and, as part of an orgy of a pot luck, cooked elk steaks, rare, on the grill. Mike, in his other favorite role of D. J., plays one moody song after another on the stereo: John Prine, John Gorka, and early Bonnie Raitt. We are all a little high from the good food and tequila. Mike's ten-year-old daughter Jamie and Jack dance cheek-to-cheek in their socks on the living room floor.

"So are we gonna do it?" Jack says when the song ends, a sparkle in his eye that says the river is always in him, whether he's standing in it or not. This fish and fiction marathon is in its thirty-eighth hour, and I have moved beyond tired now to some new level of consciousness.

I have spent too much of my life proving I can be one of the guys, never saying uncle, never admitting I'm tired, or hurting, or cold. Tonight I am all three, but the thing that makes me nod my head and say *yes*, I want to go back again and stand in that icy river, has nothing, for a change, to do with my father, or my childhood, or all the things in the world I need to prove. It is the potent and honest feeling between these men that I covet, that I can't miss an opportunity to be close to. I have stumbled, somehow, onto this rare pack of animals who know I am there and have decided, anyway, to let me watch them at their dance. I want to memorize their movements. I want to take these river nights home with me for the times when the darkness is even heavier than it is in this Michigan sky.

A flurry of rubber and neoprene, and we're back inside the Montero. Greg Brown is singing the song about the laughing river. "This is your night, Delp," Jack says, "I can feel it." Around the next bend will be Honor's scattered lights.

Moving Water

Michael Keaton

My dad shot the head off a turkey with a rifle from 150 feet at the Montour Run Sportsman's Club turkey shoot raffle in 1956. About an hour and a half later, he stubbed out a Winston, set down a pony bottle of Duquesne beer on a picnic table, picked up a .22, and shot a bat out of the air as it circled the bulb of a nearby streetlight. My dad could shoot.

I'm a pretty decent shot myself and I probably couldn't shoot a bat *into* the air if you folded up its wings and shoved it down the barrel of my twenty-gauge.

Membership of the Montour Run Sportsman's Club was made up of mill workers, railroad men, mechanics, farmers, and numbers runners. Italians, Poles, Germans—sons of immigrants. Men in hats, white short sleeve shirts, who smoked cigars, drank beer, and swore. As it applied to some of its members, the word "sportsman" in the title was probably a stretch. My father, who always taught us good sportsmanship, didn't quite fit that mold.

Montour Run itself ran slow and bath-tub cool past the sportsman's club, its banks holding deep shades of orange left over from strip mine deposits. Andrew Montour himself was a half-European and half-Oneida Indian who served as a scout and interpreter of four languages during the French and Indian War, and the idea of something as exotic as Indians fighting alongside and, in Montour's case, against Frenchmen in these western

120

Photo courtesy of Michael Keaton

Michael Keaton with steelhead, British Columbia.

Pennsylvania woods filled me with excitement. You're talking about a kid with a big imagination, and so something like this was just more coal being shoveled into an already blazing furnace.

The creek flowed under a narrow two-lane county bridge about a mile down from the club. I have always been drawn to moving water, and most summer mornings between the ages of nine and twelve I could be found sitting on the big, cool, mossy stone abutments of that bridge holding my hardware-store Zebco fishing rod, with a packed lunch at my side. And those smells. Sweet humid air, honeysuckle, creosote off the railroad ties of an old railroad bed fill my sense memory to this day, but what really transports me is the water. Staring into the water. Moving water. Water just clean enough to hold a reasonable population of bluegills, suckers, catfish, and the occasional carp. I can still feel that tap-tap of a bluegill as it sabotaged my night-crawler, nipping away at it right up to the bend in my Eagle Claw hook, then swimming away. Watching that dunk of my bobber when a catfish ate. This is what thirty years later my boy would call "plain fishin." Plain fishin' to this five-year-old was anything that didn't require a fly rod. Plain fishin' was sinking a Hare's Ear nymph or a Trude from the end of the monofilament line of his own Zebco rod. The beginning of the end of my own plain fishin' occurred after staring at on old photograph of my grandfather standing on a rock with a cane rod working a fly through a pool in the middle of a Pennsylvania trout stream. He was wearing rubber boots, a wool sports coat, and a smile. If Pennsylvania fly fishing was Christianity, to me he looked like Jesus.

It was a few years after staring at that photograph of my trout fishing grandfather that I took the money from cutting Mrs. Story's lawn and, with the help of my dad, bought a $60 fly rod and a $34 Mitchell reel, once again from a hardware store. It should be noted that Mrs. Story was generous enough to bump me up from $3 to a whopping $3.25 to cut about an acre of grass while tallying about seven yellow jacket stings per summer. I caught my first trout on a fly under a bridge in King's Creek in West Virginia, not forty-five minutes from Montour Creek. A thirteen-inch hatchery-born, planted rainbow. Over the years since then, I've become a decent angler. Self-taught and along the way generously schooled by world-class anglers, I've fished in more than a dozen countries. I've waded miles of Caribbean flats, watched the miracle of a tarpon leaping over and over again 100 yards away from the end of my line—dinosaur on a stick. I've been dropped off in the Patagonia wilderness and caught brown trout that have never seen a fly. I've stalked permit with the desperate look of a junkie at five o'clock in the morning wandering the Cabrini Green projects. I've stood slack jawed while a chrome-bright steelhead streaked back to the Pacific after a thirty-minute rodeo that left me standing there with my rod in my hand, rain dripping off my hood, and that dumb "wha' happened?" look on my face. I was left feeling like I had to lie down or check into what my friend calls the "nervous hospital." I am blessed and grateful for these experiences, and they all started on those little Pennsylvania streams.

I would get to see these creeks and rivers once I reached the legal hunting age during deer hunting trips with my dad and brothers. Crossing steel bridges over those pretty streams, I would press my nose to the side window and then crane my neck as they got farther from view. Moving water.

In the fall of 1963 the U.S. Army sent my brother to Okinawa, my oldest brother was starting a career in banking, and my brother Paul was struggling through his college finals. Me, I was going deer hunting on opening day with my dad. Alone. When you are one of seven, time alone with one of your parents is a rare thing. A cherished thing.

We crossed the beautiful Clarion River as evening set in and turned up a little gravel driveway that led to a small, two-story wood-frame house wearing the inviting glow of a front porch light. It was owned by two very perfumed little old ladies who rented out rooms to hunters. And we were hunters. It was warm and clean. A good thing, too, because as we climbed the comfortingly creaky stairs and entered our room, it began to rain. It rained for three days. We laid out our boots, gloves, long underwear, and wool hunting coats that would absorb enough water over the next two-and-a-half days to add at least another four to five pounds to my already too big, hand-me-down attire. We climbed into the double bed, just big enough for an adult and one kid who still was one of the smaller guys in his class. He turned off the light and, after the standard adjustments before settling in for a night's sleep—pillow positioning , throat clearing, blanket negotiating—my dad, who was meticulous, ran his hand through his thinning hair—hair that grew thinner and thinner as more of us were brought into the world. I remember how he smelled. Like a man. Like a working man. He smelled like Old Spice and work. We lay there. Some seconds went by and we discussed our strategy for tomorrow, the rain, etc. I threw in a token expression of what a tough break it was the brothers couldn't make it, and then after some seconds we talked about the good fortune of finding a place after not making proper arrangements, as it turned out to be just the two of us and not a party of four or five.

Then we discussed the thing we were both thinking. Normally, during our hunting trips we'd be staying in a rough-and-tumble hunting camp with a bunch of rough-and-tumble hunters or in a cheap motel, or even sleeping in the car for a couple of hours if we left early enough not to need a room the night before opening day. All the other guys we knew were doing just that, and more than likely all the guys we didn't know were, too. It's hunting. We're hunters. It's what's done. We acknowledged and accepted that we were deviating from the norm and bedding down in a very welcoming, dry, warm, and inviting guest house. A guest house that had pink wallpaper, nice lamps, clean furniture, and a cooked breakfast courtesy of two sweet little gals who were flush with what my mom used to call "rouge." Secure in our masculinity, we accepted our situation and closed our eyes for some good old manly shuteye. We lay there in the silence with only the sound of the steady rain drumming on the roof. I waited. I waited a little more. *Now,* I thought. *Drop it now.* "Dad?" "Yeah?" "Maybe we shouldn't mention where we stayed to the other guys when we see them." I waited. My mom was Irish. Laughter to her was as easy as breathing. My dad had just enough Scottish blood running through him that he wasn't exactly prone to mirth. I waited some more. I could feel the smile on his face grow without having to see it. Then a laugh. Pause. Another—this time bigger. Longer. Silence. "Good idea." He rolled over with his back to me. Pause. Then the mattress softly shook, and I could hear one more laugh from the other side of the bed before he fell asleep. *Nailed it.* Irony, situation, timed and delivered with the precision of a surgeon, if I do say so myself. I lay there with a smile on my face that you couldn't have erased with a jackhammer. I felt like a prizefighter. I felt like a gunslinger. I lay there. Smiling. Rain on the roof.

I would spend the next two-and-a-half days walking through the rolling mountains of Pennsylvania, cold and soaked to the bone. I would miss a fairly easy shot at a seven-point buck that looked at me after the fact with a look on his face that kind of said "you're kidding, right?" before calmly trotting away. Missed with the punkin' ball slug from a .410 shotgun that rests in my gun closet today. Didn't mind at all.

Some years pass and I'm thirty-seven years old, and I'm crossing the sweet little river that winds through my ranch with my own little boy on my back, his arms wrapped around my neck, his chin on my shoulder, face next to mine. Trust. We climb up the bank and I put him down. As the sun sets, we walk across a hayfield, his little hand in my left hand and my fly rod in my right. Headed home. As we walk across that field with the porch light of our house glowing in the distance, I think my chest will explode with gratitude and joy. If you're doing it right, the longer you live, the more you become just who you really are. When you've been fortunate, unless you're flat out stupid—and some would say the jury is still out when it comes to me—your gratitude should grow in direct proportion to your years.

We eat our dinner. We read our books. I kiss his forehead goodnight. He smells like grass and air and purity. Sometimes I miss plain fishin.' Sometimes I miss my dad.

Sourdough Down

Greg Keeler

I'm going to walk across the street and catch a trout. I don't need to ask my neighbors if I can fish from their back yard, though I'm sure they would be happy to oblige—as long as I don't trample a garden or snag a cat on a back-cast. No, I'll just cross the footbridge at the end of the street and fish from Bogart Park on the other side of Sourdough Creek. I've refrained from doing this for years because I believed the local myth that only kids under twelve are allowed to fish in the Bozeman city limits. It took me three decades of living here on Lindley Place to find out that the rule is just etiquette, not law.

It was August and I was at the farmer's market in the Bogart Pavilion when, over stands of Swiss chard, parsnips, and handmade jewelry, I saw a college girl with a fly rod catch a big flopping brook trout, maybe fourteen inches, by the roots of a cottonwood across the stream from our neighbors' garden.

"Nice one," I said. "I thought only kids were allowed to fish here."

"You still believe that crap?" said the girl, conking the brookie on the head with a stick and laying it on the grass beside her. "Have you ever seen it in writing?"

"Well, no, but . . ."

Photo by Greg Keeler

Greg Keeler fishing the lower Gallatin River, Montana.

"Neither have I. Only problem here is you can't false cast to dry out your fly without snagging a kid." She gestured toward the playground directly behind her then blew on her Adams, slathered it with Gink, dangled it down the same run, and hauled out a ten-inch rainbow, which she promptly conked and put in a plastic grocery bag with the brookie.

"That ought to about do it," she said, breaking down her rod and slipping it into its case. "Now all I need to do is wander over and buy me some of those fresh snow peas and new potatoes, then it's dinner for two."

"Some lucky guy, I suppose?" I said.

"No," she said, "no guy, just Madonna." She pointed her rod case at a golden retriever tied to a tree by the playground. "She eats what I can't. I had a guy once, but I wound up having to eat what he couldn't. That's no way to live, unless you're a dog. Right, Madonna?"

Madonna sat up on her hind legs, panting over her paws.

"Don't be such a whore," said the girl. "You'll get your trout."

These several years later, I still haven't tried my luck in the neighborhood trout stream. Maybe I made up the twelve-and-under-kid thing in my head because I thought that fishing near my house might be something like crapping my nest. It felt fine to watch the Gink girl and Madonna wander off to eat a couple of the locals for dinner, but for me it's more complicated.

For one thing, a friend had to tell me that this whole drainage, from the Gallatin Range down to the Missouri, used to be beaver dams; that if I were to dig down far enough in my yard, I would come to a layer of yellowish clay and sediment made from a few thousand years of beaver-chewed alder and willow; that cutthroat trout were eating caddis flies for eons in beaver ponds that ran over, under, around, and through this place where I'm sitting typing this on my computer.

Furthermore, it's hard to live by a stream for thirty-something years without getting attached to it, perhaps in an unhealthy way. For example, about thirty years ago my younger son saved his friend from freezing to death in it. They were both around six and were playing in the snow by the footbridge down the street when the friend slipped on the bank and broke through an ice shelf. My son grabbed him by the snowsuit and dragged him out. After we chiseled them out of their snowsuits, my wife and I contemplated spanking them for playing near the bridge but wound up giving them a warm bath and hot chocolate.

A few years after that, I was standing approximately where the Gink girl caught her trout, trying to abet Peter Fonda's son Justin's fledgling career in film and television by pretending to catch a large sucker out of the creek. A couple of Justin's fellow F&TV classmates knelt by the water clutching reflector screens while Justin held the video camera and I imparted words of wisdom about catching suckers on a fly rod using French fries for bait. I clearly remember squeezing ketchup from a packet onto the hooked French fry while bemoaning it as a poor substitute for special sauce and expounding on the finicky habits of Sourdough Creek suckers.

Of course the segment was a total fraud (as were many TV fishing shows in those days), because the sucker I was supposed to catch in the video was swimming in a Coleman cooler just out of camera range and had, in truth, been caught on worms about a mile downstream near the old slaughterhouse by the Bozeman stockyards.

As a mentor, I was a total flop that day because the sky kept clouding up and we couldn't get enough light, so by the time I put the sucker on the hook and pretended to catch it, it was just a stiff slab of stink. We didn't even bother with taping my rendition of a song I had written especially for the occasion:

I had fished in many waters,
And many a mile I'd trod
The day I caught the sucker
Twice as big as God.

Its lips were like an inner tube,
Its scales like a disease.
Its smell was somewhere in between
Adidas and bad cheese.

I know, I know, the lyrics are a stretch, though perhaps not as much as these from my truly bad opus, "Das Valdiz," that I wrote soon thereafter and that Gary Snyder spruced up for page fifteen of his book, *The Practice of the Wild* (1990):

Vat's dat dark ting in der vater?
Is it not an oil soaked otter?

Maybe the ultimate excuse for not fishing in the neighborhood stream came in the late eighties when a poet friend from Grass Valley, California, visited me with his son. The poet said the kid could fly fish, and he looked like he could pass for twelve, so I took him and his dad across the street, expecting to spend a lot of time helping him tie on his flies and improve on his cast.

When we got to the stream, I reached for his rod and said, "The trees and current in here are a little tricky. Let me show . . ."

"That's okay," said the kid. "I think I can handle it."

An hour or so later, he had caught and released two or three dozen trout, roll-casting in some dense brush upstream from the park with a Trude pattern he had tied. I was thinking, *Where does this little sumbitch get off pillaging my neighborhood trout?* But I said, "Dang, who could have guessed there were so many fish in here?"

"Wanna try it?" said the kid, offering me his rod.

"Uh, no thanks," I said, imagining myself tangled in shrubs with the kid offering advice. "The stream's off limits to adults."

Snyder once told me that, when he was in Australia talking about tribes to tribal people, a man was driving him through the countryside and rattling off stories faster than an auctioneer. It turned out that, in its travels, his tribe had a tradition of telling a story about each important "dreaming place" as they walked past it, and with the advent of cars (trucks in his case), the storyteller had to talk faster than the voice in an ad describing the side effects of an antidepressant just to keep up with the stories of places they passed.

Fortunately, I'm on paper here, so fast or slow won't matter much as I take you through some personal dreaming places, down from Sourdough and down from these innocent non-fishing stories of what I thought was a children's stream, to the more adult waters of the East Gallatin then the Gallatin then the Missouri—waters and stories that grow darker and more troubled as they descend through the miles and years.

I suppose my own extended childhood ends where Sourdough joins Bridger and Rocky Creek to form the East Gallatin at the edge of town. That's where, back in 1994, I used to catch and keep a few trout on Prince Nymphs as part of a futile ruse to convince my wife that I was fishing instead of spending the rest of the afternoon with another woman.

Tracing the horrors that transpired as a result of that deception requires me to backtrack upstream to Bogart Park, where a man who eventually tried to poison me threw my briefcase into the water. He was a great angler and wrote a definitive book on fly fishing in Argentina, but he was stalking a woman I was trying to protect, so he started stalking me. In his several attempts to terrorize me and my wife, with whom I was attempting to reconcile, he broke into my pickup, took my briefcase, and, in a desperate attempt to ruin my career as an English professor at Montana State University, threw it in Sourdough Creek near the footbridge, staining those pure waters with ink and worse.

To complete that story, I'll have to drive you twenty miles downstream then take a quick jog over to the West Gallatin and a nearby bridge on the old highway that crosses some railroad tracks just east of Manhattan. It is a new bridge, because in the summer of 1997 the angler/stalker committed suicide when he drove his car through the concrete railing of the old one and plunged to the tracks below while he fled the highway patrol, who were enforcing a restraining order filed by the aforementioned woman.

But let's forego the rest of these costs of infidelity and backtrack to 1980 and a little ways down from the mouth of Sourdough to the first bridge that crosses the East Gallatin headwaters. That's one of the few places Richard Brautigan and I wound up fishing instead of drinking. I took him there because: 1) it wasn't far from a bar; and 2) I had noticed that the bridge was buzzing with caddis flies when a dozen or so plastered themselves on my windshield as I drove down from Bridger Canyon the previous evening.

That was the outing where I realized Richard was no average fly fisherman because he caught and released more trout in less time than the poet's boy would catch them on Sourdough a decade later. The time was necessarily less because the landowner showed up and ran Richard and me off of his place, even though Richard made an eloquent plea in our defense.

"But we're *releasing* them," said Richard. "It's almost as if we aren't even *here*."

"But you *are* here," said the land owner, "and I want you gone."

Richard, of course, found a way to exact revenge on me for taking him to a posted stream, but I can't remember what it was because, over the years, he exacted so much revenge on me, most of which was in good fun—as is evident in this letter he wrote me:

Tokyo, June 7, 1983

Dear ⌒,

I hope this letter reaches you before you reach England. Maybe I wrote to you . . . maybe I didn't about giving my address to Scoop and Brad. Please do. And,

also about that money you owe me . . . just kidding.
There's nothing like a good hearty laugh
HO!
HO!
HO!

Love,
Richard

A mile or so downstream from that posted bridge, after Bridger, Rocky, and Sourdough Creek form the East Gallatin, is the bridge where David Behr and I launched his new mini-canoe in the early spring of 1990 for an ill-fated attempt at a fishing trip. The mini-canoe was a product of David's obsession with gear, an obsession for which he was nicknamed Gearman. Back then, he was my neighbor from across the alley (with its substratum of old beaver dams), a budding entrepreneur who had decided to make me and my fishing music his hobby, so he got me a segment, *Salmon Fly Guy,* on ESPN's *Great American Outdoors,* as well as arranging for me to be a warm-up act for John Prine when he toured through Bozeman.

This particular canoe trip was ill fated because the East Gallatin is small and crammed with car-body rip-rap and log jams. Maybe a quarter-mile downstream, our canoe got sucked under a log jam. Fortunately, that stretch of river isn't deep enough to drown a person, but I remember David standing in the shallows with his dripping cell phone (they were enormous back then), in a panic because he couldn't check out metal prices on the commodities exchange. He probably lost $1,000 worth of gear that day, but we dried ourselves off as best we could, along with what was left of his stuff, and continued fishing. We even caught a few rainbows before we took out at the Riverside Country Club a few miles downstream.

David replaced that gear many times over and continued making me his hobby for the next eighteen years. When he wasn't running his business or gallivanting around the Gulf and the Caribbean with his fishing partner, Tony Fotopoulos, looking for tarpon, bonefish, and permit, he built a web site called *Troutball* for my music and compiled a CD of my songs with the same title. He made me the mascot of the annual Whitefish Roundup on the rivers near Carbondale, Colorado. He even hired my older son, Christopher, as a techie and paid him well for years.

But, as I said before this narrative reached the mouth of Sourdough Creek, the waters grow darker and more troubled as they descend—much more troubled than a drenched cell phone. As many readers know, the revenge that Richard Brautigan exacted upon his friends grew less and less fun, until he finally retreated to his home in Bolinas, California, in the fall of 1984 and shot himself. Not so many readers know that in the spring of 2008, David Behr climbed into a treehouse he had built for his kids in his back yard in Basalt, Colorado, where he had moved a couple of years after our canoe trip, and shot himself.

I haven't even descended beyond Manhattan on the Gallatin without confronting the pain of adultery and three suicides, so I'm loathe to start another story any farther down than the bridge where David and I launched the canoe, but it's hard to avoid the house on the East Gallatin next to that bridge, the house where my friends, Sam and Carolyn Rogers, lived for years. Sam was a chemistry professor at MSU, and Carolyn was in charge of the vegetable section at a local supermarket. Richard used to call their small stretch of the East Gallatin the Little Bowling Ball and liked to fish nymphs around the car bodies stuck in the banks, and in the ensuing years, Sam and Carolyn always gave an open invitation to come and drift a Woolly Worm around the cars and log jams.

In the early eighties Carolyn even took a writing class from me at the university, where she wrote stories about her hopes, fears, and dreams, and I took heart when I read that she and Sam had persevered through some very dark times. It was only last winter that they found her abandoned car and her little shoes by the freezing waters of the Missouri near its confluence with the Gallatin.

Any more, the big water and big fish downstream aren't so much fun. The lunker trout that I occasionally catch on the lower Gallatin remind me more and more of my cat, so hooking them and watching them zigzag around in terror for a few minutes doesn't give me the charge that it used to. If the sport weren't such an addiction, I might be tempted to follow the example of an ex-fishing partner, David Quammen, who developed so much sympathy for trout that he gave up fishing altogether.

But I believe the neighborhood stream will still work for me. Last Christmas when my grandson, Henry, and his family were visiting from Alexandria, Virginia, he gave the slick banks and icy shelves of Sourdough Creek a quick glance then walked with me and his grandmother across the footbridge where his father had saved that playmate some thirty years before. Then he climbed onto the stage of the nearby bandshell and started incanting mysterious noises across the empty snow-covered park: "Gank! Wack! Pork! Heep!"

It seems that he was attempting to cast some sort of spell on the place, and, as far as I'm concerned, it worked. Any stain my briefcase or aging brain might have left on that water was exorcised then and there. That's why, on this clear day in mid-October of 2010, while the weather is still warm and I can see a few late mayflies hovering where the afternoon light comes through the trees in our front yard, I'm going to walk across the street and catch a trout.

Epic and Idyll

Sydney Lea

Like many other hyper-hormonal young men, and in fact like too many anglers until too recently, time was when I yearned to smack a big trout over the head on every outing. You can take a picture with your damned cell phone now. But I hope that you, like me, leave *that* contraption home when you head for the river. Be all that as it may, in those days you released the little ones and kept the brutes, because what peer would credit your conquests on the strength of your lying word alone?

Ego, as will be seen, is this story's antihero.

It was 1970, and I'd traveled to the Green River near Cora, Wyoming, to gather some bragging rights, even if all I'd have on return would be, precisely, my word about some titan stretched halfway along my rod. Or maybe I could get some local with a camera to shoot me and the trout's great corpse. I didn't and don't carry a camera, either, haven't even owned one for years, because I never remember to use the contraption when I ought to; even now I remain too caught up with what's going on in the *un*replicated world.

I'd scheduled six days on the water, and almost before I knew it, five had vanished. I'd caught a fair number of fish in that span, some perhaps in

135

Photo by Jordan Lea

Sydney Lea on Kenai River, Alaska.

the two-pound range, but none that answered to the fantasies I concocted back in New England. On this final day, then, I felt as desperate as determined, though the sense of urgency had very likely been there from the start of the trip. It was and continues to be a character flaw, though I've worked to check it in later life, to never be quite satisfied. If as author I took some reassurance from Auden's assertion that poems were never finished, only abandoned, still deep inside me I longed to compose an epic.

A couple two-pounders had been fine . . . well, no, they hadn't. I was working on a *piscatorial* epic, and four decades ago my visionary Green River brown would bring it to completion.

That final September morning broke into bone-numbing cold; in fact, it was snowing—not a lot, but sure-God snowing—and the north wind blew hard enough to instantly sweep away blue wings and midges, if they hatched at all. Like most people who use the long rod, I take my greater pleasure in fishing to a rise, but I've never been some dry-fly "purist." Long johns under my waders, a coarse wool sweater under my vest, I set out to swing a streamer or drift a nymph, or rather to throw all manner of each until I'd exhausted my own supply and ardor. Before that point came, I could hope, I'd lay into my monster, preferably a brown, the fish that was, as now, my favorite. Hell, I rationalized, the one I had in mind was likely too big to bother with some piddling little dry anyhow.

The water in my chosen stretch looked placid, but in fact it had the authority of massive, slow-moving things. Elephant. Ox. Freight train. Draft horse. I leaned upstream and tied on some streamer or another. Careful in my zeal not to give any fly short shrift, I made scores and scores of casts with that fly, every cast a loser, as it proved with whatever else I had in my wallet: Muddler, Matuka, Ranger, various leech patterns, on and on. I even tossed an Atlantic salmon fly or two, just to say I'd tried everything.

Nothing doing, so out came the nymph box, or boxes: Prince, Copper John, Coachman, Art Flick's deadly Stone Creeper, and, more lethal still, I'd found, a thing that I and the late Ray Hulett, postmaster of Peru, Vermont, and the best trout fisherman I knew in those days, had thrown together from remnants one late spring day. We called it the White-Ass Baboon: mallard quill thorax wrapped in nubbled gold wire ahead of roughened snowshoe hare dubbing, no wing. And as I say, every other pattern in my kit.

Nada.

After four hours of *nada*, I staggered up to the local eatery to get warm and grab a bite. The counterman suggested what he called an Eye-talian sandwich, its foamy roll sogged with tomato ooze and pepperoni oil. I remember that it somehow tasted delicious, even if in my anxiousness to go back wading I all but inhaled the concoction. I decided to pick up a quart of Gilbey's gin too, for celebration of the big fish I'd be lugging to camp, though I had no way to either cook or freeze it. Three sodden cowboys swung indifferently on their stools to regard me in my fishing regalia, then swung back, working to salt their diction with local color, or so it seemed to me. I suspected their chat about roping and mending fence and partying had little to do with the way they actually lived, and I felt an odd and ignorant mixture of pity and contempt for these barroom buckaroos. Why in hell didn't they *do* something, and not just sit there mixing drink with bullshit?

Wind and snow had not abated during my mealtime layoff. At one point, having gone back to streamers in the gale, I managed to stick a #10 hook through my septum. It didn't hurt at first: In fact, I imagined I'd snagged some part of my clothing, and only after running my hand up the leader did I find the trouble. There was pain enough, all right, when I pushed the barb through and twisted at it with my nippers until metal fatigue supervened and the steel fell apart.

What blood there was from my nose's wound dribbled onto the ratty sweater. It struck me how surprisingly little of it I'd parted with. To me it appeared almost pretty—crimson on navy blue. My principal soreness lay in having lost half an hour of fishing to that crude doctoring.

I ran the alpha to omega of my fly assortment all over again. It seemed impossible that nothing better than twelve inches could be the result of such persistence. Mind you, I had not stood in one place: I'd waded up and down that run for a quarter mile or more in each direction, even venturing into scarily heavy water at the foot of the big pool, where my fly raced through its full swing almost the moment I laid it on the current. I wasn't settling for halfway effort.

Behind the bleakness of the day, I sensed the sun sinking ever more rapidly behind me. Time for something radical. I suddenly remembered the Battenkill on chilly autumn mornings in Vermont, the leaves just starting to turn, a touch of frost on air and meadow. The spawning browns of that blessèd era would sometimes whack at a spider if we skittered it over the surface, though nine out of ten times a fish would merely slap near the thing with its tail and never come again after. But every so often, in a flurry of froth, a decent trout would actually gulp the spider, and the contest, usually in the brown's favor, was on.

In any event, I lengthened my tippet, tapering it to 6x, blew on my fingertips, and tied on a cinnamon spider. I flung it onto the river, twitched it a few times, and watched as a gigantic head immediately showed behind it. The brown did not, as I'd have predicted, if I predicted anything, slap at the fly; he merely rose in all his pomp, then sank easily back. There was no aggression there, merely an almost polite refusal.

My heart sped and lagged in the same moment. There he was, he'd presented himself, but that would be the last I'd see of him if eastern experience were any gauge. Which it wasn't. Wind behind me, I made a roll cast, flicked the spider back and forth to dry it, and set it down right where I had before.

Again, rather than slashing at the fly, the brown sipped it as though it were some tiny emerger. Then, in the manner of real trophy fish, instead of roaring off he lay low in the streambed and shook his head slowly for what seemed a long time. Next he made a brutal but very short run, gave a few more shakes, and swam deliberately upstream.

Then he took off like a bullet train.

Oh Lord, let me have him! I prayed, even though I was a more godless young man than I am an old, and even though the petition was ambiguous.

I'd bet every fisherman knows the feeling of mixed excitement and gloom when a truly big fish takes: It's a thrill to have him on your line, but you know it's at least even odds that he'll overmatch you. This brown leapt once, like a rainbow, then skittered a couple of times along the surface like a smallmouth, and finally tore away in whatever direction he chose, making a series of literally breathtaking runs, one all the way across that broad reach.

I'm just a drunk. If such an admission seems a *non sequitur* at this juncture, I mean soon to suggest its relevance. I mean I'm a *chronic* drunk, a guy who sucks down some booze in the morning before he does another thing; but I'm also one who, praise God, has been in recovery for a long time now. Primary among the tools of such recovery is living life day by day. Practically speaking, this means that even *I* can get through one twenty-four-hour period without a hit of alcohol, or if need be can make myself go without the drink for an hour, even a minute, then another minute and another.

The compulsion to take alcohol or some substitute into my body left me a considerable while ago, but that doesn't mean I can relax. I was sober quite a while in my younger years, but I went back to imagining my epic poem, my epic fish, above all, my epic tomorrow. I forgot, to quote a rather hackneyed, Zen-like formulation, to be here now . . . and I got plastered, staying that way as another significant chunk of my life went by in a blur.

Even if one big miracle a day—being sober and clean—should be enough to hold me, I must sometimes notice, say, a crab tree dripping exotic, resplendent foliage, which turns out to be a flock of cedar waxwings; or for further instance, the ramshackle structures of the veneer mill in a town just south of me when they are inverted and somehow beautified by the calm water of the stream below; or the way crystals hover before me in the subzero air as I snowshoe through an opening in woods. I don't mind platitude here: These are some things that feed what I now name my soul and they lend it a measure of strength.

Believe me, I could go on, and I will return to such matters. Let me go back now, however, to the Green River brown. Even allowing for the hyperbolizing power of recall, I don't believe in all my life I've been into a trout of such bulk again. I certainly hadn't before that day. Of course, I don't fish a tenth as much as I did back when none of five kids had yet been born, when the idea of grandchildren was purest abstraction, when fishing seemed both to define and validate my very existence during the warmer months. For all that, I have taken my share of fine ones, and although for over a quarter-century I have kept none, I've profoundly savored playing each fish before release. And—this is the gospel truth—I have all but equally relished fighting ones that in the end broke off or pulled free. For some reason, my measure of success has been getting a trout close enough to me that I can clearly make out the colorful shades and spots and lines on his lissome frame. To know such animate splendor was there seems wonder enough, and joy.

Nothing remotely like joy, however, played a part in my battle with this particular brown. I chased him up- and downriver. Tippet material not what it is now—when, as my friend Landy Bartlett lately quipped, you can practically tow a Jeep around with 6x—I was careful not to let my quarry get too tight on me.

Please, please, God. I kept at my bumbling, witless, pagan prayer the whole while.

How much time ran by as I matched wits and strength with that brute? I haven't any idea, but a good deal of it, without doubt. At last, though, he started coming my way. I still let him run when he wanted, but his dashes were becoming shorter, less magisterial.

For purposes of traveling light, I'd brought along one of those nets you can twist until the whole thing fits into a holster on your belt. Holding the rod tip high in my right hand, I pulled the net out, dipped it into the current to open the bag, and gently lifted it under Leviathan . . . who proved too long and heavy for such a contraption, collapsing the frame so that he could roll again at my feet.

I made four or five further efforts with this flimsy affair, then looked downstream to those rips. On the west shore just above them stood a tawny gravel beach, which sloped into the Green at a gentle angle. To haul my trophy onto that dry land seemed my only recourse, risky as it was: If the trout made its way to the white water, the current would steal him for certain.

By now, I was nearly dragging the poor creature, a matter that didn't concern me then. Indeed, I checked behind myself periodically to see if the brown had turned onto its side, so that I could just pinch him aft of the gill plates and carry him out.

At last I backed a foot or two onto the sand, reeled the butt of my leader through the top guide, lifted—and felt nothing.

I didn't know what to make of this until I looked down and noticed that the trout had drifted offshore, deep enough to cover its dorsal, and was finning in the pebbled shallows. I noticed the little pigtail at my tippet's end, which now trailed useless below me.

I must have tied a bad clinch knot with my impatient, half-frozen fingers. I dropped my rod on the beach, waded out to his lie, and swiped at him like a grizzly bear. A feckless bear at that. I watched the trout angle out and disappear.

What swam to mind instantly was not another brown trout but that bottle of Gilbey's in my pack. This would become a more and more common response as I went on with my life. Yet even then, had I netted the trout, I'd have toasted my own triumph to the limit and beyond, as surely as I went on to drown my defeat. There's always a reason to be soused if that's your aim.

I'm almost certain the Wind River Mountains, however cloaked in the mist and snow of storm, provided a sight to make the hike back to my cabin worth the taking. I suppose mule deer and antelope grazed in the meadows at their feet, their breath visible in the cold when they raised their heads. More than one golden eagle may have been circling above. The sage probably showed the spectral green that would tax a Corot to replicate. But that fogged-glass bottle of gin was the real focus of my mind's eye. When I got indoors, its contents disappeared, entirely, much faster than my trout. So did the rest of that day and night.

I woke up the next morning to confusion, wondering where in hell I might be and what I'd been doing to get there. I recall becoming slowly aware of Hank Williams's "Your Cheatin' Heart," though in a version performed by someone who was no Hank Williams; I had fallen asleep with the radio on, and all my damp clothing too, including waders. It took a few moments for memory to prevail.

I pinch myself today to remember that my failure on the Green in itself seemed evidence that life would have no value to me anymore, that nothing—nothing—could ever again come to good. Insane, naturally, but then addiction and insanity are very close kin: In my crazed view, I had not merely lost the best fish I'd ever had on a line; I'd lost the world.

At the same time, forehead in hands, elbows on knees, shivering like a whippet, I felt some poisonous worm boring around inside my skull. The pain in my head was largely hangover, needless to admit, but it seemed that my worm had fangs, that I could all but watch as it chewed into what remained of my brain.

Too many years would pass before that worm, some avatar of conscience, gnawed all the way through my ego, sat me flat on the floor of a Vermont woodshed where I'd gone to find a stashed jug of something, no doubt, and broke my pride but good. I would recover or I would die: Things struck me just that simply.

There is no good reason here to retrace how, with immense support from friends and family in and out of recovery, I rediscovered multiple reasons for living, above all a beloved family that now extends to those beloved grandchildren, great nieces and nephews. At that moment by the Green, suffice it to say, I had no way to imagine such a turn, no way to foresee that I'd thrive not only on the kinships I've cited, but also on what remains of that very day, the one I believed such a debacle.

It has taken every day I've lived to get me to where I find myself now.

Thinking back on that encounter, I can, as it turns out, re-envision the glory of the fish's markings, those haloed crimson spots along the underbelly. The trout's deep but streamlined shape. The flakes of snow that hit the surface and vanished immediately, and the poignant beauty in such transience. The glitter of stones on the river bottom.

And if I lift my eyes to the hills, as I must after all have done, too, I still see the whited coulees descending the mountain like angel-pale rivers, wild grazing things lit by that shine.

It was my subconscious, of course, or some other ineffable faculty, that stored these lovely gleanings for a time when they could properly impress themselves on my spirit. There they are again at this very moment, bright and compelling enough to be part of a story's happy, even idyllic, ending.

Donor

Ted Leeson

Chance, it is said, favors the prepared mind, but from time to time it may condescend to an inattentive one. Not long ago, I stumbled upon an odd little book, Vladimir Propp's *Morphology of the Folktale*, not ordinarily my kind of thing, but I ended up reading it. It was a structural dissection of Russian fairy tales, which, I discovered, rather closely resemble the folk and fairy tales most of us heard as children. Much of the book was written in the almost impenetrable shorthand peculiar to ethnographers and anthropologists, a kind of quasi-mathematical script that made for congested reading. But from what I could glean, the book analyzed various themes and motifs that appeared again and again in the stories as sort of narrative common denominators.

One of these recurrent patterns involves the hero of the tale, typically a seeker undertaking a journey or quest, or undergoing some test of worthiness or endurance. During his travels, this seeker meets, to all appearances accidentally, a mysterious figure, a wise man or a roadside beggar or another traveler, who sometimes carries intimations of otherworldly power and sometimes is more explicitly allied with the supernatural: a witch in a hut, a sorcerer, a talking animal. Just at the point when the seeker's enterprise appears hopeless and he's on the brink of giving up, this mysterious figure, the donor, appears and gives him something—a charm or a talisman, a weapon or a magic word, a cryptic phrase or the answer to a riddle. And though the seeker may not recognize it at first, this gift will allow him to go on and eventually complete his task.

The appearance of this serendipitous character in the pages of a volume I'd acquired by coincidence occasioned a reaction I hadn't at all anticipated, as sometimes happens with chance encounters, whether in a book or in life, or in this case, both. For it brought to mind something that happened more than three decades ago, though the word "happened" may promise too much; it is a very small story in which virtually nothing occurs beyond the effect it had on me. It was the kind of recollection that you are surprised to recover after so long a time, a thing hibernating beneath all that's happened since, that is unexpectedly reawakened from some chamber of the brain. You would have thought it irretrievable, but it returns suddenly, all of a piece, or at least those pieces that remain intact beyond the corrosive effects of time and the plasticity of memories themselves, which are apt to change shape under the accumulating weight of years. As it was, the recollection returned to me first, not as a scene or collection of details, but as a flash of emotional atmosphere, an abstract feeling that then coalesced into the specifics that occasioned it.

It was mid-June of 1977. Late in the previous November, the younger of my two brothers died, committed suicide, a loss for which life does not prepare you and, at the age of twenty-two, you believe unsurvivable. At the time, I was 900 miles away in the East, struggling unspeakably through my first semester of graduate school, already isolated and lonely and demoralized by an academic scene for which I was phenomenally underequipped. Confronted almost daily with personal insufficiency and the limitations of my education, I didn't think I could be more miserable until my brother's death showed me how foolishly little I understood. The funeral left me numb in the way that blocks no pain, anesthetized but still feeling, and I returned to school in a deeply unsteady condition. But there was nothing there to hold me up and no one there to fall back on, and so I just fell, face first into what seemed to me then the frigid mud of being alive, waking each morning to the same unbearable thought of bearing another day. I dragged myself through the infinity of December to May, when the semester finally ended, then crawled another few yards into the cab of my truck and drove the eighteen hours back to the Midwest and the house where I grew up.

I'd grown thinner and thinner as the year passed and returned weigh-

Photo by Robert DeMott

Ted Leeson (right) with Dennis Hess, Madison River, Montana.

ing less than one hundred and thirty pounds. At six feet tall, I barely cast a shadow, which was pretty much how I felt, substanceless and transparent, a vapor through which things passed without impediment—houseflies, beams of light, other people's words. I was spiraling inward to that territory where mourning one's loss becomes mourning one's self, if the two are ever really separable. Perhaps some fraction of our sorrow is always self-inflicted, and our grief is invariably both shallow and deep, though we may not acknowledge it. At the time it all feels the same.

I vaguely considered not returning to school in the fall, but that was farther into the future than I could contemplate. I was without a job, without the ambition or wherewithal for anything, without purpose or plans of any kind beyond thoughts of spending some time in southwest Wisconsin, where over the course of summers past my two brothers and I had taught ourselves to fish trout on the small, overgrown spring creeks of the driftless area. No one had taken us there and shown us these streams. The fertile, serpentine valleys threaded with spring-fed brooks were a revelation of a different sort, independently discovered and learned through the slow, private explorations that bring the most intimate knowing. They were among the first things in our lives that we could claim as authentically our own, and the time spent there had altered us in subtle ways with the first awakenings to an unmediated liberty in the natural world and a sense of stewardship toward it. It was a landscape that we felt we belonged to, a soil in which some part of ourselves had germinated and taken root. All anglers possess such places; this was my first. And in the months since my brother's death, I'd clung to the thought of getting back there, imagining its contours and details, the feel of the air and look of the water, trying to soothe the mind with the balm of place. I had no intentions of making some nostalgic pilgrimage or sentimental revisitation—things were too raw for that. But regardless of the circumstances, I knew that staying away would be more difficult than returning. I was deeply attached to that landscape, though as yet unacquainted with the hallucinatory logic of grief that seeks relief in re-opening a wound, the quenching of pain by rekindling it.

One evening, I packed some tackle and camping gear and, after a restless night, headed out in the early morning dark to two particular streams that had drawn us like a moth to a flame. Thirty-five years later I can bring them to mind with minute precision. I arrived at the first little creek in the ashy light of dawn. It was unusually cold for June; a thick fog hovered in the valley like smoke, obscuring the hills, distorting the shapes of trees, strangely magnifying distant sounds. The landscape, as familiar to me as the faces of my brothers, seemed alien and unrecognizable. I assembled a rod and set out through the mist-soaked meadow to fish, drawn by habit to certain favorite pools and particular meandering stretches. They were the kind of spots that fishing partners give names to because the water holds their stories, places that only a year earlier had been filled with ripe and generous days. But on that morning I found them hollowed out by loss, echoing with recollection and regret, accusation and reproach. Each bend in the stream turned to the past, igniting a chain reaction of memories that cascaded into the present and detonated in a sudden absence, each thought of then traveling forward to the same empty now. I'd intended to fish but found myself just walking along the banks, thinking and thinking back—to all the summer mornings spent sharing a pool, to all the water we knew by heart—questioning if there was something I should have known or seen or done.

I returned to the car a couple of hours later but was in no mood to pitch camp, so instead drove to the other stream I'd come to see, on a route I'd taken countless times. Each familiar mile along the way added to the weight of the morning. In the aftermath of private catastrophe, the world seems bereft of meaning yet filled with significance. Everything—a road sign you've passed a hundred times, a random song on the radio, the arc of a hillside or a quality of light—becomes piercingly electric. It crackles and grows luminous and turns into something else. You populate the world with metaphors that mirror back your own interior wreckage, people it with the clichés of loss, and compose for yourself the unremarkable poetry of ordinary sorrow. Even knowing that it's taking place does not stop it from happening. It seems not a matter of choice but a form of atonement, the penance of being alive.

I eventually pulled off at a low bridge over the small creek, wrought up and wrung out from the drive. The thought of fishing held no appeal at all, but I forced myself to rig up a rod again and walk upstream, hoping it would help me to settle down and get a grip. When the bridge was out of sight, I stepped into the water, wading wet, and began trying to fish a nymph beneath the tunnel of grass overhanging the bank. I'd fly fished a little every season for the past few years but was not much good at it and rarely caught anything. What little I knew came from a library book and from what I'd taught myself, much of which was wrong. I'd never actually seen someone fish a fly rod and understood only enough about it to know that I did it poorly, which made me impatient of my errors and acutely self-conscious.

But on the morning in question, none of that mattered. Wrapped in my own despondency, I paid little attention to the fishing, casting in deep abstraction, not even really there. I have no idea how long this went on, an hour, maybe more, repeating the motions of a fisherman without really fishing, oblivious to everything outside my own thoughts. Until suddenly, from behind me, someone spoke. The voice was so unexpected, so remote from what I'd been dwelling on, that it shot through me like a spike, one of those bolts of pure panic that registers visibly as a galvanic, full-body flinch and leaves you feeling instantly depleted and wobbly. Wet to my hip pockets from wading, I started to shiver, aware for the first time of the cold water and chilly morning air.

Turning to the bank, I saw a man half-hidden by the tall grass, crouching down with his elbows propped on his knees, not many yards away but keeping low and back from my water, in the way only another fisherman would. It was clear from my reaction that he'd startled me. And perhaps I did the same to him, for I must have looked like I felt, like someone on the cusp of unraveling, bleary-eyed, shuddering, and rattled all out of proportion to a momentary, minor surprise. Standing up, he asked with genuine concern, "Are you alright?" I managed a yes. "Are you sure?" he said. "My apologies for coming up on you like that. Thought you heard me. I didn't mean to interrupt your fishing. I saw you from back there," he explained, pointing downstream, "watched a while and got curious." Apparently I'd been standing in one place, casting over and over again to the same spot; he'd become convinced I'd marked a good fish and was working it, so he came closer for a look. "It's good water," he told me, which was true, and said that I looked to be covering it well, which I very much doubted, then added, "I was pretty sure you'd get something."

I never asked him to repeat whatever he'd said that unnerved me so. The whole incident was so remote from my preoccupations that it seemed almost dreamlike, as though from a distance I was watching two people, neither of whom was me. But I do recall one thing that struck me at the time—the way he spoke. It was not so much the choice of words but a quality of voice, soft and unhurried, with something in the tone that conveyed a graciousness or care, even a kindness, that you don't often hear in the voices of strangers. It was so unlike the tenor of my own thoughts that it caught me quite off guard, and I remember that voice distinctly because it quietly suffused the remainder of our chance meeting.

Then, hesitating a bit, he volunteered an observation that told me he was a far more experienced fisherman than I was. "Your leader seemed to be acting a little funny, just at the end of the cast. Maybe something in the taper. I might be able to tell, if you wouldn't mind me having a look." My shortcomings as an angler must have been plain to him, but nothing in his remark hinted that the fault lay with the fisherman rather than his equipment. I handed him my rod; he examined the leader for a few moments, running it through his fingers from end to end. "I think I see what's wrong," he said. "I can try fixing it if you like, but I need some things from my car. Got time to walk back to the bridge? Shouldn't take long."

The leader was the last thing on my mind that day, but the sincerity with which the offer was made drew me to accept it, and we started back downstream. I don't believe that he introduced himself, and if he did, I've long since forgotten his name. In fact, aside from his manner, I remember nothing at all distinctive about him. He was perhaps ten or fifteen years older than I was, with a thinnish face and short hair that seemed vaguely military.

His blue jeans and nondescript shirt were like my own, and judging by his speech, which to my ear was unaccented, he came from the Midwest. But in all outward respects, nothing about him called attention to itself. Clearly he was a fly fisherman, the first I'd ever run across and one familiar with the little creek, but otherwise he seemed just an ordinary person. As we walked, he talked a bit, in the same quiet and measured voice, about inconsequential things: the unseasonable weather, how few mosquitoes were about.

When we arrived at the bridge, I saw a white van that hadn't been parked there earlier and, alongside it, a pair of chest waders spread out in the grass. He opened the double doors on the back, and I could see that both sides of the cargo area had been fitted with banks of shelves and cupboards and drawers, homemade of plywood, but neatly and cleverly built. They covered the walls except in one spot, where a low table had been built beneath a window that lit the interior; clamped to the top was a fly-tying vise. In the aisle between the cabinets, shoved to the back, were a rolled up camping pad and a sleeping bag. From one of the cupboards he took two plastic mugs, offered me one, which I took, and filled both with coffee from a thermos. The day had not warmed up; my jeans were soaked, and I was still shaking from the cold. I sipped my coffee and watched as he crawled back inside and began searching through the drawers and cabinets. I was astonished to discover they were filled with fly tackle, all kinds of it: rod tubes and reel cases, kit bags and fly boxes and a great many books, wading gear, a vest and a net, and what seemed to me then an extraordinary quantity of tying materials. I'd never seen anything remotely like it, each compartment brimming with mysteries that infused the whole space with a quiet magic. And though he was the first fly fisherman I'd ever come across, I somehow understood even then that the rest weren't all like him.

He emerged from the van with a cigar box and set it on the bumper. Inside was a jumble of tippet spools, which he pushed aside to take out a tape measure, a nail clipper, and something I didn't recognize at the time, a tippet gauge. He drew a foot or two of the leader butt slowly through the gauge, stopped, and said gently to no one in particular, "Ought-17," then snipped away the rest. Choosing a spool from the box, he measured a length, cut it, and said in the same undertone, "Nine inches ought-15," then secured it to the leader with a blood knot. He continued on, the leader growing in small increments as he specified each dimension, not really speaking to me but more like a man thinking aloud, confirming the measurements to himself by putting them into words. There was no hurry about it, and between knotting each section, he spoke in a more general way, addressing me directly but never volunteering anything about himself nor asking anything about me. It was just fishing talk, as I remember, mostly things about the little creek a few yards away. Then he'd resume his work.

But the truth is, I recollect little of what he said specifically. Under other circumstances, I would have seized on every word from anyone who could tell me anything about fly fishing or trout or trout streams and would have asked a thousand questions. But while I watched him, the turbulent thoughts of the morning, still swirling in my head, would surge forward in a wave and push away everything else for a time, then subside into the calm undercurrent of his voice, then suddenly well up again. And even now, the image I have of him sitting there working and talking seems viscous and distorted, like something seen through broken water or an old pane of rippled glass. I wish I could have recalled what he said. I would quite probably have learned something, though it didn't seem to me then that he was trying to teach anything. In retrospect, though, I'm not so sure. For while he didn't offer a single word of instruction or advice, or even explain what he was doing, by the time he was finished rebuilding the leader he'd in fact communicated the whole procedure exactly, which was something else I'd never seen before.

"Maybe this will help," he said, handing me the leader. It looked to be much longer and thinner, and I wasn't sure I could even cast it. I began knotting on the fly I'd been using, almost certainly a size 10 or 12 Hare's Ear, one of the few flies I could tie and about the only one I fished. He asked if he might see it, said he had a spot in mind where the fly might be just the thing, and wondered if I'd be willing to trade for it. I must have agreed because he stepped again into the van and reappeared with three identical flies, little nymphs, maybe size 16 or 18. I see them in memory as Pheasant Tails, though I could be imposing that detail on the story now, since the pattern would become a favorite for the spring creeks as I grew to be a better fisherman.

We exchanged thanks. He said he'd kept me from my fishing long enough, shook my hand, and asked once again if everything was okay. Then gathering up his waders, he put them in the van, shut the doors, and drove off. It didn't occur to me then that he'd intended to fish the little creek but left the water to me, nor could I see at the time how the leader and flies he left me with would, over the course of summers, quietly steer me in the right direction for fishing it.

And that's about all there is to tell. Except that after he left, I realized I'd warmed up to where I wasn't shivering any more and felt just a bit calmer, a little less frayed, though even now I'm not sure exactly why. Maybe it was simply a half-hour's respite from my troubles. Or maybe it was just the sound of a voice from outside my own head, talking about things I could bear to hear, a wisp of oxygen filtering into the suffocating sadness of the morning. I'd hardly pulled myself together, but it did feel as though I might be coming apart a bit more slowly, that the interior voltage had dropped a little. Nothing was said that miraculously made me feel better. It was no fairy tale, and he was no mystical figure with intimations of the supernatural, only a person extending a small gesture of kindness. And perhaps that is the point of it all. The word "kind," I'm told, is related to the word "kin," as in "one of your kind," another human being.

When he'd gone, I stood on the bridge for a time, watching the water slip beneath it. But I didn't fish again. There'd been enough to the day. Nor did I pitch camp that evening, but instead returned to the house where I'd grown up, and when autumn arrived, went back to school, and back again for several autumns after that. In summers, I returned often to the driftless creeks and for a while kept an eye out for a white van parked at the bridge, but never saw it, and in time the whole episode ebbed into forgottenness until one day, in a chance meeting with a book, it was unexpectedly revived. Looking back now, I'm still not entirely sure what it was that he gave me, if anything at all. But that day, it seemed like something. That is the part I remember clearly.

Indian Summer
of a Fly Fisher

Nick Lyons

Even brains have their seasons. Mine turns lately on ponds, memories, books, and glimmers of better days to come, though they may or may not. The mix, rather too suddenly, has changed. I suppose I could call the fly box that I now use for pills a symbol. But I don't. It is just a helpful way to keep in one place the dozen or so pills I take daily for heart, joints, prostate, and other organs too intimate to mention. I happen to need fewer flies these days than all those I hoarded for so many years and have taken to sharing boxfuls with neighbors who fish rivers where those flies once worked for me so well; I ship many off to far-flung friends in France and England who might find them exotic and even useful. I still have many thousands, and a good fly pattern is not to be left for the ineluctable moth.

For several years, twenty-five years ago, I tied flies for my own use—the Hairwing Royal Coachman at a time when I thought it could catch everything and when I believed in the illusion of perfect simplicity; some of Flick's Grey Fox Variants, ditto; a simple marabou leech pattern or two, for a lake that held really big busters that loved leeches but that I never fished again; a few tube flies for salmon that had once, ten years earlier, worked in Iceland and because I enjoyed constructing them, keeping them was an idiot's delight. That was the sad extent of it and I confess I made some monstrously sad specimens that happily no longer exist. But I have always been a keen student of

Photo by Craig Mathews

**Nick Lyons at Odell
Creek, Montana.**

fly pattern and design. I bought, begged, and examined thousands of them, checked their attitude in a glass of water, studied the effect of water on color, insinuated myself into the trout's position, however misguided, and acquired enough to stock a rather large fly shop. I still cannot pass up an intriguing fly.

Several years ago, after we bought a summer house in Woodstock, New York, I began to fish a friend's spring-fed pond only a few miles away, and what were needed there to catch fish on a fly rod were beyond the subtlest items in my arsenal, flies that cunningly aped the naturals that hatched on some pretty moody spring creeks I had fished. I called it Bill's Pond because it belonged to my friend Bill. It was about an acre in all, with the lower end, near where it tumbled out of the cement hatchway into a little creek, warmer, filled with lilypads, favored by the bass, bluegill, and pickerel. There was a small island on which geese nested, behind which you did not want your fish to take line, and the main section, fed by a vigorous upwelling spring and numerous small springs, held trout—a lot of them and of a size to raise any fly fisher's hackles. Bill fed them delicious little round liver pellets, and the biggest of the fish, the rainbows, were seven or eight pounds; all the trout cohabitated without prejudice with a few grass carp that must have weighed more than fifteen pounds and four or five bright-orange koi—terrific moving targets to pitch to, targets that demanded you lead them like a bird hunter by just the right distance. The koi were not much smaller than the carp.

As an aging trout man, my interest was most drawn to those big rainbows interspersed with a few three- or four-pound brookies and some pretty unsocial browns that kept mostly to themselves. Bluegill and golden shiners took a fly, and the few channel cats that would take a black leech fished very slowly, Bill told me, though I never tried this, but the trout were shy of what their wilder stream relatives loved. They rejected every fly I tried. They scarcely gave them a look. All of the trout smacked their lips when liver pellets came their way, found them as irresistible as the finest escargot or goose liver pâté or just about any item on Mario Batali's tasting menu. So after dozens of fruitless tries with the world's subtlest Pale Morning Duns and Sulfurs and Hendricksons that I had patiently accumulated, there was nothing for it but to invent an imitation of what the snobby palate of these picky characters preferred.

It was not such hard or uninteresting work. I started with a little cube cut with a single-edge razor from a wine cork, rounded it to the shape and size of the natural, dyed it the exact right shade of brown with a permanent felt-tip marking pen, cut a slit in one side with the razor blade, put a dab of Magic Glue on the cut, and inserted a #10 Eagle Claw bait hook. It was done. With a few shrewd variations and modifications—like leaving a white patch of cork on top so I could see the miserable concoction on the water— I had my imitation, and over the next few years it became the standard on Bill's Pond, accounting (for me) for at least one memorable grass carp, one koi (by pure mistake), and three or four of the largest trout.

Sneer if you will. Kept from wading by an incremental loss of balance that had led to three or four murderous falls—from my two new titanium hips and burgeoning waistline, all those pills in my retired fly box, or just creeping age—I gave up rivers several years ago, embraced Bill's Pond, and sucked my memories like a bear sucks its paws in winter, for sustenance.

There is an arc to every angler's life. It differs for each of us, but we all overlap. And as the arc makes one of its last turns, we can finally see the pattern with immense clarity. Awash with memories, we see all our early bumbling and passion give way to some competence and then to preferences and choices. We see our first trout, first trout on a fly, first spring creek, first tarpon, the mastery of one or the other of the cluster of techniques we need to take a few more of the most recalcitrant trout. Each image brings a new turn of the arc and even, in some cases, leads to satiety. Some folks I know simply give it up, for golf, for spectator sports, for who knows what. One fellow I knew caught so many exquisitely difficult—and large—trout that he grew bored, just gave it over. I don't know what he did thereafter. Many, though, cannot get enough of the finest fly fishing, never grow bored, fish quite as hard at eighty, even eighty-five, as they did at forty, braving all. And a few old fly fishers, as Sparse once told me about a prominent Long Island club, simply took to a wheelchair and suffered themselves to be hauled to the ramps near the hatchery.

For some reason, I have been blessed (or cursed) with the sharpest possible memory for just about every trout I ever caught, from the first (gigged from a late-summer Catskill creek on a bare Carlisle hook strapped to a bamboo pole) to dozens of the most challenging on a remarkable Western spring creek. I can without the slightest effort conjure a certain Pale Morning Dun floating with the placid current on a placid pool, ever so slowly, and then the sudden leisurely lumping of the surface when a preposterously large brown that I had pitched to seven times finally took. And I can remember tough trout I saw good friends hook, which gave me much the same pleasure.

But memory is not merely such brief images. Any fly fisher's memories course through his veins and have colored all his thoughts, all that he is, like wine splashed through water.

Fishing and catching were always part of my life, from before memory, and probably began with my capturing what I could with my hands—newts, crayfish, frogs, minnows—prowling a rocky headwater creek. At the Ice Pond near the grim boarding school I attended, I used a long cut branch and green line, a red-and-white bobber and a threaded worm, and the simple sight of the bobber on the flat pond—first still then twitching and darting beneath the surface—always stunned me . . . and still does, when I watch my grandson's bobber. During my years in high school, I took long treks by subway and train, a massive full-service pack on my back, from Brooklyn to the East Branch of the Croton River, and fished all night and all day with Mort and Don and Bernie. There I discovered the damage a C. P. Swing cast upstream with a spinning outfit could do, retrieved just a bit faster than the current; there are grainy photographs of me, with a limit of faded trout atop a wicker creel. The sight, from a bridge over Michigan's Au Sable, of a dry-fly man casting to a rising trout remains vivid: the electricity when the fish took the fly, the explosion in my brain when I saw fully what a fly rod could do. And when I committed myself to those feathered things, it was as if I were born again, and it all became too close to a religion, which it never should be.

And then my search began and has never truly ended, not even now, to understand the architectonics of flies, the mechanics of improving my self-taught fly casting, the way in which words could become an extension of the fishing and how I wrote them and edited them, bringing all of what I had learned about words to the twin tasks, and then fishing the Beaverkill, the Willowemoc, Ten Mile River, New York's Ausable, and the Madison, the Firehole, the Beaverhead, the Gallatin, in England and in France, salt water here and south, and finally finding the greatest challenges and sweetest rewards on a spring creek that gave up some of its secrets ever so reluctantly, some never. And when I think of that creek, I always see a fly floating serenely at dusk, a great wake easing toward it, the momentous take of the largest brown my friend had ever hooked, and the twenty minutes, into the dark, that he played it to a dozen feet from his rod tip until the fish simply slipped the hook. Somehow I learned a deep slow patience on that Western river, and it sloshed through me until I could feel its stillness in me when I talked to a class of students or tried to write a decent paragraph: the feelings, the spirit of the thing inside me forever. And there are the books by Roderick Haig-Brown and Harry Plunket Greene and T. C. Kingsmill Moore, Romilly Fedden, and Ted Leeson, and John Inglis Hall's wonderful *Fishing a Highland Stream,* and a hundred more that all live inside me and release a sentence or two when I least expect and most need them.

And I have so many more memories—some of which I have put into my shaggy-fish tales, some that have a friend's face and words attached to them. G. B. Shaw's maxim that youth is wasted on the young sometimes holds, but mine, my youth, redolent with the passion with which it was lived, often as potent as that in Conrad's "Youth," lives in me intact. I love it. I thrive on it, even as I press closer to eighty and feel in my head and body and hips the price of that passion, of hard living.

A year ago I took a feeble Knox Burger, an old friend, to Bill's Pond. He had been one of the finest literary agents, outspoken, fierce in support of his authors' rights, their work, and hard on the authors, to get their best work. He had once met me on the Gallatin wearing a T-shirt that boldly proclaimed, "Honest prose and nerves of steel," his credo. He was *sui generis*, indelible. I knew him for more than thirty years, as a colleague in the tough-sweet world of books, a valued investor in my little publishing firm, a fishing companion, a frank and baldly honest friend.

Age that is only rarely kind had worked its worst with Knox. Though not too deep into his eighties, he was frail, feeble, ravished by cancer and radiation that had blasted his bones, hip operations that did not repair, his speech blurred, his eyes that had loved words for so long incapable of reading, his legs weak and unsure. He had lost much of his body weight. But age had not quite done its final act.

This was the last time I fished with him, the last time he fished. He had passed his Indian summer and was living a very cold and unforgiving winter.

I told him on the way to the remarkably fecund Bill's Pond that the trout were very picky about what they ate but that I had devised with immense cunning a fly that adequately imitated the liver pellets that Bill fed them.

He growled a word that I had to ask him to repeat. Loudly and slowly and with effort Knox said: "HAM . . . burger."

Bill put two chairs out on his low flat deck and Knox, with deliberation, threaded his line through the guides of his old bamboo rod. It was a common enough rod, a well-used Montague. Then he reached over toward his canvas carryall, could not reach it, and so I extracted a box of flies. One after the other he chose a dozen different patterns and I affixed them in turn, which he tried for three or four short, deliberate casts each. No follows, no takes. I mentioned my pellet imitation.

"NO HAM . . . burger!"

As I sat next to him, watching the water, changing his flies, I spoke of days we had spent together in Montana and the Catskills, once at a club that had recently stocked some plump fifteen- and sixteen-inch browns that were spectacularly dumb. I reminded him that he had caught a dozen of them, that a handtruck had slipped from a truck in front of us on Route 17 and nearly killed us, and how the Minetta Tavern that he loved in New York City sat directly in the spot through which the Minetta Brook, loaded with brookies, had once, hundreds of years earlier, flowed.

To each story he grimaced or smiled faintly, and grunted. He kept his eyes on the water, and I did not know for sure how much of my old friend was still there.

After an hour, Knox remained fishless. I half turned from him then and surreptitiously changed his fly to one of the little dyed cork jobs in my box. He cast once, a couple of feet beyond his shoelaces, and immediately hooked one of the truly outsized rainbows that I had seen cruising close, to whom I had slipped four or five pellets, chumming.

The fish, a plump specimen of seven or eight pounds, took off at a great clip, and Knox leaned forward in his chair, dangerously close to toppling into Bill's Pond. I lurched for the back of his belt, caught it, and never let go. Then I held tight to the loose belt and played my old friend gently back into the chair. The fish was well into the backing for five minutes, and Knox could not see that it was about to go behind the island but he kept a firm and practiced hand on the reel and the fish gradually came back toward him, a foot at a time. Fifteen minutes later Bill brought out his gigantic saltwater net, and with one scoop the old rainbow was twisting in the meshes.

Knox passed his hand slowly along the monster's sleek flank, mumbled something I could not understand, and then Bill turned the fish back.

Then the old fellow looked at me and said in deep, clear, stentorian tones, "On . . . a . . . FLY."

"Yes," I said without hesitation, "on a fly."

He who loved honest prose, who had, in Hemingway's phrase, an infallible built-in shit detector, would have berated me loudly for it. It was the only time I lied to my late friend. And I'd have done it again.

The pleasure of Bill's Pond, my continuing difficulty wading, an old longing for water of my own—these led me to investigate building a pond on my hilly four acres, a bit downhill from the house. I counseled with a friend retired from the state fisheries department, and he took soil samples, tested the pH, debated the strength of a few small springs; I asked several contractors for their views on my prospects. The reports came back quickly, bleakly: The soil was far too rocky and porous to hold water unless I packed the excavation with clay or artificial clay, neither of which I wanted. I wanted it natural or not at all. The pH was marginally okay, there was no evidence that the few springs we found could supply nearly enough water to satisfy two turtles. Rainwater and road runoff, neither reliable, the latter toxic, would help a little, and perhaps the neighbor Fisher, who owned land contiguous to where I wanted my pond, unwilling to sell me an acre or less of promising swamp, would allow me to sink a little pump into his wet hollow and thus gain a few drinks of cold water. He did. Being on a precipitous hillside didn't help. Even the local building inspector, though he approved my plans, insisted there was no hope for the pond and thought it merely a seasonal hole.

In the end, smarter than all these, I persuaded myself to believe none of them and went ahead with the contractor, who set up his retired father on a tractor for a week, and I watched the old guy chugging in and out of the hole, building a berm, carving out the rocky soil into an amoeba-shaped area, smoking a cigar out of the corner of his mouth, which his wife, I learned, wouldn't let him smoke at home, a quiet smile on his face, man and machine indefatigable.

It was not your ideal pond, though it filled for a short time from heavy rains and was actually about ninety feet across (at its longest length), and I promptly stocked it with bluegills from Bill's Pond. Bill was hopeful enough to add three foot-long largemouth bass and a couple of rainbow trout, and my friend Martina deposited a single smallmouth she had caught. When all these survived not only the first late-summer drought but also the frozen winter, I became emboldened and added a foot-long grass carp, three koi, a bucket of emerald shiners and sawbellies from a local bait shop, more bluegill, and a few of Bill's golden shiners. At least the bass would get a decent meal now and then.

The bluegill made their pancake beds that June and proliferated; several bass fry and then a few ten-inch largemouths appeared a year or so later, so they were reproducing; the trout lasted three years, grew fat, and then vanished *en masse* after an August heat wave. For the pond only had two problems: It leaked and it had no clear source of cold water.

Turtles lasted only a few months in the muddy soup and then left for more accommodating places; I got two dozen tadpoles from the bait shop and added them; I saw and heard a few frogs, then they disappeared, perhaps with the help of the blue heron that visited most mornings. I caught one bass more than twenty inches long one fall, most of its body no thicker than a plump snake's, its head huge and smiling, a sure victim of near starvation. I even thought I heard it say, "Get me out of this hell hole, *please*," before I slipped it back.

The carp, with an appetite as great as mine, kept the pond clear of green algae; two of the koi vanished, and I bought another that thrived as a younger brother or sister to the one I'd put in the first year, by then a seven- or eight-pounder. There must have been six or seven dozen stunted bluegill that came toward the dock every time I approached; a couple of brookies Bill put in one fall managed to prevail, and over the years I got down for an hour or two several times a week and watched, or tossed out bread and pellets, or some wickedly expensive nightcrawlers, and now and again cast bass bugs or bright bluegill flies, or a little jig Bob Boyle had concocted, or my pellet imitation, pure hamburger.

My eldest granddaughter showed promise and fished for a time, until she became a busy teenager with a SmartPhone, and my grandson Finn showed some interest beyond his original compulsion to pelt the pond with rocks, so we began to feed the fish together, fish now and then, knock around the odd unpromising hole a bit more frequently. We used a fly rod and something called a "noodle rod," and I proved as hopeless and hapless in interesting the boy in flies as I had been with my four children: not at all.

Finn caught bluegill by the bucketful, and one day registered some variety of Grand Slam—bluegill, golden shiner, brook trout—and then the grass carp. We had been using breadcrust, the natural not the imitation, primarily because it could be fished "dry" and because, after the great fish rose to ten similar crusts of bread, it was to him the *plat du jour.*

The carp, caught once before, a few years earlier, then a good deal slenderer, took the dry breadcrust, then swirled mightily when it realized it had been duped, sending a riot of water out in every direction, and Finn jumped as the electricity coursed through him. The noodle rod bent to nearly a circle. The fish—now twelve or fifteen pounds—headed like a freight train as far from the dock as it could get and, though the pond was small, the fish went everywhere it could go. After ten minutes of hauling and giving line, Finn asked whether we could get the fish onto the dock. I told him about the net in the shed, so he passed me the rod and raced up the hill. I stopped pressuring the fish and it rested quietly, waiting for the second act. Finn came back a few minutes later with a net I hadn't used in fifteen years that might have been rotted, large enough for stripers or blues, and in the end we got the carp's head into it and I hauled it up onto the dock—the fish massive, its scales golden and tinged with brown, its little mouth gasping. Finn wanted to drag it up to the house to show parents and sister and any other potentially interested person we could hail on the road, but I reckoned the big fellow had had enough for one day, so in the end we turned it back. I decided it was best to leave the hook in its soft mouth and was sadly convinced that the long fight had done it for the great fish.

Ten minutes later, though, some bread still floating on the water, the carp was up again, wolfing down the last of this feast.

Another winter has come, my pond is frozen solid above who knows what, and my seasonable mind turns not backward but toward April. It has not been much to brag on, these past six or seven years, not really much of a true Indian summer. But I was never much of a bragger and was generally content to love my passion with unalloyed passion, grateful for every bit of it I could get. But what comes next—more meditations on my ludicrous little pond? Whatever antidotes I can find for my most maudlin moments, mostly slapstick comedy? Another trip to my beloved West? More attention to nearby rivers? The rest of this winter near some warm and gentle flats?

The pond has survived and so have I. Certainly the arc has turned. I don't need to repeat the intensity of my youth—the long days, returning tired to the bone, always reaching for the untried and most challenging, casting until my back pained, anxious to try pike in France, tarpon in the Marquesas, tough browns in a Western spring creek. And I would prefer not to sit in a chair with a friend holding onto my belt, thank you, or be wheeled to a spot near a hatchery—though such a day might come.

A little always went a long way with me, even if it fell far short of all. And my brain remains that of a fly fisher. All of the fly fishing I ever did lives in me. Everything I do is colored by that fact. And if by good chance I fly fish in one of the best ways again, and I am determined to do so, I will not be more of a fly fisher for it. I am all the fly fisher I can be right now, and I will always be a fly fisher.

In the Nick of Time

Craig Mathews

I'm probably one of the few writers who refuses to totally succumb to computers. I still use an Underwood Standard, Model S typewriter. I don't trust a computer to "save" or to "save as" any document I type, because I have lost too many files that way. I know another man who still uses the same manual machine. His name is Nick Lyons, and he is not simply one of my best friends, but has always been a mentor and a hero to me, and on occasion a father figure, as well.

In September of 2007 Nick was honored by the World Wild Trout Symposium with its Aldo Leopold Wild Trout Award. This prestigious award is given to the individual doing the most to protect and preserve trout and wild trout habitat. That year Nick could not come to West Yellowstone to accept his award, but I did so proudly on his behalf. "We all know what Nick has done for wild trout around the world, through his publishing, writing, and teaching," I said. "He has touched me and hundreds of others, and has taught us the simplicity of seeking the truth in our work, our lives, and our fly fishing. He writes of the innocence of trout and reports on the complexity of humans, and how we have to pursue their innocence in our complex ways." There is a history behind my standing in for Nick at that ceremonial moment several years ago, and here, in what follows, is part of the record of our long and valued friendship.

Photo by Jackie Mathews

Craig Mathews at Madison River, Montana.

Our first meeting was July 27, 1980, at about 7:00 am. I had just finished a grueling sixteen-hour shift as police chief of the town of West Yellowstone, Montana. It had been a tough night at the cop shop. A few altercations between biker gang members and cowboys and a couple of "Ladies of the Evening" issues provided us with late-night troubles at a local watering hole. I came home and crashed into bed, and as I was sinking into a deep REM sleep, the phone rang. My wife, Jackie, quickly picked up the phone, and I heard her whisper, "Bud, he's dead tired," then "Okay, let me see if he's still awake." Jackie tiptoed into the bedroom and whispered, "Are you awake? . . . Bud needs you to guide a fly fishing author." In a sleepy fog I took the phone, and Bud Lilly, of Bud Lilly's Trout Shop, explained that a well-known angling author had showed up at his shop and needed a fishing guide. Back then, in what little spare time I had, I helped Bud by taking a few guide trips and tying some flies for his world-famous fly shop. I asked Bud who the author was, and he replied, "You might have read some of his fly fishing stuff; it's Nick Lyons." Coincidentally, I had just finished Nick's Bright Rivers (1977), and Jackie was reading his Fishing Widows (1974). I told Bud I'd get my gear together and be at his shop within the hour. Fifteen minutes later I was shaking hands with Nick and his son, Paul. We became instant friends.

That first day we decided to float one of the world's great "bright rivers," as Nick called the Madison River. During our drive over, Nick, always humble, explained that he was just a beginning hacker when it came to fishing rough-and-tumble rivers like the Madison. I'd read some of Nick's "Seasonable Angler" columns in Fly Fisherman magazine, as well as essays in his books, where Nick usually portrayed himself as somewhat of a stumbling-bumbling angler. But that day I was in for a treat as I watched Nick fish the river like it was his home water. He and Paul took several fine brown and rainbow trout, and during our first day astream we decided to meet the following evening to explore a small spring creek in Yellowstone Park, one Charlie Brooks had separately told both Nick and me about.

Next day, Nick and Mari Lyons joined us for an early elk steak dinner, after which we headed into the park to check out Charlie's secret spring creek. I can still see Jackie and Mari trailing behind Nick and me. The women chatted about their children and living in New York City versus West Yellowstone, and I heard them chuckling a few times about their "fishing widow" status, all the while swatting away at the hordes of mosquitoes chasing us along the main river to its junction with the spring creek. When we arrived at the recommended spot, we were greeted with dozens of rising trout, some of which were small but most of which were huge and actively feeding.

What impressed me then, and still does over the many years we've fished together since, is the excitement Nick shows for any kind of fishing. I can still see how his fingers trembled as he knotted on a dry caddis pattern; I can see his wry little grin as he anxiously chomped down on the pipe he used to smoke while fishing. I can still hear his Hardy Perfect scream as his back cast snagged Mari's sweater and she ran downstream along the river's edge taking line into Nick's backing, then jumped over a log, without once throwing the hook. No harm done—the hook was barbless—and all the while the trout riseforms intensified and became more numerous. Nick and I got back in the game. Excitedly, we cast, and cast, and cast, flock shooting into the dozens of rising trout, failing to pick one fish and cast to it, and, as a result, we did not hook even one good fish that night. But during that first evening our friendship was sealed, glued permanently by our mutual addiction to fly fishing.

During the Lyons family's short stay that summer, I ran an idea by Nick about a fly tying business Jackie and I were thinking of starting that year. Our plan was to hire local fly tiers and tie wholesale flies for several fly shops in southwestern Montana. Nick was enthusiastic about the idea, and later that year he would help us acquire our first large tying contracts with Orvis and L.L. Bean, which would carry our new business through its first years. Without Nick's encouragement, inspiration, and tireless help we would have never succeeded.

During the following years Nick and I fished together many times when he and Mari summered in Yellowstone country. Too, we became involved in a business venture partnership we both felt would make us millions. Nick had cornered the scrap fur market in New York City. We were confident that fly tiers from around the world would be calling us to supply their tying needs. Nick would prowl the side streets in the fur district of the city, making off with fur scraps left in boxes and bags along the curb for the sanitation department to haul off. He visited sewing houses and picked up valuable fur scraps off the floor. He often called to report on the pounds of priceless fur pieces he'd scored that day: mink, otter, nutria, beaver, muskrat, and exotic furs like Australian opossum. I announced to the fly tying world that Nick and I held supplies of every fur they needed to tie any fly known to man, and that we'd ship it worldwide. Nick began shipping boxes of fur pieces to West Yellowstone; more than twenty boxes arrived in the first few weeks, with many more to come that summer. We had more than 200 pounds of fur, and I locked it safely in the basement of our shop. Today, thirty years later, more than 180 pounds of fur scraps are still safely stored in our basement.

We put our fur business on the back burner, and Nick went back to book publishing, teaching, and writing, while I cranked out hundreds of dozens of flies and tried to make a dent in our fur larder. Nick began to pester me about writing an article for Fly Fisherman magazine about some of the new fly patterns we were coming up with at our little fly shop. The only thing I'd written before were college papers and police reports, but I promised Nick I'd give it some thought.

My notes and fishing log tell of Nick, some new friends, and me fishing several times during that next summer. He called one day early in June and said I should expect a call from H. G. Wellington. Nick explained that Herb owned the Longhorn Ranch, with a few miles of world famous Odell Creek running through the heart of it. He said Herb wanted to fish with Nick and Mari, and Jackie and me. He said that no matter what I had to do that day, I should put everything aside and head to Longhorn Ranch. This was the beginning of an incredible run of fishing experiences, new lifelong friends, and Nick leading me by example to try my hand at writing.

That summer on our fishing junkets to "Spring Creek," as Nick refers to Odell, as well as other waters we'd fish, such as the Madison, Beaverhead, and Henry's Fork, both he and Herb would introduce me to famous angling authors: Dermot Wilson, Ed Zern, John Goddard, Conrad Voss-Bark, Verlyn Klinkenborg, Sid Neff, and others. You find out a lot about a person when you fish together, and I had the distinct good fortune of spending many days fishing with Nick and our new friends that summer and several more that followed. We always fished dry flies, and during those times when no trout were rising we'd sit on the bank and talk about Kafka and Chaucer, Skues, Mottram and Sawyer, Marinaro and Fox, and other angling worthies.

The following winter was brutally cold and snowy in Yellowstone country. I couldn't fish due to the weather. In those long, wintry days of March when spring seemed but an insinuation, I agreed to try my hand at writing a fly tying pattern book under Nick's always generous tutelage. Nick often does this to those he cares for and touches: he leads by example, he mentors and inspires, he encourages, and he coaches his friends to write even if those people don't believe at first they can.

A wild trout is total innocence. And because we are complicated humans, we have to pursue that innocence in our complex ways. Through Nick I've come to know that this is the only way for anglers like us who are obsessed with trout. Nick and I often discussed why he and I, and other friends like Herb Wellington and Vince Marinaro, paid so much attention to what most other anglers thought were the unimportant, trivial, nonessential details of fly fishing. It seems that many anglers feel, as I once did, that thinking should be left at home or at the office so as not to impede the simple enjoyment of taking fish on a fly. Nick and I felt that if trying to solve fishing problems, puzzles, and conundrums—including developing effective flies, conquering current drag, and improving fly presentation, just to name a few—do not fascinate an angler, then he or she is missing a great, challenging aspect of our sport. As our friend, Datus Proper, realized, the big angling frontiers were long ago conquered, and the little, seemingly unimportant details, perhaps heretofore ignored, are some of all that's left in fly fishing. Shifting our field of vision to include the whole web of circumstance enhances the pursuit of enjoyment and adds a dimension of pleasure to the trout we seek and sometimes catch.

Mostly, these understandings came about as we studied, learned, and fished Herb's Spring Creek. I have video I took of Nick and Herb fishing the creek at Second Bend or Paranoid Pool or Fever Point. In one video Nick is bent over, slowly wading across the East Branch so as not to send a wading wave upstream and spook the pool's big fish. Herb waits for him on the inside corner, on the far bank of the pool where he'd been sitting for some time watching the pale morning dun emergence begin and big selective trout start to rise to impaired emerging duns, which could not escape the surface film to quickly take flight. I skirt upstream and take a position on the far bank, well upstream of the rising fish, to film the action. The trout gain confidence with each rise, and in a matter of a few minutes there are a dozen snouts and circles. I focus the camera and see through the telephoto lens several golden-bodied PMD mayflies reflecting the sunlight as they float downstream on their way to becoming trout lunch, knowing that the rising fish are as vulnerable as they will ever be on this day. I watch as Herb sneaks along the stream's shoreline, scooting on his ass trying to move closer to Nick, looking to see if Nick is concentrating, looking to see if Nick's expression is now smooth and distant and unworried, looking to see if Nick is focused and "in the zone."

I look through the camera lens and note Nick's Zen-like posture, as though he were a heron ready to strike a trout, knowing that his attention zone is small and intense as he concentrates on one single large trout feeding in a narrow current lane, hoping to entice it to eat the #16 PMD Sparkle Dun at the end of his tippet. It seemed then that all else faded away, and what remained is like a dream sequence in a movie. I looked to Herb and saw a little smile come to the corner of his mouth, for he knew that Nick was in the zone. We both recognized Nick was stripped to his purest fishing state. He needed to take that rising fish. Herb and I had both been there too, in that great vibrant place where our actions and our dreams are stirred with such passion.

Nick makes a perfect presentation. The fly lands just upstream of the big trout. We all watch as the fly slowly drifts down the feeding lane. I hold my breath and am sure Nick and Herb do, too. A big snout comes up, then a swirl, and we all watch the fly disappear. Nick raises the rod and the trout bolts upstream in a fury. Nick remains seated, raising his rod high, and gets the trout on the reel. A few minutes later he skillfully brings the big fish to shore and releases it. Herb and I quietly applaud and Nick tips his porkpie hat, but we know Nick does not really see us. He is still in his zone, and we know he'll take a couple more trout before we head back to the ranch house for lunch. A few moments later there is a bulge, then a couple of dimples, then big snouts pock the pool's surface again, and Nick is back in business doing what the stream tells him to do.

Those were the best fishing years for us, not necessarily for the fish we took, but for what we learned together, what fishing problems we dealt with and those we solved, and the complex way we pursued innocence. It's been more than ten years since Nick and Mari have made their summer treks to the Madison Valley and Odell Creek. Herb passed away a few years back, too. I'm very lucky to be able to fish the creek several times each season. I sit on that same bank at Second Bend Pool, remembering those happy, idyllic days. I take a few photos each time I'm there and send them off to Nick, hoping they'll spark him into coming back.

I still find Odell Creek a wonderful antidote to the daily anxieties and tensions of running a business. I'm blessed to have a sure and certain thing, if just in my mind, that neither fails to bring such enjoyment and serenity, nor fails to fill my head with indelible images: Nick and Herb sitting in the Suburban waiting for the duns to emerge; Dermot Wilson and Nick sitting at Second Bend Pool, with a dozen big trout rising, debating exactly what the creek was trying to tell them to do—what fly to try—which snout to cast to; Mari painting below Fever Point as the wind comes up and blows her easel down and scatters her sketches across the grass; that same wind blowing grasshoppers into the creek and huge trout racing each other to take them off the water; and pelicans circling overhead like angels of death waiting for us to leave the stream so they could move in and herd trout to shore for easy dining; avocets flying in formation and buzzing over us at the Nursery Pool as the cacophonous voices of sandhill cranes echo in the valley.

At home every morning I am reminded of those days at Odell when I look at Mari's sketch of Nick and me in the rain in 1992, and her painting of Nick and John Goddard at Second Bend Pool, for she used my photograph as a model for her painting of two sitting anglers talking over one of the many fishing problems that has fascinated anglers for centuries. Mari's stunning painting, through its colors and textures, exudes the mood of the creek as well as anything I've ever seen. And I read Nick's books every winter. His words praise wild trout for what they have meant to all of us in the past, and, perhaps more importantly, for how they will continue to fascinate us as we fish into the future.

Seeing Snook

Thomas McGuane

I started fishing around Boca Grande as a boy. My father brought me here when I was eleven years old to fish for tarpon; I caught my first one in Boca Grande Pass. For years my father and brother fished here with a redheaded guide, who died from the complications of skin cancer. My father and his friends, all clients of the redheaded guide, came to pay their last respects. The old guide was laid out in the living room of his small clapboard house, surrounded by family and friends. In the middle of it all, supported by her sisters, was his grief-stricken widow. When my father and his friends walked in, she looked up blearily, adjusted her focus, and cried, "There's the sonsabitches that killed my husband!" My father and his pals, in coats and Countess Mara ties, clutching Dobbs hats, made humble obeisance until escape was possible. "I thought those crackers would jump us," my father commented in a grave voice as his group headed for the Pink Elephant bar for an eye-opener.

You reach a point at which you have to view your life through the things you've spent so much time doing. The alternative is a perilous feeling of waste. Cancer and gulag survivors alike treasure their experiences for reasons best known to them. The rest of us have logged more platitudinous days, and it takes an effort to assign their place and value. I've spent as much of my life fishing as decency allowed, and sometimes I don't let even that get in my way. Especially when it comes to snook.

Snook remind me of brown trout—something in their covert nature,

Photo courtesy of Thomas McGuane

Thomas McGuane with snook, Florida.

their eccentric choices even in safe harbors, their sensitivity that seems de-signed to humiliate the angler when less dramatic options would get the job done. In short, snook are sleazy.

They are also hard to see, hard to hook, hard to land, and, because they are so good to eat, hard to release. But release them we do. Cold weath-er reduces them to torpor; colder weather kills them. When they're at the threshold of death, a translucent window appears in the top of their heads. Sometimes, when a snook follows your fly, then takes, you notice a quick roll up on its side, as though the fish were bringing the target in for close vision. The snook refusal has a quality of its own: a long cross-eyed follow, then a turn off. Snook just leave when suspicious, or change their swim-ming rhythm. They can also crash bait, as well as jacks or bonito. There is something touching about snook, their funny-faced striving, their sneaki-ness, their lazy travel turning into serious speed. Their heedless jumps fill us with aesthetic merriment.

The truth is, I have always had trouble catching them and felt that this was something I was going to have to work harder at. I decided to fish with a guide at least once a week, and I called on Austin Lowder, who guides here in the winter and in Montana, where he's from, in the summer. I'd heard he was effective but very demanding, and I thought I could stand a little embarrassment, as long as I learned something. I soon confirmed that Austin is not the guide for the angler who is comfortable with his bad habits or who has lost the ability to learn. As we approached a group of redfish our first day together—brick-colored tails turning slowly, a pink, wavering shape below the surface, grubbing out baby blue crabs—I adjusted my stance to face them and cast. The tails disappeared, and I had no targets. "Don't move your feet," Austin grunted, and we looked for some new fish.

There was a single fish tailing at the edge of the mangroves. In the branches above him, a dozen wood storks watched my performance. This would take a long cast. As I began, Austin's cell phone rang in his pocket. I made the throw, but a loop caught under my shoe. Fish gone. I heard Austin say to the caller, "Just missed a fish. Guy with tennis shoes."

If you fish away from your home waters, guides are an excellent investment, although, after a pleasant day together they will describe you to the other guides as a complete idiot. There are two kinds of clients: the meek and the proud. The former are happy to be insulted and abused, the latter regard guides as indentured servants. I'm a mixture of the two. I can accept a certain amount of abuse if I'm learning something, then indignation sets in and I become disagreeable. Austin's belief that a successful day on the water consists of doing a lot of little things right was a useful regimen for me. Among his assertions: Don't move your feet when approaching fish; don't talk (they can hear you); don't trail a loop in the water; don't cast overhead unless you're a long way from the fish; watch all low-flying birds (they spook fish); and so on, in an ever-lengthening list.

Austin assumes you're trying to get better, but he's a strict instructor. Your first impression from fishing a few days with him is that you have suddenly acquired attention deficit disorder.

Reaching into my tackle bag for my binoculars to look at a hooded warbler that had just appeared in the mangroves, I heard Austin say, "Put them back. You don't need binoculars." He dinged away at me for days on things like this, and eventually I conformed, though a few remarkable things stopped us both: a peregrine power-diving in perfectly still air creating a searing sound of attack; an immense stork, a jabiru that had drifted away from its Central American home—from fifty yards away we could hear it crunching crabs with its colossal beak. In any case, back to work.

A big snook lay like a black arrow in the clear water atop an oyster bar that glowed yellow in the afternoon light. I was rigged for redfish but cast anyway. The fish rushed the fly, took hard, and ran. I was forced to play him gently to keep from breaking him. After a heedless jump, he made a run for the mangroves. I had to pull hard to stop him, and I got away with it. I landed the fish and kept him alongside long enough to admire the peculiar beauty of a grown snook—the upward cast of the eyes, the beautiful undershot mouth with its sandpaper interior, the boxlike shape of the body between its ventral fins, the slight greenish cast overall, and the amber fins.

Austin wanted a picture of this fish. "Hold him like a man!" he commanded.

The next day Austin and I fished together turned out to be when a stormy northwester was rolling down the Gulf Coast. I assumed we'd have to cancel, but Austin laughed at the suggestion. We tossed gear into the skiff while the north wind tore through the usually placid bayou, rattling the palms around us. As we got into our foul weather gear, I found it hard to be optimistic. Austin called to Bill, the collector of ramp fees, "I know it's no fishing day! I just want to get paid!"

I hoped this was merely the grim joke it appeared to be, but I was ambivalent about our prospects, and my pessimism increased as Austin powered his Hells Bay skiff over an angry grey chop. After repeated lashings of forty-miles-per-hour cold saltwater, I moved back to the downwind side of the boat. I tried to look where we were going, but I was soon reduced to cowering in the noise of the two-stroke Yamaha, the hammering separations between the seat and my backside, and the sheets of wind-borne seawater.

We ran into a broad bay that narrowed and finally disappeared against a wall of mangrove swamp. Here there was no wind. Clouds scudded overhead, but we were in a place that was quiet as a church, and how very nice it seemed. Austin anchored the boat, and we got out and entered a winding creek much like a prairie trout stream, with a sandbar on one side and an undercut bank on the other. I lost count of all the snook we caught and released.

It wasn't really a story you could tell without ruining your credibility. Angling often requires eluding your fellow anglers and discovering opportunities others don't want, and here is another lesson I'd learned from Austin: Go fishing when only a fool leaves his house.

"You know, Austin, I'm thinking of writing about fishing this winter. I learned a lot. I suppose you'll be in it. Might do some good."

"I don't care. I've already got everything I want."

"Well, then let's use a pseudonym for you."

"If you're going to do it, you might as well use my name."

"I was thinking of Captain Marvel."

"Captain Marvel. . . . Hey, I like it!"

In the early years that I fished the shallows, we poled our boats from the bow; poler and angler were at the same level. Now the poler—the guide—is on an elevated platform and generally can see much farther than formerly. This should be an advantage to the team, not an opportunity for the guide to humiliate his angler, but this principle is frequently violated by a physio-social disorder known by its acronym, PIMP—Platform-Induced Moronic Phase-out, and anyone who mounts a poling platform is in jeopardy of contracting it. I've had it several times. Standing up there with the graphite push pole in hand, with all its feeling of thrust and weaponry, you stare down at male-pattern baldness and sunburn and can't help but cry out, "What're you, anyway, blind?"

"Big snook, nine o'clock, seventy feet going left!"

I looked all over the brown-and-grey-mottled bottom for a grey-and-mottled snook.

"I can't see him."

"He's right there!"

"I don't know where the f— he is!"

"He's right in front of you! He's right next to that little island!"

"I don't see any little island!"

Austin's shoulders slumped. The push pole knocked against the platform. "He's gone."

"I just couldn't see him."

"He was right next to that little island."

I was getting hot. "What little island?"

"It was just this little floating island."

"Show me the little floating island."

Austin laughed, somewhat guiltily, I thought. "Forget it," he said.

"I want to see the little floating island."

Austin ruefully poled the boat backward and pointed to a scrap of floating moss perhaps the size of my hand. I let on that it wasn't much of a landmark. I turned back to scan the water ahead.

"Let me offer this," said Austin from behind me in an abraded tone. "You didn't see the fish."

This left me speechless. But I was prepared to admit that I needed to work on seeing. Whether fishing with Austin or fishing alone, I strained to see better, and at the end of the day my eyes were worn out. Later, Austin, perhaps feeling he'd been a bit hard on me, said, "You need a prescription." I knew he wanted me to get glasses. He told me a kindly story about a citrus grower, a lifelong snook man, who had acquired prescription glasses. "Now, when I say nine o'clock, seventy feet"—a reference to my missed snook—"he says, 'Got 'im.'"

Seeing fish is the essence of shallow water angling. Anglers who see fish exceptionally well can fish successfully in less productive water than anglers who don't. Fishermen love equipment and are always looking for mechanical advantages, but there is nothing to compare with learning to see well; if you see well enough, you can walk out in the mud with no boat and catch fish. I wasn't seeing well enough.

Not long ago, in response to a spell of insomnia, I learned some of the principles of meditation, to empty my mind piece by piece. It was like the old game of jacks—cautiously lifting each jack clear of its neighbor until only the empty background remained. I began to use this small skill to see better. Seeing fish well is usually assumed to be the result of concentration, but concentration bears too much of the deliberate—too much willpower and too little intuition about the way wild creatures use surroundings and how they exploit willpower into lies for the credulous predator.

Instead of longing for sleep, I longed to see better. I began to identify the things that kept me from seeing fish—motionless fish, slow-traveling fish, fish concealed in mangrove roots, fish up light, fish in glare, fish in shadows. I continued to scan ahead as the bottom flowed toward me to the gentle lap of the push pole, and when some thought about an unreturned phone call or some email tried to elbow its way in, the old insomniac let it all out the back door. I learned to sail through thoughts as though they were clouds, and this relieved me of direct combat with intrusion. I sailed through clouds and looked into the water.

Before any real progress, however, I had another prod from Austin. We were standing on Tarpon Street in front of my little railroad house, the sun glinting off the tin roof, through the grapefruit tree. Leaning on his trailered skiff, Austin pointed down the street. "Read that sign. I think you need a prescription." It was a realtor's sign with enticements in small print. I read it aloud. He looked confused. "I still think you need a prescription." He got into his truck and drove off.

My wife said to me one evening after Austin and I had fished ten hours in a twenty-miles-per-hour wind, "This fishing you and Austin do just sounds like work." It gave me pause. My bones ached, my eyes were red, my tendinitis was aroused. There were no physical benefits—no aerobics, no stretching. It was actually probably bad for anyone who did it. Hemorrhoids, varicose veins, fallen arches come to mind. After a decade or two your dermatologist pleads with you to give it up. You consume a world of fossil fuel trying to get close to nature. A poet says to you, "I ask the fish permission to give herself to me, for I am hungry. I become the fish. The fish becomes me." The twisted sister within says, "I just want to kick fin."

I also have issues with the sun. It raises water temperatures to the point that snook want to come out of their winter hidey-holes and start busting bait. But snook are perhaps better suited to its effects than I am. My wife found on the Internet some discounted bedsheets of "thousand-count cotton." I wasn't sure what that was, but they're right smooth, and we were right proud to have them, but by the morning my bleeding lips had ruined them. I moved from SPF 45 to white gobs of zinc oxide and then to a kind of tube sock for my whole head, surmounted by a broad straw sombrero from a saddle shop in Alpine, Texas. I had become a cross between a fool and a leper, staring at tide tables. When I ran the skiff at anything over half speed, the sombrero folded back and I became a child's nightmare of Deputy Dawg, a macabre heat-seeking cartoon of not easily understood motivation.

Mostly, I fished alone.

One of the last days Austin and I fished this spring, we ran down south in Pine Island Sound to a creek with several shallow bays appended to it; left the boat tied to the push pole, which was staked into the soft bottom; and walked a bay that was almost, at this tide, dry land. We stood there silently for a long time, and nothing happened; nothing could happen because there was no water for it to happen in. The wind rustled the mangroves; egrets came and went. Off by the boat, a group of pelicans had surrounded some bait and would flap forward without taking off to scoop up a meal; tucking their chins to swallow, they looked polite and bashful. However, nothing was going on at all as we gazed at little more than bare ground. I was using all my mind tricks to keep looking and to avoid potential commentary on my eyesight.

The flat began to moisten. Austin stood beside me with his unrelenting thousand-yard stare. *What are we staring at?* I wondered. Austin wasn't saying. The tide had turned, and over time the flat flooded, at first with an inch or two; at about half a foot of depth, the snook, lazy pikelike shapes, began to come. They came steadily, and we both caught them in a string of explosive battles.

They came in such volume that it became necessary for us to stand back-to-back to manage the onslaught. We lost count of the fish we released, and Austin actually admitted it was the best day he'd ever had. My arm was lead.

I once had an episode of serious depression, and its onset was marked by a loss of interest in fishing. I believe I gave away tackle. I sold cheap my cherished Bogdan reel, which was presented to me thirty years later at a usurious price.

I marvel at people discussing depression, gnawing the topic of their own malaise like dogs on a beef knuckle. My experience of it was a disinclination to speak at all. I had the feeling of being locked in a very small and unpleasant room with no certainty of exit, and I recall thinking that it was the sickest you could possibly be and that my flesh had been changed to plaster. My business at the time was flight from expectations.

It was spring in Montana, and two old friends quite wisely arrived in my yard with a drift boat to take me to the river. I managed to say that I'd go if I didn't have to talk. As I was manifestly off my rocker, they were quick to agree, perhaps relieved at not having to hear my present thoughts. Once gliding silently down the Yellowstone, oars dipping, lines arcing out from either end of the boat, I began for the first time to picture better days, and it proved a turning point. I thought of incessant-angler pal and novelist Richard Brautigan, who relinquished his fly rod as he spooled up for suicide. Fishing, for many, is an indispensable connection to earth and life, and it matters little that the multitude that practices it is incapable of translating its ambiguities to another idiom.

A lingering, cool blow out of the Northeast dropped water temperatures again, spread foam lines across green whitecapped waters, and shrank the broad pallet of local angling geometry to a gerrymandered world of lees around islands and oyster bars. Each jaunt meant donning oilies and the continuous sting of saltwater on sunburned skin.

Mark Phillips—an Alaskan guide—and I went fishing anyway, taking a good spanking as we ran northeast to hide from the wind among the small mangrove keys scattered along the mainland. Mark told me a defining snook story as we poled out of the wind, staring into the water. He had cast to a huge snook, and the fish had followed his fly intently. Just at the moment he hoped for a strike, his cell phone, which he had set on vibration mode and placed on the gunwale, went off, and the buzz put the fish to flight. He threw down his rod, answered the phone, and endured an unpleasant conversation with a despised ex-girlfriend. Another sleazy snook moment.

We caught a couple of small fish, anchored the boat in eight inches of water, and split up to wade, barefoot for maximum stealth. We had seen so many stingrays that I spent half the time watching the bottom in front of me and the remaining half looking for fish. A cluster of juvenile wood storks were scattered on a sandbar not far in front of me, and when I stopped to watch them, a snook blew up bait in the mangroves behind them. I stole over to look, but there was no sign of the fish, and the storks spooked nothing when they flew out over the place I'd hoped to see him.

Then, farther back in a small bay, another blast. This time I was sure I could find the fish because the fish had fed in a very shallow corner of mangrove shoots. I crept over without a ripple and looked into every crevice: no fish. So I waded out of the shallow bay and was looking for new water when I noticed a faint wake leaving the area I had just inspected. This time it headed for an isolated clump of mangrove shoots that stood like a small, flooded island away from shore. Back into the bay on tiptoe and expecting only to be fooled again. Standing in perhaps six inches of water, I peered into the mangrove roots and there, nearly perfectly hidden, was my chameleon green snook.

I could only stand motionless and flick the leader into the maze of shoots. It landed a couple of feet from the fish, and as it sank he turned and struck. After several moments of close range snook pandemonium, I seized him by the lower jaw and the barbless fly fell out. I kept the fish in the water and ran my finger along his topside, feeling the thickness through the shoulders, the rigid upright fins. I then released him, and he swam off with cross-eyed, lazy insouciance. With the tops of the mangroves and wild palms tossing in the wind, the low-tide mud banks plowed up by wild hogs, this one was special.

In the end, I occasionally saw fish before Austin saw them. "Good eyes," he even said once. "I didn't see that one." It had been weeks since he'd last told me I needed a prescription.

And then for the rest of the season, with new spring breezes arising in flowering trees, I fished alone, daily. I was catching more fish than I did formerly and getting a bit complacent about how much I'd improved. There was even time to crawl around and peer at the queer, nameless fauna of the shallows. I followed a scarce banded puffer fish, a piggy-looking football with a tiny propeller of a tail that motored him along at such a slow pace that only his spines, or his benign herbivore face, kept him from being chow for some apex predator.

I looked through my binoculars whenever I felt like it. I listened to the conversation of wild pigs, quit fishing to gather oysters, took naps in the skiff, and made more elaborate lunches in the morning, sometimes at the expense of an early start.

There was no doubt about it: I was getting worse.

A Night on the Kennebago

Joseph Monninger

In the late afternoon light, in spring, Harvey is usually the first to get ready. He disappears outside the cabin, out to the porch where our waders dangle from hooks. We have learned, after thirty-five years of fishing together, to have our main meal early, so we have already eaten. We know we will not be off the water until at least nine, maybe later, and we will be cold and stiff and tired. The last thing any of us will feel like doing is cooking. After fishing is the time for drinks and talk and the orange heat of the woodstove.

"Jesus, they won't be rising yet," Ted says to Harvey, to me, to the world at large. "Haven't we learned anything in all these years coming here?"

Here is Maine's Kennebago watershed, arguably New England's best trout fishery, certainly the best for brookies. We stay at Kennebago Kamps, run by Reggie Hammond, Maine guide and friend. We make the reservation in January and jaw about it through emails for months before. It's an old business with us. We have fished together for a week each spring since we were in our twenties; we are now pushing sixty. We have been friends since seventh grade, since snapping towels and first-time beers, since Coach Gutek yelled at us to tackle blocking sleds, since Mrs. Vichedomit, the sweet-crazy math teacher, since Birdie and Sue and Cindy and Chris, girls in angora sweaters dancing in heated rec rooms to "Never, My Love" or "Mrs. Brown, You've Got a Lovely Daughter." We have been friends since before driving, friends since bike rides and dog trots across golf courses on summer nights, friends since crickets around a screen porch and late-night

Photo by Theodore Taigen

Joseph Monninger on the Cold River, Massachusetts.

Risk games, since fathers and mothers have died, children grown, cats gone missing. Friends in high mountains and on hitchhiking trips across the country, and on sports teams, even as competing wrestlers. We have played 10,000 games and remained friends, continued coming to this one spot like geese gliding into the water of the Kennebago with wings outstretched and heels cutting gunnels in the surface.

But Harvey is Harvey. A father of two, a salesman, a husband for nearly four decades, a weight lifter, a defensive end and center for the South Carolina Gamecocks after high school, a fisherman by determination as much as artistry, he haunts the water whenever he can. Little by little he has become a more successful fisherman than either Ted or I. He is an equipment guy, a man with a full vest, plenty of flies, coils of tippet. He is restless with fishing ahead of him.

"Suiting up," he says loud enough for us to hear.

"Jesus Christ," Ted says, happy with a glass of wine or a beer and a full belly. "We'll go up there, we'll wade around in the cold water, and the fish won't begin rising until an hour after we arrive."

I see Harvey shrug on the porch. Ted, joint by joint, climbs onto his feet and shakes his head. But he goes out, passes by Harvey, steps out into the chilly Maine evening, and looks up at the sky.

"Big night ahead of us," Ted says. "Fish on!"

Ted is the noise in us. The Bucker, we called him years ago. T-Bone, Doc, Papa Doc. Bearded, grey, large, he is a biology professor at the University of Connecticut, a lecturer to classrooms of 300, an expert on frogs, on oxygen use in spring peepers, a father of three, married to the same girl since the day he sat down in an undergraduate Intro to Bio hall at Colorado State sometime in the 1970s. A slashing guard in high school, a fade away jump-shot artist in the lunchtime pick-up games in the UConn field house during his athletic dotage, he's the big fun, the big drink buyer, story teller, back slapper, a beloved teacher and mentor to thousands of young people taking their first steps away from home. He's the Bucker.

And he throws the prettiest fly you ever saw. A natural. A gift. And we—Harvey and I—tell him only grudgingly, and never twice a season.

Call it cold. Call it overcast. Call it fifty-two degrees. Time doesn't matter. It could be any one of thirty-plus years. It could be sunny and warm; it could be the high alpine lakes of Wyoming, or the buggy snags of a Colorado beaver pond; it could be the New Hampshire streams near the Canadian border. Time runs together and their voices run together and here we are, single file, walking down from the dirt logging road through the rib of forest toward the Little Kennebago. "I saw one rise," someone says. Does it matter who? The soil slick under our feet, tree roots. At the water we grab branches—wading poles—because the river comes into the lake at this point and deposits dozens of submerged logs. We call it Gandalf's Pass, because we are grey men in chunky waders walking with staffs and taking large steps. Our sons have visited here and walked this passage with us, but not tonight. Tonight it's our triangle, our milking stool.

"Think I might try an Adams," Ted says, because he always tries an Adams and always says he'll try it.

Harvey, being Harvey, works his way along the shoreline, separating himself, his long legs moose-y and sure, a defensive end's legs wading through offensive linemen. He has places. He has ideas. I stay next to Ted so I can heckle him, can hear his stream of commentary about flies, trout, the political landscape, girls, women, the sweetness of a bank shot. Ted refuses to fish under the water. He doesn't like the plunk of a nymph or the feathered landing of a streamer. He's a dry-fly man, unless other people begin catching fish on something other than dry flies. Then he's a fishing pirate and a shameless borrower.

The old jokes rise. I begin laughing because nothing about any of the stories is new. Old backstory, old punchline, old characters. Down the lake, across the still water, I see Harvey shake his head at the first refrains of the old tales. The time he—Ted, this is—was working on a road crew and a blonde in a convertible stopped to give him water; the time he stole Birdie away from Harvey; the time he broke away for a long run from scrimmage at Roosevelt Junior High and waved to us on the sidelines an instant before someone crushed him.

"Do you two ever shut up?" Harvey says, because he knows we won't.

Then Harvey—usually it's Harvey, although it could be any of us—hooks the first fish of the night. We watch him, the skirt of white the fish makes when it clears the water, the question mark of his fly rod, the careful reach around for his fishing net. It could be a fish here, on this lake in Maine, or one on a river in Arizona, a bright cutthroat in Valentine Lake, Wyoming. It's Harvey fishing and what does it matter how big, how many, how why?

I catch a few. The trout begin to rise steadily, like rain or thrown sand. Ted takes a moment to retie his fly, and while he does he checks the mountain behind us. Years ago they slash cut the entire hillside and he gauges the reforestation every year. Together we have seen osprey and mink, black snakes and bald eagles, moose. Moose, especially. One year a moose ran the length of the lake as we watched and came to rest not far from us, its muzzle dripping, its bony face comical and perplexed. Another year we arrived to find a dead moose dropped down in the river, its ribs collecting grass. Ted's a bio teacher and he likes it all, holds forth on decomposition, energy exchange, nutrients.

Tonight, as the sun begins to slide behind the mountains, a flock of birds covers the water. They fly in synchronous waves, their wings bright and fluid, their ducking and bobbing like tropical fish in a rolling sea. Ted looks up. The birds make a hissing sound, almost; they sound like grainy snow blown across a driveway.

"Any ideas?" I ask him.

He shakes his head, but I know he will find out. I know he won't rest until he identifies them. He watches them, as transfixed now as he was as a boy.

Then it's the hour of the pearl. That's what Steinbeck called it: that moment, sweet and calm, when just before darkness the wind dies and the lake goes glassy. The temperature follows the sun, falling down from the sky and turning things crisp. But now one fish is fifty fish. They begin coming up, knives thrown against a plywood board, circles and splashes and an insect—which one, what size, what match?—flutters over the water. It becomes absurd for a little while. The fish can't be more eager. Ted drops his beautiful cast over them, arc, line, slow settling of the fly.

"Fish on," he says. "Oh, this is a big one."

But it seldom is. Small fish, the size of tablespoons. Down in the cove Harvey hooks one fish, lands it, hooks another. I can tell he is concentrating now. He will never brag, never claim to catch more than he does, never increase the size of a fish in its retelling. Where the truth is a beginning point for Ted and for me, for Harvey it is the only thing worth bothering to tell.

"So beautiful," Ted says, serious for a second, holding the fish quietly in the water. "Such coloring."

He stands in the hinge between lake and sky, his hand in the water as if he wanted to cup a drink. The trout rests on his fingers, and the lake covers his legs.

For a while it is simply fishing. Trout rise, cast, hook, take, splash, near miss, rise, fly, water, fog, reel sounds. For me, everything drops away. It is the only thing I do that is the only thing I do. No other thoughts, worries, considerations. Ten fish some nights; some nights forty or fifty, fish as fast as you can cast. In the big nights a certain lazy indifference invades some of it and takes part of the pleasure. Too many fish are sometimes worse than too few. One night, down on the river that connects the Little Kennebago to the Big Kennebago, Harvey and I walked into a hatch. Big fish—twenty inches, some of them—grabbed our casts among the alders. The best night fishing ever, maybe. At the end we both felt, what? An excess. A guilty nausea that the fish had been too willing, mixed with the solid memories of big fish slashing at our casts. But on this night, the one I am describing, the fishing is nearly perfect. A blend of good fish and skillful angling. Earned trout. Honorable trout. A fair wage for a night on the lake.

We have also been up here during the spring melt, when it was a job to catch a single fish. Seven days of Hare's Ears. But it is not like that this week. Tonight the fish hit in the surface film, greedy halts to a retrieved line. Probably an emerging insect shucking out of its casing like a man tangled in his trouser legs. They hit on the retrieve, not on the landing, the faster the retrieve the more solid the strike. I picture the trout down below, watching, seeing the line and fly skim across the surface like a plane going over their world.

It ends when it becomes too dark to see your fly. Ends when the fish have stopped rising. We could fish longer, and have some nights, but this night it is cold and raw, and rain threatens. We wear watch caps; when we aren't casting we have our hands jabbed down our waders, getting heat from our privates. I walk over to a small sandbar we have visited for twenty years and pull out a flask. Pass it around as Harvey joins me, then Ted. Smaller fish continue to rise close to shore. We call it Kmart fishing.

Small talk. Kids, jobs, summer plans. Bullfrogs begin to call, their voices filled with rubber bands. A pair of loons snake around the lake, let out their cackle. No one looks forward to Gandalf's Pass. It's a cold, crummy pass, and now that our bones are set, our muscles frigid, our balance is worse than ever. Some years we bring a canoe and paddle across, or use a float tube like a walker, but not this evening.

"Here we go," Harvey says, because it is always Harvey who gets us moving.

Big steps, worried balance. The logs spinning and catching at our feet. If we go down, as we never have but most surely will one day, it will be cold and dangerous and not easy to rise. We use the staves as a point of balance. The bottom of the lake swirls up and becomes a cloud of muck.

And in a little while we are back in my truck, three of us sitting across the front seat, our bulky bodies ridiculous, the Red Sox coming in from someplace warmer, brighter. The heater runs full out and is never quite enough. You can smell the lake on our boots and on our fingers and in our hair. Spring mud clings to us, and our waders make greasy sounds when we climb out. We pull off our socks when we shuck out of the waders. It is like a locker room from 100 years earlier, only calmer now, slower.

Then the ritual of the woodstove. A pint and a wee one. Ted usually with a glass of wine, a story to tell. Our limbs tingle from the cold, and little by little the woodstove fills the cabin. Do you remember? He died? Who was that, anyway? We pull out a plywood trophy my wife built years ago. It has small paper dials under each category: biggest fish, most fish, camp spirit, best dressed, first fish. Harvey, of course, doesn't lie. He serves as a referee as Ted and I trade whoppers, claiming to have hooked one at least fourteen inches. Ted eventually twists the dials to his satisfaction, leaving himself in perennial first place in every category. It's worth it simply to hear him. But sometimes, too, there is real talk: worries about a sick parent, insurance questions, retirement, investments, trouble with a grown child. We are long-standing stories to one another, cobbled tales with protagonists and themes. Each year is a chapter, or a sitcom, or whatever the intervening months have brought.

We feed the fire, have a second round. In the old days the drinking was more important, but now it's just a sideline. None of us can handle it as we used to. In our thirties we woke at dawn and fished until mid-morning, but now the breakfast talk, the second cup of coffee, is more interesting. And generally we—Ted and I—can count on Harvey to do our fishing for us, to try the lower river and to alert us if something pops. Maybe the rain begins, and maybe it doesn't, but we talk about what the run-off will do to the river, and how the fish may chase the dace up from the lower lake, and how the mergansers will point the way like arrows to the north. And later, with full bladders, one by one we pee on the cold, white grass outside the cabin, the moon a surprised "O" in an otherwise black night.

Then bed. Three bunks and the last talk, the talk we have shared since sleepovers in seventh grade, since slumber parties and raids on girls' houses, and late-night jumps into neighborhood pools. The talk that is part sleep, part memory. Little by little we leave the cabin, travel back, and it's all just fatigue and time. We go to that other country, that place only the three of us remember or care about, the land of our youth, of fresh limbs and quick muscles, where we witnessed the boy in each of us, and where that boy still lives in the others' memories, just there, just beneath the sixty-year-old, just there, one more time each spring.

The Legacy

Howard Frank Mosher

On my tenth birthday, my father and my uncle, Reg Bennett, took me fly fishing on the Esopus River, not far from our home in the heart of New York State's Catskill Mountains. It was a lovely evening in early June. We fished perhaps half a mile of river, from the old shoemaker's shop down toward the village of Phoenicia, until it was too dark to see our flies.

I'd grown up worm fishing for brook trout—still my favorite fish, but hard to catch on flies in the step-across-in-one-step, densely wooded mountain streams brookies favor. Fly fishing was clearly a different proposition. On the evening of my tenth birthday, we used wet flies, Catskill-style, with a lead fly and two droppers. My dad and uncle rigged me up with a gold-ribbed Hare's Ear, a Royal Coachman, and a third fly I can't remember.

Though not altogether easy at first, wet-fly fishing turned out to be considerably simpler than I had expected. Toss the flies quartering out across the current, let them drift downstream with your rod tip up, mend the line with your off hand to take up the slack. Quickly lift your rod a little higher when a fish strikes. Let the hooked fish tire itself out. How vividly I remember the crimson flash of the pan-sized rainbow trout that came to my flies that soft June evening. I even managed to net a few of them.

Dad fished along behind me, picking trout out of hard-to-reach spots I'd overlooked. Across the river, my Uncle Reg kept pace with us. Just at twilight, Reg did something I've never seen a fly fisherman do before or since.

He'd hooked a somewhat larger rainbow, maybe pushing a foot long. The fish ran upstream, then turned and came straight back down a short stretch of swift water, directly toward my uncle. As rainbows are wont to do, this one leaped out of the water. Instantly, and at the risk of losing the fish, my uncle jerked back on his fly rod, using the trout's own momentum to bring it sailing through the air right past him, about chest-high. As the fish flew by, Reg casually reached out and caught it in his landing net. By the time I fully realized what I'd just witnessed, he'd returned the trout to the river.

Afterward, my uncle said that netting the fish in mid-air was pure luck. He compared it to a high school baseball player facing Bob Feller, shutting his eyes and swinging and, once in a thousand times, connecting. Yet my uncle told me that his own fly fishing mentor, the fabled Catskill woodsman and angler Let Craig, had been able to perform the trick quite regularly.

In fact, when it came to wet-fly fishing for wild trout, very little that my dad and uncle did had anything at all to do with luck. They knew where those colorful Esopus rainbows liked to lie, in the slicks just below or above big rocks in the current. They knew which flies to use when, and how to give them the most natural action, enticing trout to strike even when they weren't feeding. In due time, of course, Dad and Reg explained to me

Photo courtesy of Howard Frank Mosher

Howard Frank Mosher's father (left) and uncle, Reg Bennett (right), in Quebec's Laurentians.

that the hard-hitting rainbows and ever-so-wary browns were "true" trout. Brookies, taxonomically speaking, were char. I've never really bought that, though. To me, then and now, char or no, the eastern speckled—or brook—trout is the "truest" trout of all.

The Catskills were a grand place for a trout-fishing kid to grow up in the 1950s. Evenings, Dad and Reg would tell me fishing and hunting stories, or my uncle would read to me from a wonderful, anecdotal history of the region. It was called *The Mountains Look Down*, and Reg himself had written it, though for some reason he'd never made an effort to get it published. No matter. I loved listening to my uncle read aloud about the early Catskill hemlock-bark peelers, spruce-gum gatherers, moonshiners, hermits, and trappers. They were all expert trouters, and nearly all of them were wet-fly men. Along with *Huckleberry Finn* and *Great Expectations*, Reg's unpublished *The Mountains Look Down* joined my pantheon of beloved boyhood classics.

Later, Reg and Dad and I fished together in Quebec's Laurentians. Here we used bigger, gaudier flies, with exotic names like Red Ibis, Silver Doctor, Parmachene Belle. This Canadian fly fishing could be spectacular, and the fish were all brook trout, some ranging up to three and four pounds. Once, on a remote lake in a violent thunderstorm, it seemed to be raining big brookies. That's how fast they rose to our flies.

When I finished college and got married, an aspiring, wet-behind-the-ears young fiction writer, my wife, Phillis, and I came north to Vermont's Northeast Kingdom. Thinking we'd teach for a year or two, save some money, then go on to graduate school—I was looking, frankly, for a blueprint for writing novels that doesn't exist—we wound up instead finding a home and, though I wasn't yet ready to write them, a gold mine of stories that no one else had yet discovered. Many of these stories, in one way or another, involved fishing or hunting. Not coincidentally, the three-county Northeast Kingdom was a trout fisherman's paradise.

Some local anglers used flies, though only rarely, for the huge, spring-run rainbow trout for which the Kingdom is famous. Hardly any of my new neighbors had ever seen a three-fly rig before. Some thought it must be illegal.

I, for my part, began to experiment with dry flies. Immediately, I caught more and bigger fish, especially those lunker brown trout disdainful of anything larger than, say, a size 20 Adams. Dry-fly fishing, however, seemed more like work. I still loved to find a new brook, hike up it to where it wouldn't hold a trout, and short-line my way back down with a Coachman or a red-legged grasshopper fly, fished wet. If that didn't work, well, a nice, firm garden worm would usually do the trick. I'm no purist, and, while I'm on the subject, I like to eat fish as well as catch them, especially freshly caught brookies.

When our son, Jacob Bennett Mosher (named for my fly fishing uncle, Reg Bennett), turned fifteen, he and I began going north to Labrador and Ungava, Quebec. This was fly fishing of an entirely different order. Wet flies, dry flies, streamers—it didn't really matter. Many of the rivers we fished were teeming with gigantic brook trout. In late August these fish, resplendent in their matrimonial colors, turned fiery red halfway up their sides. One afternoon under a boreal, blue sky, on an unnamed river that might very well never have been fished by anyone before, Jake hooked a two-pound brook trout on a muddler minnow. Instantly, a laker upward of twenty pounds seized the hooked brookie and refused to let go. Eventually, Jake handed me his fly rod, waded into the river, and came out with the lake trout in his arms and the brookie still clamped in the laker's jaws.

Photo courtesy of Howard Frank Mosher

**Howard Frank Mosher
and son Jake, Montana.**

By the time Jake and I started going to Labrador—we went five times, until I finally ran out of outdoor magazines to con into sending me—my Uncle Reg was in his early nineties. His wife, my aunt Elsie, had died ten or twelve years prior. Recently, Reg had fallen for a much younger woman. I'll call her Margaret.

It was, to say the least, an unusual courtship, even for January-May relationships. In her mid to late thirties, trim and athletic, Margaret seemed to have appeared in Reg's life from nowhere. He was hopelessly infatuated by her. Even fly fishing his Catskill Mountain streams took a back seat to this new romantic preoccupation. When Margaret married a man her own age, informing Reg only after the ceremony, he was devastated. A few months later, Margaret's marriage ended as suddenly and mysteriously as it had begun. My uncle located and hired a divorce lawyer to represent her. What, wondered Reg's friends and family, could possibly be happening to him? Personally and professionally, my uncle and mentor had always been a man of superb judgment. None of his behavior in regard to Margaret seemed to make sense.

On my last trip to the Catskills to see Reg, a month or so after that glorious afternoon on the Labrador River where my son, Reg's namesake, caught the brookie and the big lake trout, I drove my uncle to the little village where he had been born and raised. There we sat in a pull-off, looking down at the stream where, long ago, I'd caught my first trout, though not on a fly.

"Howard," Reg said. "I have something important to tell you."

He paused, and the pause lengthened into what seemed to me like a prolonged hesitation. For Reg, that was unusual. Once my uncle made up his mind, he rarely hesitated.

Reg thought for a moment longer. Then he nodded and said, "Well, Howard, you'll understand." After another brief pause, then he said again, with quiet conviction, "You'll understand."

A few weeks later, Reg died, becoming a part of his beloved Catskills, where he would now remain for all time to come.

The envelope arrived by registered mail a few days after my uncle's death. Inside was a copy of Reg's will, naming me as his principal heir, the recipient of his home and property. Like Pip's legacy in *Great Expectations*, it was an unexpected and valuable inheritance, particularly for a scrambling writer with two kids approaching college age. I had also inherited most of the contents of the house, including Reg's extensive library, with several first editions of Hemingway and Fitzgerald, his antique fly rods, and his manuscript of Catskill stories. Still, as the leaves blew down that fall, and the Green Mountains of Vermont turned grey for the winter ahead, it was a sobering time for me. I had inherited, besides a house, a responsibility. Reg had devoted his life to education. One way or another, I would use the inheritance for our children's education. And one way or another, I would find a way to publish Reg's great stories.

One evening the following week, our phone rang. The caller identified herself as the executor of Reg's will. "Of course," she said, "as you know, there is no property. Reg gave it all away."

It was true. A few weeks before he died, Reg had turned over his house and land to Margaret. I was as stunned by this disclosure as I had been a week earlier in learning that I was to be Reg's heir. Indeed, he had given Margaret every last possession except for some furniture, fly rods, his books and the manuscript of *The Mountains Look Down*, which would still go to me in accordance with the provisions of his otherwise invalidated will. But when, still in a state close to shock from my conversation with the executor, I called Margaret to inquire about the fly rods, first editions, and unpublished manuscript, she informed me that some months ago, Reg had given them all away, as well. She didn't know to whom. I was welcome to come and look through the house—now her house—Margaret said. But I would find nothing.

What distressed me most was the missing manuscript, *The Mountains Look Down*. Despite his own disclaimers, Reg wrote beautifully. Where were those true stories chronicling the history of his hometown, and mine? I feared that they were lost forever, and that loss, for me, was unbearable to contemplate. Maybe, like Boswell's famous journals, the missing manuscript might turn up in a notions shop in France. Or a roadside boutique in the Catskills. I doubted it, though. All trace of Reg's stories seemed to have vanished as completely as the Catskill hunters and fishermen he'd written about so lovingly. How could I fulfill my promise to my uncle to find a publisher for *The Mountains Look Down* if I couldn't locate the manuscript?

Fast-forward fifteen years. At sixty-five, I was still an ardent fly fisher-man. Also, I was still writing fiction, often about fly fishing and fly fishers. I had just published my novel, *On Kingdom Mountain*, set in the early 1930s in northern Vermont. In it, the feisty heroine, Miss Jane Hubbell Kinneson—a fine angler herself, and the owner of three wilderness ponds containing a unique sub-species of brook trout—is determined to protect her mountain fastness from development, especially from a new, four-lane superhighway that would bring "civilization" to the last frontier of Vermont.

I'd been out on the highways of America myself for the past two months, slogging from city to city on an author's tour for the new novel. Late one af-ternoon, on the final leg of the tour, I found myself in Albany. With two or three hours to kill before my event that evening, I decided to go for a walk.

I suppose that it was natural, as I headed west on Broadway, to find myself thinking of my Uncle Reg. Although he'd never attended high school a day in his life, in his thirties he had put himself through SUNY-Albany— then Albany State Teachers' College—where he eventually earned a master's degree. While Reg's house and property had duly gone to Margaret—I did not contest the transfer of his property, which I believed, and still do believe, my uncle sincerely wished Margaret to receive—I had, over the years since his death, searched high and low for the missing manuscript. I'd located a few scraps and pieces of it, but long after I'd recovered from the loss of the legacy, the fate of those Catskill Mountain stories gnawed at me like the eagle sent by Zeus to eviscerate Prometheus anew each day. The madden-ing disappearance of those tales of Let Craig, the Chichester fly fisher *par excellence*; Grammy Moon, the local witch who could conjure a trout into jumping right out of the Esopus into her frying pan; and dozens of others remained a great disappointment in my life.

Distracted by these reflections, I walked farther than I intended to. I was surprised to find myself on the SUNY campus, just outside the university library. Recently, I'd been looking, in a desultory fashion, for a novel about a Canadian con man, a book I'd read decades ago and then lost track of. *What the hey*, I thought. Now that I was this close to a large library, why not try once more?

I went in, poked around in the fiction section, scanned some *New Yorker* and New York *Times* reviews from the fall of 1977, when, I was pretty sure, the con man book had been published. Nothing. Then I checked the baseball scores and standings in the Albany *Times Union*. I was thinking about baseball, my uncle Reg Bennett, and, fleetingly, the missing manuscript, when the dimmest of recollections flared up in the recesses of my mind. An eerie feeling passed over me. It was as if some part of me knew something, something of tremendous importance, that I hadn't yet consciously processed. I walked over to the information desk. How far back, I inquired, did the library's files of SUNY-Albany master's theses go? The young man on duty at the desk wasn't sure, but after I explained what I was looking for, he punched the name I gave him into his computer, made a quick note to himself, and told me he'd be back shortly. I still don't know what I expected him to find. Probably nothing.

At length, the librarian returned with a cardboard box, which he placed on his desk. "Is this, by any chance, what you're looking for?"

The flaps, as I recall, were fastened with twine. Inside, wrapped neatly in plain brown paper, was a hefty manuscript. The title page read: *"The Mountains Look Down: A Study of a Mountain Village. A Thesis Presented to the Faculty of the N. Y. State College for Teachers in Partial Fulfillment of the Requirements for the Degree of Master of Education. By Reginald R. Bennett."* What followed was, as nearly as I could determine, a word-for-word transcription of Reg's missing manuscript. It began with the stately, assured cadences I remembered from my early boyhood when Reg first read me his stories: "In the winter of 1863, a man came west from the Hudson River, traveling by easy stages, and slowly, with horse and sleigh, to the foothills of the Catskills." I could scarcely believe it. Searching for one book, I had found another, one that was infinitely more precious and personal. I had found the book whose stories, nearly sixty years ago, inspired me to write my own.

They were all here, just as I recalled them, tales of Catskill fishermen and hunters, moonshiners, ginseng diggers, ox drovers, and famous guides and storytellers. Here were the sagas Reg had read to me when I was five and six and seven, about fabled fly fishers and town-team baseball players, about Hermie the barn burner, Jingle the hermit, and Grammy Moon the mountain witch. The stories that I had supposed to be lost forever.

The manuscript was about 500 pages long. The librarian ran off a copy for me, for which, as I recall, I paid thirty dollars—surely the best thirty dollars I ever spent. Then I walked out of the library, into the cooling early evening, with my legacy.

How do you know when you've finished a story? In real life, after all, stories tend not to have well-defined endings. There is always one more thing to happen, one more thing to tell. A few weeks before Reg died, up on that mountainside looking down on our hometown, just before he told me that he had something important to say, and then apparently changed his mind, he asked me a question.

"Howard," Reg said, "Do you think Margaret loves me?"

It was a question that I could have answered in many ways, each of which would have been truthful. I could have said, "Yes, as much as she loves anyone." Or, "In her own way, I'm sure that she does." Or, "I can't see into Margaret's heart. But I have no reason to think otherwise."

I am far from proud of some of the things I did and said and thought in regard to the bitter matter of my disinheritance. But I am glad to report that, in reply to this question, I said, without hesitation, and meaning it as much as I've ever meant anything, "Yes. I know she does."

Looking off down the valley, Reg nodded. I believe that this may well have been the moment when he made up his mind what to do with his property. Certain mysteries remain, as they are apt to with true stories. Where *did* Reg's fly rods and first edition books and great Catskill manuscript go? Why did Margaret get married and divorced in less than a year? What was the exact nature of Reg's undeniable love for her and hers for him? Was she a surrogate daughter? Were they lovers? I'll never know. The point is, Reg had trusted me to understand his decision.

The point is, at last I do.

September 23, 2010

Jake Mosher

It isn't the first mountain snow, fall morning with heavy frost, or cold, north wind that turns my thoughts to Montana's long winter each year. It isn't strings of geese or raucous, southbound sand hill cranes, or even the absence of pre-dawn songbird notes. Instead, it's late-summer days just like this when, with only subtle hints of what's coming, nature goes out of its way to show me what's going to disappear.

There's no wind, and the temperature is already approaching sixty degrees, though the sun hasn't been up for more than two hours. Heat waves pulse between me and the lodgepole pine ridge on the western edge of the meadow, the forest blurring to a blanket of dark green tipped steeply toward timberline, where jagged peaks carve a broken horizon in sky a deeper blue than it was a month earlier. I shiver as some residual instinct as old as man tells me to lay in winter meat, chop wood, chink walls, and brace myself for rougher times.

Today, I'm doing something else. I blink hard and focus on the beat-up handle of my beat-up Battenkill fly rod. A new, size 10 grasshopper, complete with yellow legs and a splash of red behind its wings, is buried to its barb in the cork. Myriad fissures spread through the soft wood from the hook, testament to the fact that the wrapping of any fly holder that may have been on this rod gave way before I was born, and the best way to fish the woody, northern Vermont brooks where I grew up was with a long pole, monofilament line, angle worms, and hundreds of Eagle Claw hooks clipped and un-

Jake Mosher with steelhead, Idaho.

clipped into this handle. I shiver again and start across the meadow.

The creek is an odd combination of exactly as I remember it and brand new. I've fished it once a year, always on days like this, for well over a decade. I remember where its pools are and also the pockets I unwittingly kicked trout from without casting to. I remember individual fish, encounters with elk, moose, and once a martin, and wolf tracks where they crossed a sand bar. I know on a level similar to my sense of approaching winter that it's going to be a perfect day, though I can't predict everything that will happen.

I suppose that's why I'm here. To mark time, to ease into a new season, to celebrate doing what I've loved from the time I was three years old and felt the first magical tug of a trout. Stripping line from my reel, I realize its ticking is the first sound I've heard louder than the swish of boots through dewy grass, and in a millisecond also realize that wouldn't have been the case three weeks earlier when summer had a stronger hold here. I shrug off a chill, false cast three or four times, and land the hopper downstream at a forty-five degree angle, close to the opposite bank in a patch of quick water. It's gone almost as soon as it hits, vanished in a swirl of color, as a ravenous brook trout finds it faster than my eye can follow. I jerk the rod instead of lifting it, reflexes reacting before I feel the fish, and I miss him.

I cast again, not as well this time, but the trout returns and is hooked. He heads for his undercut bank—that shady overhang that's kept his mottled back darker than fish living midstream—but is turned with firm pressure from the rod and brought skidding toward my feet.

There's nothing prettier than wild brook trout at the onset of fall, when they take on their spawning colors, and this ten-incher sports crimson his full length. The edges of his fins are outlined in a rich white, and the haze of blue around the spots on his sides is the shade of similar spots on the mourning cloak butterflies I remember from the week I learned to fly fish on a stream in upstate New York near my grandparents' house thirty years ago. As I bend to wet my hands before handling the fish, memories of that week flood back, coming as the smell of early morning coffee, the sounds of water fed by snowmelt, excitement only a boy can feel doing something he loves with men, and the gentle curl of brown trout laid in a wicker creel on a bed of the spring's first grass. Holding the same rod I did then, the years between shrink, and I remember my father teaching me to cast, his hands wrapped around mine to guide the rod, our arms moving together, the white Coachman settling a few feet upstream of a limestone ledge, bamboo suddenly endowed with life and the weighty pull of a good fish.

I breathe deeply, realizing I've been holding my breath, unsure of how long. The shadow of a male marsh hawk flicks by, and I'm grateful for the company. Vivid memories of long ago from the other side of the country and the other end of the solstice aren't unwelcome, but like my sense of encroaching winter, come with a certain uneasiness, and I'm glad to see I'm not totally alone here.

Jarred back to the present, I gently work the fly from the trout's mouth, my eye again unable to follow him as he torpedoes downstream.

I pivot, strip more line, and throw dry-fly-style, this time toward a run broken by granite boulders. The hopper touches down, swirls in an eddy, and bobs toward me two or three feet before the next trout has it. It's another male, smaller than the first though no less colorful, and full of fight. I give him the run of his pool, not because I have to but because that's partly why I'm here—to savor the day and be certain it yields enough memories to help me through the months ahead.

Working upstream, perhaps not casting to every pool though certainly hitting most of them, those coming months begin to fade from my mind, leaving me entirely in the moment, my existence confined to the arc of my rod on the cast, the few feet of water visible to me, a sense of wild country all around, and the never-ending thrill of feeling a fish.

It takes an hour to reach the first stretch of woods where the creek falls more sharply, its pools darker and deeper, the pungent odor of pine mixing with the less definable scent of the forest. High water from above-average snow last winter has eroded more of the roots of a great fir sitting on a bend where there's always a good fish. I creep up on my hands and knees, careful to obey the only cardinal rule of brook trout fishing and not be seen, pull my line in until the leader knot comes grudgingly through the top guide, my fly less than two feet off the rod tip. I reach out and dangle it down into the fork of a water-worn log that has surprised me annually with its unwillingness to wash away in the spring. The hopper meets the surface, skips sideways on the crest of a wave, then heads under the fir as I give it line. I know right away the trout that comes for it is a big fish. He holds effortlessly in the current, bolting when I stand, sucking the leader knot back through the guides, taking line from the reel, the rod jumping twice before the fly is torn loose and he's gone.

I've experienced very little in life as defeating as losing a big fish. I've been knocked out in a boxing ring, had home runs hit off me as a college pitcher, and missed a handful of shots at trophy big-game animals, but the moment my rod dies and my mind wraps around the fact that a hell of a trout is gone has a unique ability to drain my energy, soaking deep into my soul. It's pointless to keep my fly in the water, but I can't bear to lift it and complete the loss. It twists under the fir and tangles on some root I can't see, where, with a disgusted jerk of the rod, I leave it as though it's somehow to blame.

Not wanting to fish in the woods anymore, long strides carry me up an elk path a quarter mile to the next meadow, where the stream forks for the first time, a tributary cutting a narrow seam to the north, heading away toward a narrower crease in a distant mountain. At the confluence, I stop to tie on another fly and decide to follow the tributary at least to the timber. I wonder why I've never done it before, the loss of the fish giving way to excitement of the unknown—albeit 200 yards of tiny, meadow brook.

It's been a wet summer and the grass has grown tall, folding over the water from one bank to the other. At an oxbow, I spot what looks like enough of an opening in the timothy hay to sneak a fly through and land a lucky, blind cast into the brook. I can't see the fly, but the splash of a fish signals a strike. He's well hooked, and on a short line I extricate him from the leaning sage he's gone under, swinging him up onto the bank. He's the better part of a foot long, thick through, with a lower jaw beginning to hook, mimicking in miniature the big brookies I caught as a teenager with my father in Labrador. I've plucked him from water barely wide enough to turn around in, taking him for a few moments out of the stream he's driven up to ensure that in coming years some of his offspring and I may meet.

As I'm thinking about it—time again seeming an abstract dimension that I realize, with quickened heartbeat and shorter breath, is going to pass all too rapidly—I notice an obsidian arrowhead jutting from mole diggings near where the fish continues to flop. With the trout returned to the brook, his V-shaped wake gone upstream, I peel the point out of the ground and rub it clean. Well made and thin, expertly knapped long before this stream saw its first brook trout, it's missing only the tip, left perhaps in an elk rib a thousand years ago. A treasure to me, I smile thinking how puzzled its original owner would be that I don't rework it, look for a suitable willow shaft, and put it to use as it was intended. I'm careful to get it all the way down to the bottom of a pocket in my jeans, looking up in time to see a cow and calf elk melt into the timber 100 yards from me, once more feeling as though the time that's passed between their departure and that of the Indian who made this point may be as brief as summer here. As if on cue, a faded fritillary butterfly drifts by, offering three or four tired wing beats before floating to the ground. Behind me, a single, pearl-grey cloud hangs low in the north sky—the first of many that will eventually drive all butterflies to ground.

I find one more pool to fish in the tributary, flailing the hopper down through grass to the surface, and the trout that comes this time is scarcely larger than the fly, though he somehow manages to hook himself. He'd better be careful, I think as I release him, wondering how it is he's survived this long with fish like the last one I caught so nearby.

Cutting back to the main stream through low sage and blue bunch wheat grass, I flush a meadowlark. It flies straight away without offering me a view of its yellow breast, a sight I connect more with the snowless, south slopes of March than this time of year, anyway.

Grasshoppers, including giant red- and yellow-winged locusts, leap away with every step, the air alive with the crackle of wings. One of them sails over the brook, lands on a strand of bending grass, and is picked clean by a jumping fish, whose over-zealous launch carries him wide, forcing him to twist back on himself, taking the hopper on the way down. The image freezes in my mind and I know I'll never forget it.

It's half a mile to more woods and the shell of a Model A rusting among ragged blue asters and pink-topped fireweed. Hard to imagine someone driving in here ninety years ago, coming by car to this remote corner of Montana, where, in stark contrast to the rest of the state, there are no roads today. I tug at the driver's door, and as usual it moves only enough to send a garter snake zipping under the frame. There's a story of why it's here I'm sure, and the one I want to believe today involves a fishing expedition and a long, long walk home. That sits better with me than the gathering clouds and the possibility that this vehicle belonged to a backcountry trapper who didn't make it out.

There are three pools in the 300 yards of woods between the Model A and the next meadow, and they never hold as good a fish as they look like they should. They must lack cover, I think each time I fish them, watching my fly float untouched through a Currier & Ives run. Today, the first two pools are predictably barren, but in the third, a cauldron-shaped hole patchworked by sun feeling its way through the pine, I nail a good cutthroat. A true native who has withstood the onslaught of the more aggressive brook trout, he's been relegated to one of the least desirable stretches of water yet has grown to a solid thirteen inches. Like the leaping brook trout I saw earlier, he's one I won't forget.

Twenty black angus are waiting at a rail fence in the next meadow, clustered under a group of squat pines where I usually stop for lunch. Even though they scatter like wild elk, they've been there long enough this year to force me to look for another spot to eat. I pick a group of rocks on the north side of the opening where I can sit with something against my back and face away from the billowing clouds. My sandwich bread is dry before I finish, all moisture gone into air devoid of humidity. I've attracted a grey jay and toss half the remaining crust in his direction. He flutters down from a stunted spruce whose lower limbs have recently been raked clean by a bull elk's antlers, cocks his head to look at me, picks up his meal, and eats it with the same speed that the fish I've caught find my fly. The remaining piece of bread I place in the middle of my chest, lying down, arms at my side, eyes closed. Only a few seconds pass before I feel the bird hop onto my shirt. I can't help laughing, and as my stomach moves so does this camp robber, flying away with his lunch.

I've brought an apple, and its flavor—fall in New England—is out of place here. For the second time today, I look at my fly rod and remember fish from long ago, rainbows this time, caught in a river full of red, soft maple leaves. For an instant, I can smell it—decaying vegetation, damp air, iridescent scales scraped off in a metal sink. As quickly as ants find my apple core, it's gone, and I stand, still not looking north, and head back to the brook.

Two hours later and another mile and a half upstream, well above the third fork in the creek, I enter a meadow where every visible rock has been turned over recently by a bear seeking insects. The earth beneath one of the larger stones is still damp, and just as I realize the bear must be nearby I see him pigeon-toeing toward a rotten fir. He goes at the bark with gusto, claws ripping long chunks of orange wood onto the ground, inspects his handiwork with close-set, beady eyes and a nose that misses nothing, and continues on out of sight. I stare after him, trying to decide exactly what color to call him—the rare cinnamon or more common chocolate. He was cinnamon, I tell myself, though I know it could have been the way the sun played off his sleek coat. Either way, he looked as though he'd put on good weight and should winter well. I like to think of him sleeping inside some crevice high on one of the mountains that ring this brook, alpine fir limbs gathered all around him as snow piles to six feet and higher. I've seen this country in the winter, viewed from a highway thirty miles away on top of the Continental Divide, when it appears in soft shades of blue and white, barren except for a few hardy fur bearers and snowshoe hares. If I see it this year, I know I'll think of the bear.

I've got less than a mile of fishable brook left and tell myself I have to slow down. I've got to draw out the day. I'm not ready to come to the beaver swamp where the main channel divides into slender fingers shallow enough to freeze solid. It seems mere moments ago that I made the morning's first cast, and as badly as I want to add more minutes to the day, I've no better luck doing so than I do slowing my progression toward the final pool. I'm there in an hour, standing downstream from the last bend deep enough to hold a trout, a severely mangled grasshopper fly saying I've caught an awful pile of fish today. I strip line, start to cast, then have a better idea.

It's been years since I've thrashed the grass along a meadow brook trying to catch a grasshopper in my hands. I'm as quick as I was the last time I did this, I tell myself, swiping at a fat hopper perched on the uppermost leaf of a sage bush. I feel his body against my palm but my hand doesn't close in time and he flies away. It takes a few minutes, but I get one, his tobacco-colored spit staining my skin. I hold him tight between my thumb and index finger, crawl up to the edge of the bend, and toss him into the middle of the brook. He kicks twice for the opposite bank before the best trout of the day has him. It's a fish I really want to catch, better even, I think, than the one I lost far downstream in the woods.

I crawl back to where I've left my rod, check the knot on the fly, pull line from the reel, and begin false casting from my knees. I know the trout may have seen me when he took the live hopper, and also that I've got to make this cast perfect. I strip more line, watching the fly sail further from me, instinctively realizing when it's time to let it drop, which it does lightly, touching the surface before any of the leader.

Three things happen simultaneously. Clouds swallow the sun, a cold, north breeze touches my cheek, and the big trout sips my fly with the delicate kiss of a fish sure of its target. And then all hell breaks loose. Icy rain slaps me in the face, the trout explodes, bulling upstream into a side channel less then eight inches deep, and I have an acute sense—one any man who spends much time in wild country develops—that I'm not alone. Even as I follow the fish on foot, jumping over sage, stumbling in and out of the deep trails cut by cattle in early summer when this land was more marsh than meadow, I'm looking over my shoulder, scanning my backtrail, certain I'm being watched.

In thirty yards, the fish is out of brook, yet like salmon I've seen in Alaska, still attempts upstream movement. He twists and shivers, red gills flaring, square tail slashing air as I leap headlong off the bank, my hands pinning him to the soft bottom before he's able to orient himself downstream. For a second, I'm less aware of another presence, but by the time I've got the fly out and the trout walked down to deeper water I can feel it again—something sizing me up through the rain that's falling in earnest now, shielded from view by its curtain, or the timber, or the mist sailing toward the brook from the mountains.

With an indignant toss of his head, the free trout vanishes beneath the pocked surface, gone so entirely that even my muddy shirt and rod lying twenty feet away don't fully convince me that I caught him. I stare until my vision blurs and water runs off the brim of my hat, only then remembering that the muted snap I heard diving off the bank onto the fish was the tip of my Battenkill catching and breaking between boot and sage.

It's broken two guides down from the tip—a ragged fracture that won't be mended. In a rush of memories, as though the bamboo is freeing spirits confined to its hollow, six-sided core, I see my grandparents' house again, remember the names of brooks I fished as a boy and thought long ago I'd lost to the currents of big waters in the Rocky Mountains, see a late-fall Vermont landscape from the eyes of a kid crushed at the thought of fishing season ending, and can almost feel the spongy moss growing six inches deep along rivers in Labrador where this rod was tested by fish who'd never seen a fly or a man. Like a lion dog I once watched snarl at the night, I whirl around, fixing my eyes on the treeline behind me, seeing only the smudge of pine through slaty rain. And then I'm walking at double-time, moving past the places I fished much more recently, memories from today mixing with those from the past until they run together in a realization that much of my life has been spent in close proximity to a trout stream.

By the time I reach the woods where I lost the good fish, it feels as though there's snow mixing with rain. I don't see any flakes yet, but the prickle on my arms tells me they're only a few degrees away. I push on through fleeting thoughts of trying the pool once more, broken rod and all, deciding my memory from this year is of a trout that got away and that's all right. It isn't dark in the woods, but it isn't light, either, the trees taking on definition only where they join sky above me, their trunks a conglomerate of black masses. I'm not as convinced I'm being watched as I was further upstream, but am not totally at ease, either, and want to get down into the last meadow before true night finds me.

I don't quite make it. An enveloping, western darkness falls twenty minutes before I reach the first pool I fished, though it's stopped raining now and I can see a planet shining in the north. Winter isn't coming tonight.

At the tent where my day began, it takes some earnest searching to find wood dry enough to start a fire. There are spruce here, and their innermost limbs have been protected from the brunt of the storm. They snap to force from my hands and, with coaxing breath and careful flame, begin to burn inside the circle of stones where I've had small fires for fifteen years. In time, I'm able to add larger limbs of pine and fir, until eventually a sphere of light and heat keeps the night at bay for twenty feet in all directions and my clothes begin to steam dry.

I don't know how long I sit and watch the flames or how many logs I add or when it is my eyes first close. Like coming to the last pool of the day, I realize only that, inevitably, time has passed and I must sleep. I reach inside my pocket for the arrowhead, fingers wiggling through the hole it's sliced in my jeans, which allowed it to escape, feeling loss and gain and exhaustion all at once. I crawl inside my tent, zip the door behind me, burrow into my sleeping bag, turning toward what's left of my fire and the orange glow of coals through canvas.

I'm not entirely conscious now, but I don't think I'm in full dream. I can see the brook, in the meadow above the second stretch of woods, I think, near where I ate lunch. Somehow there's a pool I missed, and it looks like a damn good one. I start toward it, stepping over a log capped with British solider lichen, a Vermont moss that I realize is out of place here, also understanding that my unbroken rod isn't right either. Go with it, I figure, as I begin to cast, aiming the fly toward a seam in the current. It lands where it should, the fish comes hard, and I struggle to stay with the image, my body falling toward deep sleep. Just one more, I think. Just one more.

A Shell Game

Craig Nova

I don't think I am different from most fishermen, at least in one regard, and that is the fact that, at least in the beginning, I spent a lot of time avoiding a central, if not critical, question: "Just what the hell am I doing out here, on this stream, with these fish?"

Of course, like many serious matters, the initial impulse doesn't seem like that big a deal, but as time goes on, as you spend more time on various streams, as you buy more fly rods, fly boxes, waders, wading boots, zingers, nets, not to mention flies, books, maps, GPS devices, fly tying equipment and materials ("Genuine Australian Possum"), hooks, and vices, and as you spend more time writing letters to friends who have been to Montana, Alaska, New Zealand, Austria (where, I'd like to add, I have been myself . . . terrific fishing, but expensive), this question, so long avoided, so neatly squirreled away, becomes more pressing and, finally, it requires an answer.

Some easy answers come to mind, but they are all pretty thin. It keeps you out of bars and trouble, and that blonde down there on the last stool, with her legs so becomingly displayed from a bar stool, might be avoided (if you are, say, married) if the Green Drake hatch is on its way.

Next, fishing is a hobby. This answer isn't even worth considering. . . . It puts fly fishing in the same realm as building a three-masted, square rigged ship out of kitchen matches.

No, when you go through all the cheap answers, you have to dig deeper. And so, in ascending order, I thought, before giving an example of some of the answers in a practical circumstance, where these answers are ap-

Photo by Robert DeMott

Craig Nova with spring creek rainbow, Montana.

plied, I would list, in order of importance, what I have discovered.

First, when you are on a good stream and the fish are rising to, say, small white flies, and the water is green, it is not like looking at an Impressionist painting, but being in one. This is profoundly, if not spiritually, satisfying. It is not like watching the natural world, but being in it. Also, one obtains more profound satisfaction, since this circumstance (green water, white flies, rising fish) makes you feel your humanity in a larger sense. You have the sensation of communicating with trout. When was the last time you communicated with a gazelle? Or a spitting cobra?

Sooner or later, though, I have to descend even deeper to, as Melville was fond of saying, "the lower layer." This is down in the depths where most people don't want to go. And when I need a guide for this journey into the depths of the powerful and the unseen, I turn to Marcus Aurelius.

In this passage, when he speaks of "tool, vessel," etc., I take this to mean he is referring to trout, although of course he could be speaking of almost anything made by, well, some mystery we don't understand.

"Every instrument," says Marcus Aurelius in paragraph forty of the sixth book of his Meditations, "tool, vessel, if it does that for which it has been made, is well, and yet he who made it is not there. But the things which are held together by nature there is within and there abides in them the power which made them; wherefore the more is it fit to reverence this power, and to think that, if thou dost live and act according to its will, everything in thee is in conformity to intelligence. And thus also in the universe the things which belong to it are in conformity with intelligence."

So, as far as I'm concerned, the time on the stream, in touch with the vessel (trout) that has been made by that mysterious intelligence in the universe, is not just wasting time. It is a moment of profound peacefulness.

And then, you know, it is fun.

But now we come to the real depths, the Ninth Circle of motivation. I am a novelist, and so I claim a particular license to spend time on a stream, and, as I promised, here is an example of the various principles I've mentioned, not as abstract notions, but in hard-hitting practice. They are lurking here, just as surely as a large trout against a bank, but they combine to help with a practical matter, too.

Writers, and novelists in particular, are a superstitious lot, and this is so because they have so little control over what happens when they sit down to write. One day, a book will unfold like going to the movies. No effort seems necessary at all, so easy and so much fun, so satisfying and effortless that it is a sort of joke, and a cosmic one at that, that a writer gets paid for having such days. This doesn't happen that often, and it's been my experience, too, that such days turn out to be an illusion, since the pages done under such circumstances turn out to be pretentious, silly, and outright delusional. I will look them over and wonder just what the hell I could have been thinking.

And the reverse is true, too. The novelist will start the day with a mild depression and the sense that not much can really be done with the new book. It is so flawed and resists any attempt to fix it. Maybe, the writer thinks, the entire thing is the product of some bad mood, indigestion, or just another screwy idea that should be left alone. My experience has been that sometimes the best work is produced during those days when a writer is mildly depressed. Or, the lesson I've learned is that if you try to elbow Tolstoy out of the way—that is, you shoot for the moon—nothing good comes from it.

So, of course, when I finished work in the late spring or early summer, and had had one of those days that is way up or way down, I'd go to a stream I liked on the western side of Vermont, where, in the evening, a pool was almost always dimpled by rising trout. But the difficulty with the place was that, while it was fairly predictable, often it seemed dead, or if it was filled with those rings of trout taking a caddis fly from the surface, they would be picky and hard or impossible to catch.

Under these circumstances, the superstitious novelist sees this as a sign, a sort of fishing version of what is wrong with the book he is trying to write, that the inability to catch the fish, the frustration of the moment, the defiance of them (which is the way the writer sees the essence of both the fish and the book), are signs of how the writer is not up to the task at hand. Getting skunked, as they say, when you are worrying about something else always seems more significant than otherwise.

Of course, as time went by, and as I managed to get through one book and then another, as the children got a little older and the difficulties I faced with them (showing them how much I loved them) were partially solved, I came up with a solution to the sensation that not catching fish on a bad day was an indication of general failure. And, in this solution, I discovered something as totally unexpected and beguiling as a book that begins to work out contrary to all expectation. Or should I say, in this solution, I came across another mystery and one I think about all the time.

The landscape of Vermont north of where we lived was a series of small valleys, all of which had rivers of various sizes that ran down to the Connecticut. One of these, the Williams River, was very poor water, at least in the lower and larger sections. It got too hot in the summer, and hot water can't carry much oxygen, and so it was not a good river for trout. Still, the water looked good, here and there, and I discovered by accident that one hole in this river was filled with fish, just stiff with them.

Frankly, I don't know how that occurred, although I suspect that perhaps a driver for the Vermont stocking program was in a hurry or had extra fish to get rid of, or for some other reason (maybe a flat tire) found it necessary to dump an entire load of nine- to twelve-inch trout into this pool. I don't know if that is what happened. It is a guess, but whatever the reason, the place was filled with fish, and when I had had a rocky afternoon someplace else, and I couldn't stand that feeling of incompetence on steroids, I'd make this pool my last stop of the day. I guess many comparisons could be made about this stop, both biological and chemical, but maybe it is best to leave those to the imagination. I can't say that I felt exactly guilty about going to this place, but it sure made me feel better.

Hatchery trout are dismissed as being "canned fish." Of course, what you want is a wild fish, one that really lives in the stream, and one that has encoded, in its genes, every stone, rock, and possibility for the hatch of insects.

Anyway, one day, just before dusk, I went to this pool on the Williams. It was a kind of elbow pool, in that the stream washed out of some rubble and hit a bank and turned to the right, if you were facing downstream. Mostly, the Williams River ran through farmland, and above this pool there was a farmhouse. It sat about fifty yards from the stream, on a knoll. The house had a wide porch, white siding, and green shutters. The underside of the porch was painted a light blue, like a Vermont sky on one of those soothing summer days that takes the sting out of winter.

The afternoon I was fishing that pool, a woman was out on the porch, where she sat on a chair and seemed to be shelling peas. I wasn't close enough to hear the rattle of the hard peas as they fell into the bowl, but I imagined I could. Every now and then, as the woman dropped a green pod onto a newspaper on the grey floor of the porch, she glanced up from her work and watched. Her glance was not interrogatory, not curious, but utterly neutral, as though I were a robin tugging on a worm.

Anyway, I stood in the water at the head of the pool, in the rubble, and fished a Hare's Ear, quartering down and across the stream. The Hare's Ear is made from rabbit and imitates a nymph or the underwater stage of a mayfly. I used to tie them myself, with what is known as a spinning loop to make it look buglike. One of the things you learn is that some materials, like rabbit fur, when wet, have a movement that is lifelike and suggests anxiety, or at least the desire to get its business done quickly.

If you just let the Hare's Ear swing down, out of the rubble, and then let it lift a little off the bottom, it drives the fish bananas. The entire presentation, as they say in fishing circles, isn't more than a couple of inches, really, but it is an important couple of inches. It is a fatal movement that suggests the nymph is about to hatch.

From the head of the pool, I did this and caught some fish. A lot of them. Not big, between ten and twelve inches, but their lack of size was compensated for by numbers. So I stood there, reeling them in and letting them go. The woman on the porch shelled her peas. The sky began to get a little pink. I began to feel better about getting skunked on more demanding water and, in fact, began to think that the book that was giving me so much trouble might, just might, work out after all. Abbey and Tatie were getting along better, and they liked to play a game called Hop on Pop—that is, on a Saturday morning I heard a sort of rumbling sound and then the bedroom door opened and there they were. A small thing, of course, but it lingers.

A pickup truck pulled up with two guys in it, and they looked across the dashboard as only a certain kind of countrified character can, which is to say with a mixture of hostility and inertia. I was not sure I wanted these guys to know that this pool was stiff with fish, even if they were hatchery fish, since, of course, the men would show up with a Styrofoam cup of worms, some Eagle Claw hooks, and a couple of large baggies, which they would fill with fish and then either throw away or maybe, at best, take home and freeze to eat. If that happened, and the pool was killed, what would I do on those days when I was filled with doubt and self-loathing?

I reeled in the line. Then I cut off the nymph, dug around in my fly box, and appeared to think a long time, a very long time, about what would fix those trout. The brooding and thinking seemed to increase the interest of the guys in the truck. Maybe, it seemed, they were going to see if there really were any trout here after all. I appeared to be tying on a very small fly, so small of course that it couldn't be seen, and this was so because I didn't tie anything on at all.

I started casting, and under these circumstances, with no fly to worry about hanging up on a tree on the bank, I made it look like a Joan Wulff demonstration tape: I shot the line on the backcast and the forecast, used what is known as an extension cast. The line made a lovely shape in the air, at once serpentine and hopeful. I made it look good. In general, I tried to make it appear that if I couldn't catch fish in this pool, why then, it was impossible. Of course, I caught nothing. The guys in the truck watched for a while. They opened a couple of beers. They drank them slowly, and they seem to be waiting for the pay off. With this kind of display, they seemed to be saying, a fish is about to be caught. They finished their beer. They opened another. One said something to the other, who shrugged, and after a while they stared with a sort of dismissal perfectly mixed with disappointment. I had failed them. Then they started the truck and drove away.

I tied the Hare's Ear back on and started reeling them in again. One after another, which, of course, I let go. The fish were just mesmerized by that quarter-inch or half-inch or inch twitch as the fly comes out of the rubble at the head of the pool. Under these circumstances, it felt like we were in it together, and that we were both inspired. The possibilities for the book looked up, too.

But here is where the mystery comes in. When the truck drove away and I started catching fish again, the woman on the porch stopped shelling peas. The sky now was pink, and the water appeared like a piece of tinted foil. The fish made that crown-shaped splash. Then she waved.

Now, I think about that wave a lot. Had she seen someone else do this? Or had she simply known what I was up to? And the essence of this, as far as I'm concerned, is the surprise that comes in writing books or catching fish, or in anything else that has an unpredictable quality, or in those activities where you constantly search for and never get control. Of course, I thought I was doing this as a sort of disguise, but, in fact, the woman was there all along, and our communication about it, or hers with me, is one of those things you never forget. Something said, and said beautifully, without a word being spoken.

I got into my car and drove home. The house, as I drove up the driveway, had a golden light in the windows, at once domestic and almost surreal in its perfection, like a painting by Magritte. I put my fishing things in the closet where I kept them, sat with a glass of beer at the table while Christina made dinner.

"Well," she said. "You sure seem happy. Did a pretty girl give you a kiss?"

"No," I said. "I was just thinking . . ."

"Uh-oh," she said in that voice she used when we played a game (that I am untrustworthy and that she is the one who sees things clearly). "Not that again . . ."

"Maybe I can do something with this book after all," I said.

Her voice instantly changed from the light and the playful. "Oh, that's lovely," she said. "It really is."

So when I am stuck with a book or have other problems, I think of that woman on the porch, her bowl filled with green peas, her hand in the air: just a couple of movements back and forth, as precise as a haiku.

Inside, Looking Out

Margot Page

If the truth be told, I am only a virtual angler these days. I am un-astream.

Virtual anglers (who are most commonly editors and writers in our field) are rarely found near water. More often than not, they are seated in front of a computer at an office or home desk, typing or thinking about being near water. Or, when lucky, both. Nowadays, my answer to the question, "Are you fishing much?" is always "No."

I am steeped in the sport, with connections that run from genetic to personal to professional. I am the granddaughter of a fly fishing writer and editor, the former wife of a prominent angling author, an angling publishing and communications professional, and a founding advisor of a national non-profit breast cancer survivor program that uses fly fishing as therapy. But over the past decade and a half, for personal reasons, my chances to actually get on the water and fish have faded away, and, truth again be told, I self-imposed a ten-year hiatus from the angling world in order to raise my daughter and find my own, singular identity as a professional in another world that had nothing whatsoever to do with fishing. So I have been, for quite some time, inside, looking out.

Photo courtesy of Margot Page

Margot Page hooked up, Alaska.

One chilly, rainy November day in 1983, while working at my new job in New York City, I heard the faint drums and earnest brass of the annual Veteran's Day Parade marching down Fifth Avenue and ran to stand next to the grimy window. Just minutes before, I had received a phone call informing me of my grandfather's death, and on that morning the military music honoring the grizzled veterans who had fought for their country seemed particularly to honor my grandfather, who, as a teenager, had lied about his age and proudly driven ambulances (despite his near-blindness) bearing the wounded and dying over the ravaged French landscape of World War I, and whose unending stories of those adventures had lulled me into quiescence in my girlhood. Now, one of the last lions of the Golden Era of fly fishing was gone, and a veteran's band was marking the moment.

My grandfather's real name was Alfred Waterbury Miller. He was also known by another name, his writing pseudonym, Sparse Grey Hackle. When I was laid up in bed as a child, my grandfather would arrive to rescue his granddaughter from sickbed boredom. He was then already an enormously old figure to his grandchildren, formally dressed in three-piece tweeds and courtly both in manner and speech. Deac, as we called him, sought to distract his granddaughter, me, from her fevers and respiratory distress with long and detailed stories of his World War I adventures. These tales would inevitably veer into longer, more convoluted discussions of ballistics, which were even more torturous to a twelve-year-old than being imprisoned in bed. After trying to follow his narrative, I drifted off into my feverish, headache-y daze, and Deac would take his satisfied departure, paternal duty done.

My Grandfather-with-Three-Names had large blue eyes that were further magnified by his memorably thick wire glasses and baby-smooth skin, remarkable in such an old man. Because of his bad eyesight, it took him rather a long time to focus on the face of whoever got a chance to insert a word in edgewise into his famous monologues, and then he would gaze vaguely at you while he digested your brave interruptions. Following that, there was a delicate clearing of his throat, *ahem, errrrr, ahem*! and off he went again into an unstoppable Sparse tale, continuing his narrative line undisturbed.

I knew vaguely that my grandfather and my grandmother enjoyed a queer hobby called "fishing" (it was never referred to in the family as "fly fishing"), that they wore queer, baggy clothing while "fishing," and that they went up often to the Catskills on weekends to "fish." On Sundays, en route back to Darien, Connecticut, they would stop by our old carriage house and drop off a couple of dead trout, which my parents would enthusiastically grill outside. Luckily, the kids got steak.

Sparse's classic book, *Fishless Tales, Angling Nights*, was published when I was a senior in high school, in 1971, by his editor, friend, and fellow Anglers' Club of New York member, Nick Lyons. Nick and Sparse, I learned later, enjoyed sitting happily at the club in downtown Manhattan telling stories for hours, both unaware of Sparse's smoldering pipe ashes on both of their clothing that were mixed in with fresh and ancient food stains. Actually, I am not sure how much talking Nick got in, but I do remember hearing that many of Sparse's tales ended with Nick being called "Bub" by Sparse, through teeth tightly clenching his pipe.

Twelve years after Nick published Sparse's book, the reason I was standing next to the dirty window overlooking the Fifth Avenue parade was that Nick had taken in Sparse's thirty-year-old granddaughter, (me), who had left magazine publishing and couldn't nail a job in advertising. "I think we might have some work for you to do," is how I remember Nick kindly inviting me to join the nascent Nick Lyons Books as the fourth member of his team, not long after he had left Crown Publishing to start up his own publishing enterprise.

I began with Nick on a part-time basis, eager to help him in any way I could despite a temporarily crippling back condition. Upon my arrival at

Nick's first office on Fifth Avenue and 26th Street, I had to immediately lie down on the floor after being forced to stand on the crowded subway ride over from my apartment in Brooklyn. "Is she all right?" I overheard Nick whisper in a worried tone to his partner. I could only imagine the dire thoughts running through his head about his new hire while I lay flat next to my desk, fighting tears.

The first Nick Lyons Books shared an office space with one Henry Cekum, an importer of dark Maharini furniture, which was stacked in teetering mounds in his wing of the office, often overflowing into our shared entry space. These pieces smelled noxious, perhaps because of preservative chemicals, and the malodor funked up our office air to the point that I worried about toxicity. Rosa, Henry Cekum's assistant, who padded around the office space in sloppy slippers, oozed a sensual laziness that Nick later described as "looked as if she had just come from having sex for ten hours."

One morning, Henry Cekum arrived at the redolent offices distraught over something. He was carrying a shotgun. Nick quickly assessed the dramatic situation and gallantly sent us all home for the day. The gun was not fired, but soon after this incident we were looking for a new office space. For Nick Lyons Books' second home, we located a gigantic loft space on Fifth Avenue and 21st Street, where Nick sublet out a few rooms in the front to an architect, and we took over the back two-thirds of the floor. The four desks, single copy machine, and several bookshelves were dwarfed by the loft's truly cavernous space, ringed entirely by huge windows, and our voices echoed hollowly as we called back and forth to each other from our tiny islands in this empty architectural ocean.

I was now working full-time for Nick, having come to the realization that my advertising job search was a misdirection of my editorial interests and skills. My job included creating press releases, writing jacket copy, working with authors on promotional efforts, digging up media contacts, and hawking our published wares, i.e., books. In those days, we still used typewriters; all the material I worked with was typewritten—that is, except for Nick's handwritten notes and his precious contacts list. But usually, Nick banged away on his vintage Royal typewriter, producing a happy, furious clatter.

And my writing education! That jacket copy, those press releases, were written to catch someone's attention, to make them stop and think a moment about the meaning of the words on paper, to stir interest within a brief three seconds in the new book that we, at Nick Lyons Books, had fallen in love with deeply enough to spend a year creating and publishing. I mimicked Nick's style as best I could, mixing the most important points with splashes of color, depth, snap, and, here and there, sprinkled judiciously, just the right word, never achieving, of course, Nick's artless polish, his elegant rhythm, and delicate use of the English language.

Under Nick's experienced and prosaic eye, I learned to (somewhat) rein in my natural instinct for lushness and my grad school love of Virginia Woolf-ish semicolons, and began to get the hang of the simple but rich sentence. It was Nick who encouraged me, as had my grandfather, to write, write, write. *Oh, I could never be a Writer,* I thought to myself. *Not like Nick or my grandfather. Oh no, no, no.* Such big footprints to follow and I was too timid to fail. But inside, peeking out, was a former tomboy bookworm who had always, very secretly, hoped to be a writer but was not yet ready to expose herself. I possessed enough inner drive, though—during the hot summer of 1983 when I lived in an un-air-conditioned SoHo loft—to write with the feverish intensity of a new, if naïve, lover about my pre-New York adventures as a hippie in the 1970s and my transition to a magazine editor in Maryland.

I mustered up the courage to show Nick some material I had written, an inchoate mess about a dream, as I remember. He kindly refrained from commenting specifically on the screed, but must have sensed my pulsing ambition, for he proclaimed one day, "It would do you good to get on the boards." "What are the boards?" I inquired. (The "boards" is a term for the now-archaic process of pasting type on "boards," which is the way dinosaurs used to make books.) My hopeful heart leapt at his words of advice. It was embarrassing to have shown Nick my scribbles, but not long afterwards he gave me more sage words about writing, ones that I have never forgotten: "Never throw anything away." And indeed I have saved nearly all of my notes, finding certain phrasing, narrative fragments, or jotted-down memories most useful twenty and thirty years later.

By his own example, Nick taught me how to edit, pare, and streamline, how to find the primary threads of my own writing and that of others, and to remove unnecessary tanglers. I can say I even approached baby-level ruthlessness about editing, but Nick also taught me by example how to edit words on paper with respect and kindness for both the writer's ego and for the many individual voices and styles that could have arguable merit in a piece. This respectful attitude was a critical lesson, and I went on to become an editor who tried not to impose my own style on writers' work.

The firm of Nick Lyons Books grew quickly, and soon we hired more staff and moved in more furniture. Our vast office space became less echo-y. Nick sent me through a graduate course to learn about selling subsidiary rights, which I added to my skill list, finding additional ways to promote books through first- and second-serial publication (selling excerpts to magazines) and other avenues. At that time, audio and digital rights to books were a nonstarter in the publishing landscape; today they are nearly everything. I worked with books by many established angling authors and helped spotlight such emerging writers as Walt Wetherell, David Quammen, and Verlyn Klinkenborg.

Nick also supervised my introduction to the art of fly fishing itself (the skill had been imparted by my grandfather to only the male line of our family, i.e., my brother), asking the legendary Joan Wulff, upon one of her visits to the loft, to give me a quick casting lesson with her orange-yarned "Fly-O." I kept the Fly-O right next to my desk and picked it up while pondering a press release strategy or a book summation, casually flicking it back and forth. Nick watched me out of the corner of his eye while he clacked away on his ancient machine, offering an occasional gentle correction. *Flick, flick, flick. Ten o'clock, two o'clock. Ten o'clock, two o'clock. Flick, flick, flick.* Somehow, the mesmerizing casting movement helped me think straight and write better.

Nick seated me next to one of our authors at a dinner party, and he wrote a poem for us when Tom Rosenbauer and I married a year later, a few months after the sudden illness and death of my mother at the young age of sixty. Nick stood by me during those difficult months, generously giving me family leave so I could be at her bedside, and then afterwards he paternally eased me back into the world of the living.

When I would whine upon occasion about my work or my writing or my personal life, Nick would ask me, "What are you, a mouse?" His challenging query always made me square my shoulders and sputter a denial that technically, no, I certainly was not a mouse; but I did feel mouse-y inside. Indeed I was afraid of a great many things back then, including subways, bad men, not being good enough, and loneliness. The truth is I didn't know what or who I was. Buck up, Nick was saying to me. Be strong. Live life.

Upon leaving New York City and my brief but life-changing career with Nick Lyons Books in 1985 to marry Tom, I found public relations work at the American Museum of Fly Fishing, located in my new hometown of Manchester, Vermont. The small museum was housed in a historic house off the picturesque village green. To get to my office aerie, I had to climb the stairs from the museum's galleries and pass through the archives of hundreds of priceless, vintage bamboo fishing rods—Leonards, a Garrison, a Thaddeus Norris—and gleaming fly reels—Bogdans, Hardys, a Hewitt, and Vom Hofe—plus shelves of antique, gold-gilded nineteenth-century volumes, and myriad nets, creels, tackle boxes, flies, and stored artwork (one piece even drawn on birch bark). One of my favorite artifacts was the breathtaking turn-of-the-twentieth-century Livingston leather fly wallet that featured vintage flies and delicate pen-and-ink sketches. Outside the windows in front of my desk waved heathery hemlock branches that filtered the strong southern sunlight into beautiful lacy patterns on the piled manuscripts, folders, and photographs on my desk.

By the time I became editor of its quarterly journal, the *American Fly Fisher*, in 1988, my lovely pre-school daughter was attached to my hip. Fortunately, Brooke was content to play on the floor of the stacks or in my office for a few hours while I desperately tried to publish a magazine. As editor, I became familiar with more luminaries of the fly fishing world through their biographies, journals, and memorabilia. There, in my museum office, I could time-travel back to the respective worlds of angling notables whose passion for the natural landscape and for angling endured through the writing, photographs, memories, and relics they left behind, frozen mementos of a time and avocation past.

Since the journal featured no advertising and there was no budget to actually pay writers, part of my job was to convince them to write for zero money. Luckily, up-and-coming writers learn early that writing for a living is an oxymoron, and during my tenure, some very talented writers, including Gordon Wickstrom, Dave Klausmeyer, and John Mundt, were willing to contribute highly researched, fascinating pieces to the journal in exchange for a prestigious, scholarly notch in their belt. *Quid pro quo.*

It was clear during the early days of our marriage that, in order to see anything of my husband, I needed to learn to fish, not just wave my Fly-O around. I picked up the technical skills quickly from my husband/private tutor, and for about a decade we fished together happily on our little rivers in Vermont, on the broad waters of the West, in the wild saltwaters off Cape Cod, and in the tropics. Fly casting was always a joyous experience for me; it made me feel close to my grandmother (dubbed "Lady Beaverkill" by Sparse), a beautiful natural caster herself, a skill which I had witnessed on the only occasion we ever fished together, in 1986. That day on the Battenkill, she pulled up her battered, patched old waders that were tied together with string, put on a jaunty sun brim, and strung up her priceless Garrison bamboo rod, made for her by Everett Garrison himself (at the request of his friend, my grandfather). With Tom's hand to steady her, she sturdily positioned herself between the rocks, calmly eyed the stream, began her gentle, expert casting, and promptly hooked a fish, which she played with grace and pride. It had been more than a decade since she had last been on the water.

I never mastered, or cared that I didn't want to master, the bug end of things. Just tell me what to use or give me an Adams, and then I can get to the parts of fishing that really fire me up: casting and catching fish. My genuine and primal delight in the actual hunting and catching of fish always surprised my suburban and urban selves. It was as if an ancestral, muscled huntress exploded out of my soul, trumpeting, "Stand aside, wimpy, I'm putting food on the table tonight!"

When I lost my mother and became a mother myself just two years later, I experienced that profound time in our human existence when the joys and sorrows of life become very real, and I felt driven to experiment with writing so as to honor and describe them. My first public writing was in the form of a brief letter to the editor that sang the praises of our local fire department, and then I wrote a longer, more impassioned one about pesticides in children's food. Emboldened by seeing my words "on the boards," I began to think I would very much like to see more of my words on the boards, and so I started taking notes during my adventures to record the specific, immediate, and accurate details that I required to weave a story.

From these real details, short essays revealed themselves. It was a format that I was comfortable with because the structure came naturally to me. My first published pieces appeared in our small local weekly newspaper in essays about my early motherhood experiences to my hospice volunteer work to the challenges of balancing marriage, parenthood, and fly fishing. There also existed in Vermont a brave daily newspaper that devoted the entire, large last page of its Sunday special section to personal essays . . . complete with commissioned artwork. O, imagine the decadence! I screwed up my courage and submitted an essay, which they published, along with artwork drawn specifically for my piece. Then they took another piece and another, and so on, giving me the opportunity to test my chops with regard to voice and subject matter. *Click* went my secret, hopeful soul.

In those years, women anglers were still a phenomenon on the water, as the fly fishing world was then almost completely male-dominated. As I wrote about and published my experiences and thoughts, my essays on being a woman in the fly fishing arena began to garner some interest because they came from a unique perspective: I was a female angler who could write. Additionally, I was of the opinion that the women who were just then starting to enter the sport in increasing numbers were just as legitimate as the tweedy men who had owned the sport for centuries, though their angling interests might lie in more varied areas or levels of the sport (i.e., they did not have to love marathon fishing or entomology to be considered real anglers). My opinion was, I am fairly sure, considered strident and potentially militant by some back then, but despite growls and grumbles from some of the die-hards, the angling world eventually adapted to the valuable expansion of conservation resources and passion that the growing population of women anglers brought to our sport.

In 1989, one of my pieces got to the editor of the New York *Times'* "Outdoors" column, which had been written by Nelson Bryant for many years. He was taking more frequent, well-deserved breaks, so the *Times* had started using alternative writers. Miracle of all miracles, my piece was accepted, and so I became the first female contributor to that column, writing for it occasionally over the next several years. The editor, Susan Adams, told me, "You won't get rich writing for the *Times*, but you might get famous." Well, certainly the former didn't happen, and the latter not so much either.

Nick and I had stayed in touch over the years of my marriage, and he wrote me generous letters of support and praise about my writing. We began to talk about me putting a book together, and by 1994, I finally had a thin collection of fly fishing essays that could form the spine of a book. I wrote new material and wove all the pieces into a narrative that became my first book, *Little Rivers: Tales of a Woman Angler*, published in 1995.

The summer of that same year, 1995, I was called in as an advisor to help Gwenn Perkins, a professional angler, and Dr. Benita Walton, a reconstructive surgeon, hone the model for a brilliant idea they were developing. Over the next year, our small group of co-founders and advisors, all women, gathered on Vermont living room couches and at kitchen tables to birth a unique retreat program that would use fly fishing as physical and psychological therapy to help women recovering from breast cancer. We named it Casting for Recovery.

Casting for Recovery was founded on the principles that the natural world is a healing force and that cancer survivors deserve one weekend—free of charge and free of the stresses from medical treatment, home, or workplace—to experience something new and challenging while enjoying beautiful surroundings within an intimate, safe, and nurturing structure. The brilliance of the idea lay in the marriage between our gentle sport's therapeutic casting motion, the quality-of-life education and support we provided, and the overall respite from the rigorous cancer journey. It was tremendously moving during our early test retreats to witness how local breast cancer survivors received our love for them.

For the next four years, the Mothers of Invention, as I like to call our original group, refined the Casting for Recovery model, the basics of which are still in place today in its greatly expanded and successful national programs. Casting for Recovery was powerful magic from the very beginning, and that magic and its life-altering gifts have never waned. At this writing, seventeen years after conception, Casting for Recovery has served over 5,000 women across the United States.

When my marriage ended, the fishing pretty much ended too. My last major angling expedition came when, newly single, I traveled to Alaska with three other women anglers the summer I separated from my husband. I remember the four of us, giggling madly and jet-lagged, driving around Anchorage's frontier utilitarian kitsch with its sophisticated but salty neon glow just after landing at the airport. We were looking for a sex shop in which to buy a small rubber, ummm, toy, to which we would attach a colorful fly, just one of the trinkets we hoped to present to deserving guides at our destination, a fishing lodge near Dillingham.

The summer of 1997 was one of unprecedented warmth. Daytime temperatures stayed in the nineties, and one brilliant day the porch thermometer at the lodge read nearly 100 degrees. The side channels of the powerful, wild rivers had become rocky, sandy roadways, and the streams had shrunk to Vermont-meadow size. Yet the crimson sockeye and giant King (Chinook) salmon still forged their way up the shallow rivers from the ocean to spawn, driven by irresistible ancient instincts, with dorsal fins gliding above water like pink triangle sails.

One morning, during the flight in the refurbished Sikorsky helicopter from our lodge to a small, privately leased, world-class river where we would fish for ocean-fresh Kings, I felt as if we were being transported through the air in a floating living room. The floor-to-ceiling windows on either side of the seats placed us nearly atop the breathtaking landscape that passed below—complete with grizzlies feeding—or smack into the glorious mountains that rose thrillingly above the helicopter's rotor blades.

At the sight of the untrammeled majesty of the Togiak National Wildlife Refuge and its miles of bouncy tundra, meandering streams, and rock-pocked mountain slopes, tears began to roll down my cheeks. I wept uncontrollably that day at the magnificence of the natural world, and then again, helplessly, many other times throughout the trip. I wondered why such powerful, transcendent beauty affected me so, and also why 5,000 miles away from the source, I felt closer to my pain than the previous week when I signed the legal separation papers. How can a human heart hold all these impossibly indescribable feelings of awe, gratitude, and sorrow while experiencing vast, pure, wild landscapes of such glory and power?

I have been since told that humans often react with tears when encountering divinity.

These fishless days as a communications professional, I am married to my computer. It is my constant companion, both in and out of the office, and though our relationship has been more successful than some other human relationships in my life, I frequently feel as if I am being sucked into the screen. I fear I've become a drudge, a desk monkey, an office slave, an armchair angler, a grind, a paleface, a prisoner, an angling theorist.

But with me still are poignant, comforting memories of those years when I was outside, looking in. I can easily call up soothing visuals: the dazzling diamonds of light on the water; the soft palette of foliage before the sun burned off the morning mist; or the dark, massive pods of stripers streaking towards me off Monomoy Point, Cape Cod, as I positioned my electrified body at the ready to make the only six casts I would be given to reach the underwater, high-speed, piscatorial fleet.

And the sounds and the sensations: the crash of saltwater waves; the gentle gurgle or intense rush of flowing rivers; the slap of water against a drift boat or its cold pull and surge against my legs; the vast and perfect silence of the Alaskan wilderness; the songs of hidden bird life along watery corridors; the delighted, excited hollers of my companions when they glimpsed or hooked their quarry.

And I remember fondly even the uncomfortable times: miserable, raw fishing in rain and wind; having to pee in buckets or off the sides of boats; getting sun stroke on a Bahamian flat; leaving my hand-built rod on the top of my car while blithely driving home, never to see it again.

These memories form my rich life tapestry, interwoven personally, professionally, and generationally with the world of angling. It is hard to believe I won't again be outside, someday, looking in. After all, the waters have trickled, meandered, and raged through my life thus far, carrying me from shore to shore, adventure to adventure, to be with loved ones for a while and then swept onward.

As we know, water is the source. Its salt is in our tears. It flows through our veins and hearts. Its healing powers are carried deep within our souls. Its gift is the divinity that drives us to our knees with gratitude and wonderment. And tears of salt.

May

Datus Proper

"And yet, at the very least, [the angler] will have his wholesome
and merry walk at his own ease, and also many a sweet breath of
various plants and flowers that will make him right hungry and
put his body in good condition. He will hear the melodies of
the harmony of birds. . . . And if the angler catches the fish with
difficulty, then there is no man merrier than he is in his spirits."

—From manuscript of *The Treatise of Fishing with an Angle*
(1450), modernized translation by Sherman Kuhn,
in John McDonald, *The Origins of Angling* (1963).

Fat of the Land

Fertility is fragile still, hyaline wings and blue petals and aspen rustling
her crinolines, daring you into the dressing room. The buds have opened
on twigs nearest the sun. You can walk through limbs with perfect leaflets
brushing your face, whispering, quaking in a gust. You can stand by pale,
living skin. Alone among trees on our farm, the aspen has a bark that turns
sunlight into energy.

The hot days will be next, and then things with strong stalks, barley,
and partridges. After that will come deer, pheasants, and me hunting the
deer and pheasants—walking oil fields, all of us, sun's energy stored in fat.
Now is when we build up the deposits. "Joys of spring," my wife Anna calls
them, using an Irish-ism for rambunctious males. The feeling can come at

any time, but in May it scarcely lets up. Every man is a fathead now, thick sunny–yellow joys between skull and brain.

May brings the first summer clouds, too, big fluffy ones and polka dots, clouds rain-streaked and sun-sparked, guerrilla clouds rushing down to fluster the pond and move on. There is soft murmurous thunder, no heat, and barely enough rain for the hay. For a farmer, these clouds do not amount to much.

Water is on the way, nevertheless, as sun thaws the high country. Three hundred inches of snow have fallen up there since September. That's four times my height, but I wasn't wading around in it. Nothing could make a living there but blue grouse eating fir needles, snow sifting quietly. The grouse are following snowmelt downstream now to mating season, and the water is liberated, too. Molecules that made a snowflake in January are bounding down the slopes, surging toward the Missouri River, headed for New Orleans.

Melting snow makes this a bad time to walk on the highest peaks, but a good time to see them. They will hide behind their foothills in summer—a trick of perspective—and you will need the mind's eye of an Albert Bierstadt

Photo by Anna Collins-Proper

Datus Proper on Thompson Spring Creek, Montana.

to separate high, bare, distant mountains from outriders that are below the timber line, but much closer. Postcard exceptions are the Tetons, 100-odd miles south of us, which seem to spring from Jenny Lake. They do not, however, look remotely like *tetons*. He must have been a lonely trapper who saw femininity in those icy crags.

Here at home, spring makes white peaks stand above shoulders draped in dark firs. The clouds help, too. I see these mountains every day, sweat on them sometimes, and take them for granted till they dress in gauze—peaks above, peaks beside, peaks peeking out.

Energy and the Stream

Our spring creek is separated from this rowdy season by a filter: dirt, miles of it, through which the snowmelt must pass before reaching us. The river to our east is running over its banks while here, just two fields away, the spring creek remains almost as low as it was in February.

The stream is waking, nevertheless. Midday sun pulls up mayflies; mayflies pull up trout; trout pull an angler out of the house. None of us are sun lovers, exactly. Trout and flies are usually most active under mild grey skies, and so am I, but in May we need warmth to beam over the mountains and get us going.

Everything in the place rises and shines, now that the sun has its strength back. Brewer's blackbirds perch atop alders and catch light in beady eyes. Little saurian heads lift from the robin's nest on our front porch. Worms climb toward the warmth, and mother robin catches them for her brood. A pintail drake stands tall on a green peninsula, looking big as a goose, with the light reflecting from his white breast. Four, five, six yearling deer splash across the stream in their new red summer coats. The mature does are back in the brush somewhere, waiting. Soon they will nurse dappled fawns with the sun's milk.

For those of us who live in air, the stream's workings are harder to parse, but sun is the source of energy there, too. Warmth is reaching into the bars of mud below my wing-dams and pulling up watercress leaves the size of mouse-ears. Water buttercup (*Ranunculus*) and three kinds of pondweed (*Potamogeton*) are sprouting from the gravelly bed. These are the plants that anglers like to talk about—big ones. I cannot even see the specks of algae that feed the mayflies, which feed the trout, which in turn feed the herons.

Anna and I enjoy fish dinners too, but not from this spring creek. The trout taste like their food chain.

Geology as Destiny

Sun is universal, geology, individual. I could walk from here to the mountains and fish under the same light, but in an utterly different stream.

The spring creek is flat, silent, and meandering, though nothing stands in its way but soft black soil. The mountain stream is steep, noisy, and direct, though it must push aside boulders.

Insects in the spring creek are small, individually, and divided into few species, but these few are so successful that the biomass is great. The mountain stream has more species and some of the individual flies are large in size, but the biomass is smaller.

In the spring creek, you see big trout feeding in water that barely covers their backs. In the mountain stream, most trout are small, even in the deepest pools.

Geology accounts for the differences, and geology is a hard language for me, though I grew up hunting carnelians and geodes. I can spot a chunk of petrified wood with rings in it from the time before Genesis, but I can't tell you much more than that. Our teachers should have given us children geology as poetry, not grammar. We needed order but not an order so hard. Geology squeezes human history between layers of rock and human culture into a thin layer of sediment above the strata. The world's greatest epic ends like all the rest, heroes dead.

You need some distance from geology to see what it means. I climbed a ridge last week, for no bigger reason than to spy on the mating season, and saw the whole story. The small of it was a cock grouse strutting on a fir needle stage. I crawled toward him, wondering if he would take me for a rival, but he seemed more inclined to court my blue visor. He could hoot with his bill closed—which struck me as a good trick—but he did not recognize the big picture spread at our feet.

The glacial lake was 2,000 feet below us, thousands of years back in time, and still aqueous when clouds lent their shadows. I imagined races of giant trout cruising below me in what was, geologically, the Recent. I caught vertigo from both altitude and time. And then I hiked back down to reality, if that is what the Present is.

Dig far enough into our home acres and you find the old lake hiding in gaps between rocks and particles. There is a little of everything down there, from old river gravel to fist-sized lumps of a conglomerate with veins of chalk. This is not the pure white stuff of English chalkstreams—I have a piece of that for comparison—but calcium carbonate in any form does good things for trout water.

Our fertility starts in ancient seas. To keep from being eaten, small soft creatures evolved hard exoskeletons, died in their time anyhow, fell to the bottom, were compressed into limestone strata, rose with the Rocky Mountains, washed downhill during some other May, and are now building the chitin of a mayfly's exoskeleton. This is the small picture—the one with consequences for trout and me.

- The geology produced a fertile stream with relatively even flows and temperatures.
- The stream in turn produces a nutritious soup composed of living diatoms and fine particulate organic matter.
- The organic matter nourishes large numbers of a few species of mayflies that roam the stream's bed for food.
- The mayflies attract trout that, though not so specialized as the insects, do well in spring creeks.
- The trout attract people of an angling culture that used to be small, but is today flourishing.

You would not enjoy a broth of fine particulate organic matter. Its parts are less than one millimeter in diameter—so small that you (or at least I) cannot say whether they are animal, vegetable, or algal. Yet from this chowder springs the beauty of the mayfly.

Even people who are squeamish about other insects learn to love this one, which preys on no other living animal and is preyed upon by all. In its winged form, the mayfly does not even eat. It mates, lays eggs, and dies. It is perfectly innocent, which is to say perfectly stupid. It sits on your finger without protest until you, in order to study it, drown it in alcohol and put its wing under a lens.

Look away from this death, if you are not made of coarse particulate organic matter. I don't know how mayflies feel, but I know how they struggle when they are caught by alcohol or spider. I know how they look on their mating flight, too, dancing in the sun. The only emotions involved may be mine—yet I know when mayfly nymphs want to leave their husks. I can feel it happening. They are under water and I am breathing air through screen doors, but we get the same message. Sky darkens. Breeze stirs. Weather lifts the nymphs. I hatch too, emerging from this husk of a house.

The Trout's Economy

Trout are in the recycling business. Sun warms the meanders; insects hatch; fish make gentle circles on the glassy surface. The scene seems lazy, and poets over the centuries have been soft observers, choosing not to look beneath the surface.

The stream is busy converting sunlight into life. Dip a fine-meshed net in the current and it comes up full of mayfly nymphs, mayfly subimagoes (duns), mayfly adults (spinners), midge pupae, occasional caddis flies, and other aquatic insects of the season. I cannot measure the thermodynamics but suspect that our marshy creek is the best food factory on our property—more efficient than grass, alfalfa, trees, barley, or brush. And the abundant nutrients produce intense competition.

Trout are the largest predators that live in the stream full time, yet they subsist on insects almost as light as air. To catch enough mayflies, the fish must occupy feeding lies—positions in which trout can spend little energy while intercepting food drifting with the current. This is a riskier diet than that of, say, a garter snake, which can catch one sculpin and then take a long digestive break under the porch. Every mayfly caught in the surface film exposes a trout to predators from the air-breathing world. The reward is abundant and nutritious, but it selects for the supertrout—the one in a thousand that learns to eat often without being eaten even once. Survivors of this food fight become bigger and stronger than fish of the same species in a hard rock stream.

There is a painting that reminds me of a spring creek trout. The subject is a cavalry officer from Kipling's time. He lounges on a couch, uniform elegant, pose insolent. He is alone because no solid Victorian would let his daughter near the man. Even in repose, he seems to be challenging you to a duel. He died in Africa, run through by a spear.

Herons spear the spring creek trout; you accept a challenge that, in real life, your prey did not intend to offer. You do not rush. You do not look over the side of a pool to see if there are trout present. (There were, till they saw your hat.) You stalk upstream along the banks, eyes focused far ahead, looking for the ring-on-water made by a trout taking an insect. You tie on an imitation with a hook—an artificial fly that looks like the natural and will behave naturally on the stream.

Then you enter the water and kneel in it, keeping yourself below the fish's line of sight. You wait until your prey is feeding steadily. You cast, aiming for a spot upstream of the trout's lie, and your fly drifts downstream. If the trout does not take, you wait for another rise before you cast again, and watch your fly disappear in a dimple on water.

What follows is shocking in a scene so placid. Your prey feels itself caught, bolts upstream, and flings itself out of the water three, four, five times. Do you know the sound of a rainbow trout vibrating in air? You can hear it above Humility Creek's gentle flow, much like a mallard's wing beats.

Sources

Fly fishing attracts us because it is close to nature, which is to say, archaic. Early in the second millennium, however, fly fishing evolved at least three times—in Macedonia, England, and Spain—as a way of getting around the fragility of a trout's natural food. Mayflies and other winged insects would not stay long on a hook, but they could be simulated with feathers cast on a horsehair line tied to a wooden rod. Over centuries, the technology evolved into polypropylene dubbing, nylon leaders, and carbon fiber rods. We perfected what we loved and we loved our whispering lines, even as we made them shiny and plastic.

Of course, protein could be produced more efficiently. We could, for example, raise catfish in a pond and net them out. But we do not want efficiency. We want to stalk like Bushmen and cast with an eye-hand coordination that evolved to guide spears. We want to catch beautiful fish under the rules of fair chase, which give our prey a chance to evade capture.

Though I grew up near the spring creek in Montana, I did not see it till

I had fished a chalkstream in England. The two are chemically similar and must have resembled each other physically once, because both flow through fertile bottomlands. But such lands are as good for agriculture as for trout, so it was inevitable that both streams would be affected by human works.

The Montana spring creek is still in its original channel, though the banks were damaged during a few decades of grazing in the twentieth century.

Much earlier, a section of the River Itchen had been moved upslope into a new channel dug by muscle power. The stream's original meandering bed became a water meadow for sheep, which produced wool for the clothing of the resident monks.

In both places, the changes made economic sense. Montana was new, spacious, and lightly populated, so even fertile land was cheap. Montanans, therefore, let cattle use the stream as a natural watering trough. Call this *laissez-faire* agriculture.

In England, however, fertile bottomland had to be managed intensively—first for the sheep and later for fish. River keepers learned the needs of trout, insects, and the stream itself.

In the Abbotts Barton water, where I fished, the artificial main channel of the Itchen no longer had sweeping meanders like those of the Montana spring creek. In compensation, there were man-made sidestreams called carriers, which—unlike most irrigation ditches in Montana—provided good fishing. One of the carriers was about the size of Humility Creek, but with banks in better condition.

Do not conclude that nurture had triumphed over nature. Nature still provided the cool clear alkaline water, the weeds and insects growing in it, the partridges nesting on the banks, and a snipe winnowing the twilight. The wildness of the place came as a surprise, given its history. Humans had lived there forever, as we know time, and yet you could wander in water meadows with the stars coming out and look for a way around the soft spot that swallowed a horse. You could circle the duck's-nest spinney twice before spotting a faint path back to the fishing hut.

The hut had no name on the door, but it was one of a line descending from *Piscatoribus Sacrum*, where Charles Cotton and Izaak Walton met on the River Dove—not far away as Americans measure distance, but far off as we measure time. This was my refuge: a squatter's shack for one Montanan in a half-wild remnant of what England used to be.

The Itchen had been saved by its value on the market. In Hampshire, chalkstreams became important to anglers in the nineteenth century, and by the time I got there, fly fishing was a substantial part of the Itchen's economy.

In hindsight, the 1970s may have been the end of a golden age. Not that the British economy has collapsed since then. On the contrary, it has grown, and the population with it. What has been good for the post-industrial economy, however, has been bad for the rivers. Postwar agricultural prosperity may be harder on the chalkstreams than all the wars in history, because of the widespread use of herbicides, pesticides, slurry, fertilizers, silage, and spray irrigation, and the draining of water from both rivers and aquifers.

With one-sixty-sixth of England's population—and three times the area—we Montanans can afford to use some of our abundant land to buffer our streams. We have more time, too, and history to learn from. We could get our priorities straight in Montana. We could.

In old Hampshire, time may be running out. There are many streams, but not enough to do all that they are called upon to do. There are big streams, but none too big to suck dry. A modern society has the power to plunge its beak into the aquifers and drain them of trout, angler, and snipe alike.

As well demolish the Winchester Cathedral. The Itchen runs by its side; Izaak Walton lies under its floor. At this level, all anglers are English.

Consider snipe, which tastes good and whose feathers make good trout flies. Humans learned of these virtues when the shotgun slimmed down to a graceful design. The hunting would have been as difficult then as now, but there were many more snipe in the early nineteenth century, before the marshes were drained, and a few determined hunters were up to the slog.

By then, too, it was possible to buy small, graceful hooks on which to tie the snipe's feathers. The Snipe Dun pattern appears in John Turton's *The Angler's Manual*, published somewhere in Britain in 1836: "Wings & Legs: A full Snipe's underside wing feather. Body: Blue Rabbit's down, twisted on yellow silk. Silk: Yellow."

Americans were interested in bigger game then, but in Britain it would have been natural to eat your snipe in October, save its feathers, and use them to dress flies for May.

This is very broad ecology, so do not pin me down. I have, in fact, reasoned backwards from present facts to what may be history. The snipe and the trout fly seem to have evolved together, as human artifacts.

What I know is that the Iron Blue Duns in my Irish/English fly box are decent representations of a Montana mayfly of the same genus (*Baetis*). Both hatch, moreover, in the same merry month and are accessible to the same peripatetic anglers. An angler from Hampshire could fly one-third of the way around the world today, Iron Blue Dun on his leader, exposing himself to jet lag but not nature shock. He would find the same fish feeding during the same blustery weather on what looks very much like the same insect.

The next two months would present no great surprises, either. After the *Baetis* peak in Montana will come *Ephemerella* and *Centroptilum* mayflies, which correspond to the same Old World genera. Only in late summer will there be a fly—genus *Tricorythodes*—that would surprise a chalkstream angler, and then not for long.

In this case, then, culture agrees with nature across seven time zones.

Flying Fishers

I am not sure that the great horned owl on our chimney catches trout, but it could, and it would not let me know. It is a philosopher by day and a predator of things that quiver in the dark. One day, perhaps, I will get accurate information from the pellets—regurgitated inedible parts of the prey.

The osprey, on the other hand, is no spook. It is a shotgun. It thinks fast, fixes the target with both eyes, and lets go, more in faith than certainty. The plunge seems life threatening to both fish and fish hawk. Once in every few tries, however, the osprey emerges and flounders off with a trout flopping in locked talons. The victim is likely to be a bold young rainbow that was too far from cover, rising for mayflies.

And after all that work, the osprey may lose its catch to the bald eagle, which Benjamin Franklin called "a bird of bad moral character . . . too lazy to fish for himself." I watch eagles flying over the farm looking for prey, but in May I seldom see them eating anything except previously owned trout and young ground squirrels. Eagles plunder the osprey, gourmandize the gophers, and perch to recover. I cannot swear that I hear the sound of burping.

Eagles do not, unfortunately, deter the pelicans. They too are a formidable spectacle, massive white triangles soaring out of the Cretaceous. There is no other species that I would rather watch—at high altitude. Fortunately, they make several passes before splashdown, giving me time to hit the "save" key on my laptop computer and bound out the door. Usually they decide that this creek is not big enough for all of us.

I have watched the pelicans at work, however, on big water where they operate like a fleet of trawlers—clumsy at all but the one thing in which they specialize. They surround their fish, push them to the middle of the circle, and scoop them into capacious pouches. We did not know how effective the method could be when I was growing up. Pelicans were scarce then, and therefore valuable, and we did not imagine how abundant they would become.

Kingfisher is merely the squire of fly fishers on this place. He is built for survival on short rations, small and bright and perky. Well, semi-perky. This particular kingfisher does not sit on the end of a limb and brag, like kingfishers in places with fewer raptors. He perches in the willows by our screen doors, looking for small fry, and when he spots prey, he flits. The word was made for him. He reaches a vantage point over the stream and hangs there, body motionless, wings moving like a hummingbird's. You can line the kingfisher up with a peak in the distance and find that they are equally steady.

Kingfisher is a rifleman aligning his sights. The shot always comes close, I suspect, but does not always hit its tiny target. Perhaps one try in four succeeds.

Somewhere along the banks, there is a better hunter than any of us. The heron moves in sun time. It gets from one place to another, but you cannot keep up with its slowness. Your attention wanders. Then when you look again, the great gangly bird has a squirming trout or a duckling shrieking for its mother. Sometimes you spook the heron from sedges where baby mallards hide, but it sneaks back, skinny as Don Quixote and far more deadly with a spear.

Heron is the teacher. He does not hunt on general principles and neither do you, his student—not unless you want a humility lesson. You stalk one particular trout till you can see its fins. You note that it is taking duns in the surface film and then you offer the fly it expects to see. Your weapon reaches ten times farther than that of the great blue heron, which means that you are one-tenth the hunter. You lack the infinite stealth and the spear that strikes faster than a trout can move. But you know how to learn.

I spent yesterday with the heron, though not by intention. It was on the pond when I woke up, almost invisible but for a horizontal beak against vertical cattails. Ducks stayed away from that spear, as usual, but one pair of mallard drakes may have been distracted by their mating duel. I doubt that either was clever enough to push its rival toward the heron. An hour later, though, I saw a white blob and went out for a look. The blob was the belly of a drake. Its neck was broken and its head twisted back under the body. Placement of the body—on the bank near the water—fit the heron's method, but I wrote the case down as not proven.

Then at midday I hiked out to see if the trout were rising. They were not, perhaps because the sun was too bright for mayflies to emerge. By the Echo Pool, however, a rainbow glistened in death. The heron stood back from its kill, no longer interested. The trout had two stabs on its back near the head—deep punctures made by the lower beak. Those were the fatal blows. Underneath, behind the throatlatch, were two smaller stabs made, I guessed, by the parted beak when the heron lifted its prey.

The rainbow was about as big as they get in this stream: twenty-two inches long and three pounds ten ounces in weight after being drained of blood. I had caught the same trout in some previous year and trimmed its adipose fin as a marker for research. I had tried to catch the trout this spring, too. It rejected me twice.

I opened the fish's stomach and found nymphs that were recognizable individually, near the front, and just excreta near the vent. A few midge pupae were mixed in, but most of the trout's calories were coming from two mayflies: the olives (*Baetis*) hatching now and the sulphurs (*Ephemerella*) due soon. Altogether, the nymphs would have numbered into the thousands. The great blue heron's needless kill was not unusual. In winter, when the weeds die back, it regularly spears fish that are too big to swallow, and by spring, most large surviving trout carry the heron's brand. One fish—the record holder—had four healed beak marks. It may have had a lie in water deep enough to blunt the force of the stabs.

Many trout run downstream to bigger water for the winter months, and the heron may have something to do with this migratory pattern. The big bird kills because

- it is a predator, hard-wired to hunt; and
- it has nothing to lose.

The energy budget is important to understanding. Heron spends time stalking a pool and—having sunk its investment—might as well strike, even if its prey is too big to eat.

Most other predators on this stream kill only for food. They are, however, not virtuous but thrifty. The osprey, for example, wastes energy in its dive and might even be drowned if its talons lock in a big trout. Owl, pelican, and kingfisher also have something at risk.

I don't. My energy, like the heron's, has been invested since before I see the trout rising. I have the desire, too—same tense neck when I see the trout and same eager strike.

You know what I mean, Mr. or Ms. Predator. I'd rather have you here than the heron because you might release your big trout, if you do not intend to eat it. But the feeling is there. I am a heron. You are a heron.

The Meeting Place

Three lives come together in a circle on the water. A mayfly nymph climbs from the gravel, swims toward unaccustomed light, and is beginning the winged life when a trout pulls it down. Another fly then floats by, but this one has a hook in it. Trout rises gently. Angler swallows deep.

These are matters of life and death. The mayfly might have finished its sun dance, but for the trout. The trout might have stored fat for the winter, but for your fly with a sting. And you there, at the top of the food chain: What brings you here? What drew you to the edge of the stream?

You are here to walk, but not for the exercise, and to sweat off some flab, though nobody could pay you to work this hard. You are here to crouch in cold water, cast to a trout, and catch it or put it down, then stretch the cramp in your thigh and move on up and up where the stream runs small and its fish never saw a fly they didn't like.

You keep going because your prey believes in you. The trout is still dappled to hide when you pass, still swift to flee from your clumsy feet. The mayfly believes in the trout, too, and unfolds wings clear as air. You kneel by the river, shoot your line, and hit the ring of the rise. You and fish and fly meet where you have always met, in that window between stream and sky.

Life After Fly Fishing

Le Anne Schreiber

Ihave not done any real fly fishing for more than ten years now. By real, I mean standing on the slippery stones of a streambed, securing my footing as best I could while water coursed a slow or fast detour around my ankles, knees, or thighs, casting hopefully toward a spot I imagined a trout might like to visit, perhaps call home.

Many hopes attended every cast. I hoped not to snag an overhead branch during the back cast, but if I did snag, I hoped to snag a flimsy leaf, not a stout twig, and if a twig, I hoped the line would not triple-wrap itself around it. I hoped my leader would survive its flight without a wind knot, without a slap-down landing, and that my fly would alight with grace, sly and enticing.

And then, of course, there were those last, best hopes—that a trout would bite; that I set the hook at the exact right moment; that I keep the line just taut enough, not too tight, not too slack; that I play not bully the trout to my side; that it arrive in my hands tired but intact, lip-hooked so it could be released with one quick flick of the wrist.

I always fished alone, but was never lonely, never wanted for companionship. From the moment I set foot on streambed, I was engaged in an unspoken, unbroken conversation with my father, the first provider of my rods, boots, flies, and passion for fishing. Welcoming but not willing it, I felt his encouragement riding with my hopes on every cast. Both before and after his death, the communing was no less real for being phantom. In fact, that phantom communing was a large part of what made stream fishing the only real fly fishing for me.

Year after year, from mid-April to mid-September, I pulled on my waders and picked up that conversation several days a week, the frequency made possible by the convenient flow of the Roeliff Jansen Kill within easy walking distance of my home in Ancram, New York.

And then I moved. Not far, just five minutes up the road, a short ride instead of a short walk from the stretch of the RoeJan that I had considered my private bend in the stream. I moved in May and easily could have extended my unbroken streak of trout fishing seasons to thirteen, but I had become smitten with another body of water, a pristine, spring-fed, twenty-six-acre lake called Snyder Pond.

In truth, I was far more than smitten; my commitment was so great, I might as well have married Body of Water #901, the formal designation by which Snyder Pond is known by the New York State Department of Conservation, which allowed me to build a home on a twelve-acre peninsula that jutted into its western flank.

The lake is about a half-mile long, nestled between two wooded hillsides, and because there is no public access, and no inflow from less protected waters, Snyder Pond has remained as unsullied as a latter-day body of water can be. When I became the person living closest to Snyder Pond day in and day out, I became both its worst potential despoiler and its self-appointed twenty-four-hour security guard. That first summer, I left the lake only to run the most essential errands and then rush back to make sure it was still okay.

That meant forsaking the stream, but at first I didn't realize that also meant giving up fly fishing. The lake was home to many large bass who cruised among the lily pads, leaping in vain for dragonflies darting above, mating, laying eggs with flicks of tail too quick for even the speediest fish. I bought a second-hand canoe and tried my luck, hoping to lure the frustrated bass with a lazy drift of fly.

Every cast brought a bite, but not from bass. Bluegills sucked in the flies, inhaling them so deeply that extraction required deft wielding of long-nosed surgical pliers inserted through their dainty mouths into delicate in-

Photo courtesy of Le Anne Schreiber

Le Anne Schreiber on her favorite water, New York.

ner recesses. More often than not, the bluegills died in the operating hand, which utterly defeated the point of fly fishing.

I started using flies too large for bluegills to swallow, drawing on a small supply of balsa-wood poppers my father had tied decades earlier. Bass loved those poppers. The strikes were thrilling, and although the catch often arrived in my hands festooned with long, garnet lily pad stems, I was able to release the hardy bass in good shape. The only problem was that, except for the instant of the surface strike, this fishing did not feel good.

Fishing with poppers from a canoe had little in common with my afternoons afoot in the stream. Take casting. There was none of the elegance that sometimes made the cast its own reward on the stream. If fly casting for trout had been a waltz, this popper casting for bass was a polka.

The popper didn't float down; it plopped, which was okay, because causing a commotion isn't the liability in bass fishing that it is in trout fishing. Bass often like a commotion, and I often caused one, not just with plopping and popping sounds, but with the banging, splashing, and cursing that accompanied my frequent attempts at one-fisted paddling to correct the course of my windblown canoe while clutching my rod, its line drifting under the boat, in the other fist.

In the stream, when the wind shifted, or I spotted a fish rising, or a hooked trout changed direction, I could respond with a little careful footwork or a body swivel. Compared to body management on the stream, canoe management on the lake was so time-consuming, aggravating, and noisy that I seldom experienced the quiet attentiveness to my surroundings that I now realized more than ever had been the heart and soul of fishing for me, and the medium of those unspoken conversations.

By mid-summer of that first year on the lake, I stopped fishing.

I beached the canoe and bought a used kayak, so small and tippy that many of my visiting friends could not manage to get in or out of it without capsizing. It suited me perfectly, though, because that kayak, unlike the canoe, felt like a natural extension of my body, the way a fly rod had felt like a natural extension of my arm. It was light, as easy to maneuver as feet are, and I was as close to the surface of the water as I had been in the stream.

The best time for kayaking was the hour before sunset, when the lake's surface turned glassy, offering an unruffled view of whatever was gliding, scuttling, rising, or diving beneath me. It was also the hour when deer or raccoons came down the hillside to drink at the water's edge; when beavers, muskrats, and minks cruised, their wakes visible in the surrounding stillness at a 100 yards' distance.

In calm water, the kayak could be maneuvered with short shallow strokes, so little disturbing the peace that I could come within fifteen feet of a beaver dining on the lily pads, observe how he delicately plucked a pad with one hand, brought it to his mouth to nip pad from stem, then dexterously rolled the pad into a cigar-shaped tube before munching it in two or three bites.

I left the fishing to wading blue herons who high-stepped through the reeds, to a pair of huge mossy-backed snapping turtles who prowled the shallows where bluegills made their nests, and to a migrating osprey who splashily announced his return every spring with dazzling beak-first plunges into the lake from high above.

The unspoken conversation with my father resumed, although now it took a simpler form, its gist not much more than, "Wow! Did you see that?" The presumption had changed. When I fished, there had always been an element of striving, which gave my father's part of the conversation the tinge of encouragement. Now that the layer of striving was stripped away, what was left was a presumed sympathy of perception and response—the pure gold that allows conversations to be unspoken.

Though obscured, that vein of gold had been there all along. After all, the reason both of us loved trout fishing had little to do with catching fish. What mattered most was that getting wise to trout demanded a sharp, focused, moment-by-moment attentiveness to our natural surroundings. Without a defined goal—catch that fish, track that deer, hunt that mushroom—it is hard to maintain that attentiveness. With a goal, it is easy to get so caught up in striving that you forget the goal was devised as a means.

Now, in those hours before sunset on the lake, my goal was attentiveness itself. I wanted to see and hear everything, see not only what was happening below, above, and on the surface of the water but also what was budding, leafing, flowering, or bearing fruit on the banks, hear not only the splashes and plops but also the whistles, hoots, warbles, and shrieks that issued from the forested hillsides.

During my first year on the lake, I was treated to a generously large catch of "Wow, did you see that!" firsts—the first osprey plunge, the first sight of a beaver cruising with a hitch-hiking kit on her back, the first sight of those mossy-backed snappers mating among the lily pads, roiling and snorting, their massive heads submerging and surfacing within feet of the kayak.

Some of those firsts have yet to be repeated—the June day several dozen great white egrets spent an afternoon fishing on the lake, the September morning a female moose trotted through the marsh, the moment a bald eagle swooped out of a tall maple overhanging my dock, its dangling claws coming terrifyingly close to my awestruck head before the third, shuddering wingbeat launched the eagle's ascent.

The lake continues to surprise, but looking to it only for firsts, like looking to a trout stream only for fifteen-pounders, is a bit like trying to survive by cake alone. Inevitably, as my seasons on Snyder Pond accrued, repeats became my daily fare. In the kayak, I became more of a scientist—a cataloger and identifier.

Every spring, I anticipated the day of ice-out, when the lake regained its fluidity, the way I had once anticipated the opening of trout season. The date was less certain, though, sometimes arriving as early as March 9th, sometimes as late as April 5th. A couple years, when winter had tried my patience too long, I tried to force it off the lake by launching my kayak as an ice-breaker of the last thin layer that stood between Snyder Pond and the first spring migrants—ring-necked ducks, who were being welcomed at other, shallower, already watery lakes and vernal ponds.

My observation of annual repeats on Snyder Pond had begun with ducks, and spring duck-watching set the template for many other kinds of observation. First, with the goal of identification in mind, I simply noticed shape, size, and color, which was usually enough to find a match in a field guide. That done, I started to note behaviors, like which ducks paddled in pairs; which seemed to prefer group dates; which dove for their food, which dabbled; which dabblers only seemed to slurp with their bills and which did a vigorous head-dunking, rear-raising bob for their meal. I looked for a champion among the divers, counting their seconds underwater while eyeballing the distance traveled, and gave the unofficial crown to a certain female merganser.

As my observations became more detailed, I began a strange *pas-de-deux* with my shelf of field guides, which had expanded considerably. Whether the quarry were fish, fowl, turtles, mammals, or insects, I would observe first, then try to confirm in the guides only what I had observed, without reading further. I literally flinched if I accidentally read about some aspect of appearance or behavior I had not yet noticed or had noticed but not registered as significant, identifying.

I was trying to reinvent the wheel of naturalist observation in part because I wanted to do my own noticing, in part because I wanted to hone my skills, but mostly, I suspect, because I wanted to slow down the process of learning, fearing that once I had noticed everything that could be found in field guides, my interest would flag.

I need not have worried. I soon learned that if I temporarily exhausted my capacity for observation on one front, as I did with ducks, there was always another layer of Snyder Pond life to compel and focus my attention. Dragonflies alone posed enough of an observational challenge to keep my eyes and mind alert every May through September.

When I first tried to sort the dozens of dragonfly species that taunt the bass on Snyder Pond, there was no field guide to confirm or direct my observations. I could have bought a four-pound, 829-page dragonfly textbook for a hefty price from Cornell University Press, but I decided not to. I would let my observations build from a base of pure know-nothingness, drawn in by the obvious allure of dazzling color and aerial acrobatics.

Willed ignorance, anathema to me in most of its manifestations, was in this instance the route to perceptions I might not have arrived at by any other means. Unguided, I simply began noting everything I could about a dragonfly's size, shape, color, flight patterns, mating behavior, and preferred perching and egg-laying sites, and because there was no possibility of marshalling the information toward an identification, there were no preordained notions about what was important to observe, what not, and, most importantly, there was no end point to observation.

When a field guide was published two years after I began my dragonfly watching, I was gratified to learn that many of the varieties of behavior I had observed were indeed traits used to identify different species. I was just as gratified to learn that other kinds of behavior that had captured my attention received no mention.

Professional classifiers give priority to information with a clear connection to species survival—information about feeding habits and sexual reproduction. They confirmed, for instance, my own observations that in some species, the female deposits eggs while flying in tandem with a male; in others, the male hovers nearby while the female does the depositing; and in still others, the female deposits alone and unguarded.

The field guides had nothing to say, though, about the death dance I saw performed several times by a species of small gold-bodied dragonflies that show up every September. The dragonfly, showing no apparent weakness, does a perfectly vertical headstand on a flat surface, holds the position for a few seconds, then flops on his back; he repeats the headstand and back flop four or five times until finally he does not rise again. The oddest part of the behavior is that the dragonfly, when choosing his platform, seems to prefer the outstretched palm of a human hand to other equally warm, equally flat surfaces like stone or wood.

Tutored by dragonflies, I took the silences in field guides as my license for purposeless observation. That's how I came to spend many hours one early June day last summer patrolling the lake in my kayak, watching blue-gills swim tight circles above their nests; noting the behavior of redwing blackbirds in the marsh, using those behavioral clues to locate two of their reed-woven nests among the cattails; crossing to the other shore to inspect a patch of flowering wild irises at water's edge; then stilling my kayak against the rocky bank and settling in for a prolonged session of dragonfly watching.

A large territorial male was guarding a stretch of lily pads that extended about twenty yards to each side of my kayak, shuttling back and forth at a speed that made the binoculars around my neck useless. He flew nonstop, never perching, deviating from his straight-line flight path only to chase off the occasional male intruder. His speed made it hard for me to do more than keep him in blurred sight with constant side-to-side head movements, as if I were watching a tennis match on fast forward. A few times, though, he caught light when passing near, so I was able to see a pattern of three mark-ings on each long wing and coppery bands ringing each segment of his dark brown abdomen.

I tried to see his face color, but never could, even after he had shut-tled past me more than a hundred times, always within a foot or two of my nose. When I paddled a few strokes to get a less myopic vantage, he shifted his flight path to make the same nose clearance. I paddled again; he shifted again. He was apparently as watchful of me as I was of him. I stayed near for about half an hour, saw him get lucky with a female, hook up and fly with her in wheel position before returning to solo flight.

Finally, I needed to rest my eyes. As I sat in the kayak, stilled against the bank under overhanging tree branches, I happened to gaze up and see a beige splotch on the underside of a green leaf. I reached up to inspect the leaf, and a beige moth fluttered onto my hand then settled on the sky-facing lens of the binoculars still hanging uselessly around my neck. There was a slight breeze, and a redwing blackbird *creeee-ed* in the marsh.

And then it happened. I entered a state, welcome but not willed, and welcomed only after the fact, because for its brief duration it was state of blessed self-forgetfulness. My observation of the life humming around me had become so close and mesmerizing that it stopped being observation and became existence. I was neither observer nor observed, just part of and inseparable from the hum. The felt quality was less of merging than of stepping through the windowpane of looking onto a plane of pure, enmeshed being.

The state was rare but not, during these years on Snyder Pond, unfamiliar. Words are inadequate to the experience, which in its essence is wordless, unmeasured by any consciousness of time passing, and dispelled in the first heartbeat of returned self-awareness. With the second heartbeat comes a rush of overwhelming gratitude.

Both the scientist and metaphysician in me believe the state emerges from a literal change of focus. When my mind and eyes, tired from a prolonged effort of selective concentration, widen their focus, intending only to rest, I am taken by surprise at the broader view—all that I have filtered out rushes in, fills me with a sudden blast of appreciation for what is, all of what is, around me. What I apprehend in these states is a vibrancy—the world a mesh of moving, changing parts whose interconnecting particularities are indistinguishable from the humming rippling whole. It is a moment of profound delight, felt also as a moment of profound clarity.

No conversation, spoken or unspoken, accompanies these states. Afterwards, along with gratitude, there is hope and a wish. I hope my father found his way to this vibrancy. I wish it upon everyone.

My way in remains the quiet attentiveness to natural surroundings I first associated with fly fishing. It is an indirect route, but I know if I don't intensely narrow my focus, fixate on a dragonfly's wing, a bird's call, the veins of a leaf, I might never arrive at the moment of broadened vision.

Dithering over Dogs

Paul Schullery

When I walked into the little fly shop in Juneau that day in late July, I was pretty sure my fishing trip was already over. I'd spent much of the previous two months in the Yukon and Alaska, where I'd sampled what was, by my standards, an amazing array of fishing opportunities. The idea that here, just pausing for a couple days on the way south with my wife through the Inside Passage, I would show up at the right time for some fishing, felt like an extreme long shot. But I had to ask; who knows, maybe there was a little trout pond within reach.

So I asked the friendly guy behind the counter if there was any fishing right then, and he gave his head that slow sideways shake that, far from meaning "no," meant, "I can hardly believe the fishing here right now myself."

One of the places he sent me was Sheep Creek, a small stream that falls off the steep green slopes on the east side of the Gastineau Channel just a few miles south of town. There, he told me, right by the saltwater, I would find a hatchery that produced a strong run of chum salmon, just then in progress.

Now and then over the years I've done some pretty determined griping about our odd condescensions to and mistreatments of the non-sport fish that share our favorite waters with the fish we are so passionate about. But the Sheep Creek salmon were a reminder of a different kind of discrimination—the equally ancient and equally peculiar bigotries of taste we exercise among the sport fish. Chum are victims of an almost bizarre disapproval

248

Photo by Marsha Karle

Paul Schullery catching a chum salmon, Gastineau Channel, Alaska.

among sportsmen. They are big, strong fish. Their life histories are every bit as dramatic and heroic as the other Pacific salmon. They take flies as serendipitously and demandingly as most other fish. And they are beautiful. Imagine for a moment that fishing had never arisen as a human pursuit. Imagine that we didn't have any interest in catching fish, much less eating them. If there were no fishermen and the only reason we went to salmon rivers was to admire beautiful creatures, the chum might well be our favorite. With their flanks jaggedly streaked in complicated non-primary colors, they are among the most strikingly patterned animals we're likely to see outside of the tropics. The subtle variations on burgundy, olive, cream, and green are enough, but they're complemented by other shades that almost defy labels. Some observers even claim to see blue (well, okay, maybe the off-slate-blue of certain riverbottom rocks, on an overcast day, seen through a foot of glacially tinted water).

But all this is not enough for us. There are stories of anglers catching chums and abusing them verbally and physically, mostly for not being some other fish they would have preferred to catch—like those stunted souls who pitch whitefish up on the bank rather than return them to the water. This foolishness has to do with many things. As it happens, chums do have a lower fat content and less colorful flesh than the others, so their market value has been historically lower—though why these things should bias sportsmen, especially non-meatfishers, against them isn't clear. Chum also have a reputation for not jumping, though that hardly makes them unique among Pacific salmon. The reasons for our dislike of chum go on, each with its accompanying "but" to suggest that, underneath our stated reasons, we don't like chum because, well, we never did. They're chum, right? Dog salmon? Dogs?

The folklore of the name is another accumulation of imagined grievances. When I first fished on the West Coast in the 1970s, I was told that they were called dog salmon because they tasted so bad that Indians just fed them to their dogs. Whoever enlisted Native Americans in the anti-chum slander certainly didn't care what Native Americans might actually do or think, but the literature seems to suggest that historically Native Americans might feed the meat of any species of salmon to their dogs if the meat was for some reason—time of year, efficiency of preservation, and so on—sub-par. They knew their fish, and made the most of each species.

Another more authoritative part of dog-salmon lore has it that the chum were called "dog salmon" because they sprout noticeably dog-like fangs during spawning. The guys standing next to you along a river are hardly the best place to acquire a comprehensive overview of a story like this, so I'm sure I've missed additional dog-salmon nomenclature lore. Whatever combination of forces gave rise to the name, it couldn't help any fish's public relations to be called a dog. I wonder how differently this would have gone if those teeth had inspired everyone to call them shark salmon, or even wolf salmon, instead.

The name "chum" probably hasn't helped the unread angler's opinion of the fish, either. For most fishermen, the word is associated with the junk meat we toss into the water to attract fish. But according to Robert Behnke's masterful *Trout and Salmon of North America* (2002), the word "derives from the Native American Chinook language word for 'striped' or 'variegated' and is descriptive of the streaks and blotches found on the body of a chum as it nears spawning time."

If I had to guess why the chum's other common name, "calico salmon," hasn't caught on more than it has, I'd propose that it's too pretty and descriptively appropriate to appeal to the people who already prefer to dislike the fish and need to give it a suitably insulting name. Besides, how many right-thinking, chum-stomping, manly men would be caught dead fishing—anywhere near home at least, considering the exotic appeal of the calico bass—for something named "calico?"

So often these prejudices come down to quirks of local culture and availability. Many Americans look down on the carp, whose comprehensive introduction in North America has led to many unpleasant complications in native fisheries. But some of the United Kingdom's most passionate and literate anglers enjoy the sophisticated and vastly rewarding sport of carp fishing (the fish is not native there, either, though it has been around a lot longer than here). These Old World experts, recognizing just how savvy and wary carp can be, reverse our own biases and refer to carp as "salmon, with brains."

In contrast, while I and many like me look at the grayling with little short of reverence, there is a long tradition among many UK anglers—they are known as "thymallophobes"—of treating that magically beautiful fish as a pest. They hate them with an inherited bitterness the match of any of our chum loathers. We're fishermen; why should I expect more of us?

I was lugging along all this cultural baggage, and probably other complicating notions, as Marsha and I drove down to Sheep Creek that day, but in my case it was completely swamped by something else: my lifelong dream of finding myself, fly rod in hand, standing within casting distance of an immense number of really big fish.

This, too, gives me pause. Some of our most venerated angling writers have described the progression of the typical fisherman's engagement with the sport. According to their formula, which varies somewhat from writer to writer, we all start out as nearly barbaric little fish vacuums, mad to catch anything of any size by any means. We grow from that into self-competitors, seeking to best our own previous record by catching the most fish possible, or the largest fish possible. And we finally arrive at a stage that is invariably portrayed as the wisest, in which we care only to catch the most difficult, challenging fish. By the time Edward Hewitt gave us his version of this prescription for an angler's life journey in his *A Trout and Salmon Fisherman for Seventy-five Years* (1948), the prescription had taken on a slightly bullying tone. Hewitt, who is now remembered as much for the confidence of his pronouncements as for his angling expertise, clearly believed that if you were serious about fishing, you must follow this course or prove yourself a boorish lesser creature.

Luckily, most of us don't buy into that narrow a code. A day with bluegills has a glory of its own. There is no shame attached to it (except maybe a little if you can't catch them).

As much as I love difficult fishing for selective fish, I have never lost my affection for hog heaven. In fact, that affection has been intensified by many years of wilderness fishing for easily caught trout. The more the better. The more and the bigger, the better yet. Nothing suggests the joyous complexity of sport in nature better than the bewildering process by which we define its success and failure.

Being mostly an inland and highland angler, I had few opportunities for exposure to those occasions my world-traveling friends told me about, in places where there were fabulous numbers of very large fish within easy reach. I had heard about situations like Sheep Creek, and I could imagine nothing more exciting than the chance to see if it was, indeed, possible for me to get tired of it. Apparently not.

At high tide, the tidewater stretch of Sheep Creek was barely any length at all. It poured from the mountainside almost directly into the hatchery operation, then under the road and immediately on into the saltwater. As the tide went out, the creek was left in its channel, twenty to thirty feet wide, which wound across the wet, dark rocky ground and grew longer and longer until there were a few hundred yards of it. The rocks didn't dry because it rained lightly most of the time we were there.

The tackle-shop guy said that the salmon hit only on the incoming tide, and the locals all seemed to agree. As many as a dozen anglers would be scattered along the creek or bunched up near the steadily climbing "mouth" of the creek. Fish splashed and rolled almost everywhere. The carcasses scattered here and there demonstrated that these chum were typically about thirty inches long, and their substantial depth from dorsal to belly led me to believe that they probably weighed between ten and fifteen pounds. I know that's nothing unusual to many globe-trotters, but I'd never hooked even one fish so big. A bunch of gulls and ravens—and a solitary pigeon, of all things—picked at the carcasses, especially closer to the hatchery, where the dead fish seemed thickest.

And that's another thing—the "h" word. This whole fishery was made possible by a hatchery, the bane of modern wild trout enthusiasts and the curse of native aquatic ecosystems all over the world. During my long, rambling trip through the Far North, never once had I paused and said to myself, "Golly, I just hope I can find some intensely artificial fishing situation where all the fish are the result of aggressive human manipulation of the environment!" Whether fishing for roadside grayling or salmon and trout somewhere in the bush, I'd never found any Alaskan fishing as grandly circumscribed and aesthetically compromised as this. Looking up from my casting for fish whose lineage was downright agricultural, I could watch enormous cruise ships going by just a mile or so out in the channel.

I suppose I must have underestimated my flexibility, because at the time none of this was a problem for me. The raw excitement of the scene simply overrode concerns about anything else. This was Alaska; just look at those mountains. These were incredible fish; just look at them, and look at where they've been since they left that hatchery. And this was still incredible fishing. I knew I'd think about all the navel-gazing aspects of it later, but right then was no time for ruminations. There was too much of the real thing to soak up. I could save the intellectualizing for later. Right then, coming upon this fabulous scene put me in a category of sensory overload best characterized by a comment made by a man with whom I once dug ditches, who described some similarly overwhelmed soul by saying, "That old boy don't know whether to shit or go blind." Hereinafter, this will be referred to as the SOGB syndrome.

While Marsha alternated between taking pictures of all things Alaskan and dashing back to the car to read or paint as the next squall came through, I stumbled over the slick rocks down to the nearest part of the stream and started casting, but I was too overcharged to stay in one spot. Figuring there must be some reason that the other fishermen—all of whom were fly fishers, I was surprised to notice—were standing where they were, I overcame my SOGB syndrome just long enough to think for a moment. It seemed likely to me that the fish in somewhat deeper water were much more likely to have the opportunity for deliberation required to notice and take a fly, so I looked for deeper spots. I also imagined, correctly, that the people gathered at the stream mouth were casting over a larger concentration of fish that were holding in the quieter depths there. I also imagined that the fish out there might be fresher than the ones up near the road, some of whom were obviously dying, if not rotting, as they held in the riffles.

It was impossible not to hook a fish, though not necessarily the way you wanted. Snagging was unavoidable. With so many fish holding in the current together, a fly drifting through them would eventually hang up on some fish's snout, fin, or side, whether the fish wanted the fly or not. At the slightest hesitation of the line or feeling of weight, I had to set the hook, and off the salmon would go. In direct violation of received wisdom, a few of these fish did either breach or even jump completely clear of the water, but most of the struggle consisted of frantic knuckle-knocking runs. I went through most of my modest stock of freshly purchased florescent chartreuse and pink egg-sucking leeches, the flies most highly recommended right then, intentionally snapping them off in a number of the obviously snagged fish so I could get back to casting.

And here I was confronting an inflexibility of mine that didn't evaporate even in the face of such a thrilling abundance of big fish. I became nearly obsessed with fair-hooking one. I was not willing to completely abandon my sense of How This Is Supposed to Be Done, no matter how exciting it was just to be randomly connected to one of these wonderful animals after another. I was more disappointed every time I discovered that the fly was just hung up on a salmon's dorsal or some other inappropriate part of its person. Seeing that one or two of the other fishermen had an obvious and enviable knack for fair-hooking fish after fish on their flies, I figured I owed myself no less.

Local rules and customs in the parts of Alaska I visited were fairly casual about the fair-hooking issue. Hog Heaven is often like that; when there is so much, who worries about details? It did seem that some of the other fishermen at Sheep Creek might be there just for the undeniable excitement of playing and releasing these big strong fish, without any particular concern for where they might be hooked. Everybody was having a great time, and it was all the same to the fish.

I finally dragged a couple of strong and apparently fair-hooked fish right to the wet rocks at my feet before they broke off or got free, and then I landed one that had the fly embedded in the tip of its snout. Earlier in my trip I had been told that, according to local practice and tradition, if the fly is within a few inches of the mouth, it's regarded as a fair-hooked fish, but I ended the day with the feeling that I still hadn't done this right.

As we drove back to town, I was still shaking with the excitement of having participated in such a magnificent nature spectacle, hatchery and cruise ships notwithstanding. I had a sleepless night in which vague, porcine fish shapes wallowed and slashed ceaselessly before my eyes. It was as if I was worried that something—an earthquake? the Endtimes?—would prevent me from going back and standing there at the edge of that rolling tide of fish and casting and casting until I could once again haul back on the vibrating weight of the world.

But we were back at Sheep Creek the next morning, Marsha for more dashing and reading, and me for more fish. It was still drizzling, and I immediately went down to the mouth of the creek so I could fish out toward the deeper water.

Having no success with alternatives, I put on my last pink egg-sucking leech, and on the first cast a small Dolly Varden, probably following the salmon to eat their eggs, took it. On the next cast, the fly was taken by a twenty-nine-inch chum who acted a little tired and didn't run as hard as many of the others, but whose golden sheen was beautiful when the fish was stretched out on the dark wet rocks—and who held the fly well inside its mouth.

For the really dedicated worrier, even a fair-hooked fish provides the opportunity for a little creative agonizing, because it is well known that if you cast precisely and often enough into a pod of big fish you will eventually manage to swing the fly right into a fish's mouth, effectively snagging it in the mouth. The fish's willingness to participate in the process being an important part of the idea of sport fishing, mouth-snagging fish provides its own interesting intellectual diversions for thinking about how sport works. Ultimately it's imponderable, though. Salmon aren't the only fish that require the fly to be presented for their convenience; many choosy trout have a narrow and precise feeding lane. Intention and volition are hard to measure under those circumstances. In that last instant before the fly goes into the fish's mouth, there's always room to wonder if even the most stodgy and uncooperative salmon may have welcomed it, or even lazily popped its gills a bit, just to speed the fly on toward its gullet. I find wondering about things like this a lot of fun, but I gather that most people don't.

My final fair-hooked fish of the trip, a thirty-incher, fell into that category. As I fished, I had a good look at him only fifteen or twenty feet from me. The water was murky from all the rain, so as he sank or rose in that one spot, he would fade into the grey water and then materialize back into the light. I had the luxury of choosing a nearby position on the bank that would allow me to swing the fly right at him, and after a few easy sweeps of the line I did in fact feed him the fly. How he "felt" about the offering is unknowable. But I can tell you that even in the magnificent buffalo-herd/passenger pigeon biological storm of this kind of fishing, for all the excitement of just being there connecting with these powerful animals on any terms, I still found a special thrill in that first clear sight of the line running tautly down from the tip of the rod through the water to the front end of that fish.

There is a range of temperament in our approaches to fishing that is as broad and diverse as those of us who fish. I call it the Waltonian Spectrum. When we are on the water, our contemplative impulses range from the intense to the nearly absent. The reposeful anonymous anglers pictured in ruffled-sleeve elegance in eighteenth- and nineteenth-century engravings, sitting under a tree and fiddling with tackle or gazing serenely at the stream, occupy one idealized end of this spectrum. Vincent Marinaro laying comfortably on a lawn along the Letort in the 1940s, his nose inches from the surface as he studied the tiny insect life floating by, may seem at first glance like those quiet ancestors in the engravings, but his contemplation was much more aggressive and demanding. (It was not better; don't fall into the Hewitt Fallacy of thinking that you're entitled to imagine that certain neighborhoods on the spectrum are necessarily classier. It's a spectrum, not a ladder.)

From these fishermen studying so obviously to be quiet, we move along the spectrum, past various types of ease and athleticism, concentration and disengagement, delight and dismay, generosity and greed, altruism and competition, until finally we encounter people caught up in special SOGB moments, when so much is going on that all contemplation must be deferred.

But anywhere on the spectrum, for all but the least attuned of us, contemplation must come, even if it never develops beyond a warm memory of a given day's fishing. Judging from how often absolute strangers we meet feel compelled to tell us a fishing story as soon as they learn that we are also fishermen, contemplation in one form or another is just what we do.

I fished over those chums in 1998. It took me three years to publish a book about that summer in Alaska, and when I did I didn't even include the chums in it, partly because I was still engaged in poking at the memories. And here, fourteen years after those rainy days on Sheep Creek, all I have to show for my many hours of contemplation is this breezy little gloss on a very complicated set of memories. I find it comforting to realize that I am nowhere near done contemplating, remembering, and dithering over those dogs. As long as memory holds out, a day's fishing is never really over. What happened that day never loses its capacity to surprise and excite us again. Maybe we won't get all the way back to the SOGB syndrome just on the memories, but we'll get close enough.

Local Knowledge

W. D. Wetherell

Pristine beauty, if you can find some, does wondrous things for the soul, but lately in my trout fishing I've become more involved with wryness, weirdness, wackiness—qualities that the nearby Mascoma River has in spades. It's a perfect example of a twenty-first-century American trout stream—sick in some respects, healthy in others, but never fully one or the other, and so dynamically schizoid in all kinds of interesting ways. Having done the pristine thing for two weeks in British Columbia, I was home now and in the mood for something nastier.

"The mouth of the Mascoma?" Ray Chapin said, when I called him with an invite.

"It will drive us crazy, but that's just what I need."

The Mascoma works hard and plays hard in its thirty-mile run down from the hills. Rising in a rocky pond on a remote, forgotten plateau in central New Hampshire, the private domain of an Internet baron, it spills through a logging dam built a hundred years ago and becomes a trout stream, home to native brookies, or rather the former home—acid rain and/or global warming has completely done them in. The stream picks up a few small tributaries, accepts the tea-colored ooze of various beaver ponds, flows under rude bridges built by snowmobilers, then enters civilization behind a road of tarpaper shacks reminiscent of Appalachia at its poorest. A half mile downstream it decorates the opposite extreme, a tony New England boarding school pupiled by twelve-year-olds whose parents live in Bogotá and Dubai.

Photo by Ray Chapin

W. D. Wetherell with brown trout, Vermont.

It enters the first of its three towns—an old New England mill town, with old industrial dams—and then a second mill town, with more old dams, before it flows through a fine brown trout pool (run-ups in the spring, three and four-pounders) into manmade Mascoma Lake—beautiful, but with all those abandoned mills upstream, signs stapled to the birches warn about never eating the fish.

Into Mascoma Lake with its summer homes, and then out of it again, flowing under a causeway built by the Shakers in the nineteenth century, then spilling over yet another dam. The next three miles run through a pretty patch of woods, flanking a bike trail on the abandoned grade of the old Boston & Maine. It looks like a picture perfect trout stream here, and would be if the lake water spilled from the bottom of the dam rather than the top; great structure, great hatches, but the water's far too warm. It's one of New Hampshire's rare fly-fishing-only stretches, and the stocked fish are enjoyable enough while they last. Once upon a time there was more challenging fishing to be had here, and celebrity fishers down from nearby Dartmouth included Ernest Schwiebert, Jack Hemingway, and very possibly the young Norman Maclean.

Having passed one high school, the Mascoma now passes a second, loops under the interstate highway, cavorts through Lebanon's venerable old downtown, trips over two more dams, cuts around the airport's runway, then runs past the site of an old electrical generating station, yuppified into the "Powerhouse Mall," complete with an L.L. Bean outlet, past which the river slides and splashes in its channelized bed, providing a frisson of authenticity to the pricey yellow and orange kayaks stacked outside the store's entrance. Sensing the end is near, the river chunnels through the Route 12A bridge, licks the backside of another mall, disappears into scruffy woods, flows past a homeless man's improvised wigwam, passes a sewage treatment plant, widens beneath a canopy of jungle-like vines into a modest delta—and then finally enters the Connecticut in a bright, wide-flowing pool.

Things become even more layered and interesting here. The sewage treatment plant funnels in its wastewater with a heavy smell of chlorine. Big Wilder Dam, built in the 1940s, is only a mile upstream, and its releases, flowing unpredictably, drown fishermen with some regularity. Railroad tracks follow the riverbank over in Vermont—Amtrak's "Vermonter," like a silver ghost from another era, races by twice a day. A hundred yards downstream, the river is spanned by the huge I-89 bridge—high, even lofty, but truck vibrations run down the pylons, and if you're fishing near here with your buddy, you often have to shout. Withal, this is probably the most reliable place in the valley to spot a golden eagle. We see them all the time, gliding high over the traffic as if monitoring it then finding a dead elm further upstream where they can sit in dignity and brood.

As I said, a fascinating and complex river, the Mascoma. What brings us to its mouth is not its signature blend of rural decay and rural endurance; its gallery of post-industrial relics; the temples of consumerism scarifying its banks; the carbon-culture monument rising just downstream; the rich social, economic, and natural histories flowing with its waters; its Shaker heritage; nor even the ghost of Norman Maclean. What brings us here is its trout.

The junction pool ("the Big Box pool," Ray calls it) where it enters the Connecticut can offer some of the finest trout fishing in New England, though the important qualifier is *can*. It often doesn't. The flow has to be right from Wilder Dam (at 4,000 cubic feet per second the trout hug the bottom with their mouths zipped; a cfs of 12,000 can drown you), the evening has to be well advanced (if you can still see the sun over the Vermont bank you're here too early), and, the water being so prolific with insect life (the sewage treatment plant ripening it just right), you have to be shrewd with your choice of flies. If all these stars align, you can catch eighteen-inch trout fat as rugby balls, and there are stories, which I have no trouble believing, of rainbows and browns pushing eight pounds.

Plenty of locals know about this, but the weirdness and danger keep most of them away. New Hampshire and Vermont share responsibility for the Connecticut, which means both states ignore it, and probably none of their fisheries people even know these trout are here. So it's all about benign neglect—and my experience is that trout, while deserving all the TLC we can give them, often grow very large under benign neglect.

It's a tailwater fishery—that magic phrase—but not quite the classic kind, since the water spilling from the dam is often so warm. As to where the trout actually come from, this is one of the mysteries we've never been able to figure out. Both the Mascoma and the White are heavily stocked, so it's reasonable to assume some of the fish were planted upstream, and, not liking the neighborhood, headed downstream toward the glitz. But we catch smaller than stocked size, too, so it's likely that at least some natural reproduction is going on, particularly with the browns.

The dirt road down to the pool is just rutted and spooky enough to deter non-initiates. Some bait fishermen had already parked there—as always, their goal seemed to be getting their tailgates as close to the water as possible without sliding in. We're usually glad to see bait people—we're very forgiving of anyone engaged in an activity not involving computers—but one bunch was on their cell phones and the other had their radio blaring with country rock. But what the hell. The Mascoma mouth is a stew of complexities and everything goes into its pot—even golf balls from a riverside driving range, yet another feature I forgot to mention.

"How's the fishing?" Ray asked the bait boys as we readied our canoe.

"Caught an eight-inch rainbow," the oldest, most grizzled of them said, beaming.

"That's great!" Ray said, genuinely pleased. He's a gentle man—no one else I know could have avoided sounding condescending. "Well, we'll just duck under your lines here if that's okay, get this baby launched. Nice talking to you!"

("Eight inches?" I mumbled, being the cynic I am. "He's adding two inches—that means six.")

We paddled upstream, found a rocky terrace near the bank, got out, cushioned ourselves with life preservers, then, as is our custom here, sat sipping cognac while we waited for the hatch to start. Around the next bend but plainly visible was yet another layer of interest. The old railroad bridge to Vermont that the log drives used to smash apart every spring. The wide bay where the White River brings in the water off the Green Mountains. The semi-shabby, semi-quaint townscape of West Lebanon, complete with church steeple, old warehouses, Greek Revival-style homes.

And the light was the kind you often get here in September—beautifully filtered, the trees burnishing it up—and it was so wistfully pretty we expected the trout would appear earlier than usual, just to let their rise forms stir the color even more.

"In fishing, local knowledge is everything," I opined, sweeping my arm around. "A visiting fisherman would never find this, not in a million years. It's camouflaged. It's a tailwater in disguise."

I say "opined" because that's what we do while we're sipping cognac near the Mascoma mouth—opine on a lot of subjects, starting and ending with fly fishing.

"So," Ray said, after a detour through politics, sports, and kids. "You had a good trip to B. C.?"

I nodded. "People who rave about Montana being the last best place haven't seen British Columbia."

"Trout?"

"As common as perch."

"Salmon?"

"Sockeyes everywhere—the biggest run in a century. It was hard not to step on them."

And it was funny out there in British Columbia, speaking of local knowledge. I fished seven rivers and creeks, spent a lot of time exploring, and the only other fly fisher I encountered was when I was climbing out of the Skagit on my last afternoon. B. C. anglers are well spaced out. And yet I missed finding locals to pump for advice; I can do this shamelessly, and on many trips it's paid off, taking me to waters I never would have found on my own.

"Local knowledge," I said, in case Ray hadn't heard me the first time. "Out there, for instance. Probably we're the only ones in a fifty-mile radius . . . normal citizens I mean . . . who know that enormous clouds of flying ants passed through the valley on Monday afternoon. It's reasonable to assume there are still some around. For instance—right there."

Out in the center of the current, like a golden keg shoved gently upwards from the bottom, the water fattened, bubbled, and thinned. First rise of the night—and much earlier than usual, with the sun still on the water, giving us time to do serious business with those trout.

Or not. For while our cinnamon ants looked exactly like the naturals, the fish could tell the difference. Time and time again I would maneuver the canoe into position, Ray would present his fly perfectly, only for the trout to bulge toward it then shy away. Fake! They could have been shouting this out loud, their disappointment was so palpable.

So it was back to usual, which meant, after a few more paddles up and down the pool, tying on skinny Light Cahills above fat White Wulffs while waiting for the Mascoma mayflies to appear, starting with the creamy ones at sunset, then the white ones at dark.

Ray and I have pretty much expunged the word "caught" from our fishing vocabulary, replacing it with (when it comes to assessing a fishing day) the more evocative word "encounter." We encountered dozens of trout that night—rises over toward Vermont, rises back toward New Hampshire, rises splitting the difference right in the river's middle. One of Ray's encounters became more personal, and he was actually attached to a trout, to the point he had to coax it over to the canoe and gently detach it. The problem with "catching" a trout here (to use the old term for a moment) is that, with the time taken to bring it in, with darkness rushing on fast, you probably won't have time to "catch" another, so you end up wanting to catch one and not wanting to catch one at the same time—a contradiction only a fly fisher can understand.

But this was all remarkably enjoyable. Most of the hatches we've seen up here were midges or caddis, and to have this many mayflies on the water—so beautiful with youth, their wings upright and stately like miniature swan boats barging downriver—provided the classic fly fishing moment: trout greedily sipping and duns hatching fast.

The bait boys over on the bank had sheathed their cell phones, turned off the stereo, built a bonfire big enough that its flames stretched across the water and licked our canoe. Time to give our Wulffs one last pass through the pool before darkness shut us down. Turning back upstream, we saw a surprising, even extraordinary sight.

Backlit by the bonfire, their shapes hunched low, two men were launching a fishing boat down the bank, despite the fact it was now pitch black. Night fishing!—we could see the silhouettes of their rods. No one does it up here, and certainly not at the Mascoma mouth, where the interstate bridge takes on a weird, shimmery, overpowering sort of presence; the looming, hungry-looking trees on the banks get you thinking of Algernon Blackwood's terrifying story "The Willows"; the dam's sudden releases can drown you—and, in any case, it's against New Hampshire state law.

Unless they were smugglers ferrying contraband to Vermont (maple syrup? maple candy? maple scotch?), these fishermen knew something Ray and I didn't: how to catch monster fish there at night. This obviously wasn't their first trip—they moved too quietly, too smoothly; this was their long-practiced routine. Were they fishing bait for big browns? Using minnows? Using mice?"

"Yeah, mice," I decided. "Live ones. They strap hooks to their undersides and douse their fur in phosphorescence."

Were they going after big bass, not trout? Big walleyes? Giant pike? They were gone downstream by the time we got to the bank. This was one Mascoma mystery we weren't going to solve.

Things were turning rowdy around the bonfire—the bait boys had been joined by the man from the wigwam, the Gallo was being tapped, and the shapes ringed around the flames made me think of hobos from the old days—but the light helped us to load the canoe on our car. We bounced our way back toward pavement.

"Did you hear they're building a mall here?" Ray asked.

Yes, I had heard; the developer's plans had been in the paper, but I wasn't going to mention it unless he did. The Mascoma mouth is about to become an even more complex stew than it already is, complex enough, most likely, to prevent us from ever coming back.

Ray lives in Vermont, so we took the interstate bridge home. I craned my head just enough to see the bonfire down below on the bank with its generous scoops of red, then, further out on the river, a chartreuse, firefly-like flash that came from the night fishermen setting up. It made me jealous, that last light did. Not just in the way I've always been jealous seeing any fisherman go out, no matter how much fishing I've done that day myself. Jealous in a deeper way. I could brag about local knowledge all I wanted, but these were men who had more of it than I had, and really, when you considered all the layers, my thirty years living here barely counted—I was a beginner; I hardly knew anything at all.

Fishing Together

Robert Wrigley

I'd had one of the best fishing days of my life the day before, having fished from mid-morning until dusk, using a single pattern, something called a "Spruce Moth" our guy at the local fly shop suggested we might give a try. It was one of those days when everything is just about the fly, when reading water and making the ideal presentation seem almost incidental. I couldn't remember how many fish I'd netted and released—thirty-some cutthroats, maybe a dozen of them fifteen inches or longer, hefty and sleek.

The next day, a whole lot of nothing for most of the morning. The fish were feeding. A couple of times my little Spruce Moth drifted alongside something that might have been the real item—the actual wingy bug the dry fly was an imitation of—and a cutthroat slurped or seized the moth and let my now seemingly half-assed simulacrum float by. We'd started out the day with a two-mile walk up the trail from the end of the road, then a scramble down a narrow, rocky, might-as-well-be-a-game-trail chute, to one of our favorite holes on the river, where my wife caught a couple of beauties and I grew ever more baleful. She's a beautiful woman who becomes even more beautiful when she's happy, and nothing makes her happier than landing a fine trout. I love it when she catches fish, in other words. A good thing, since she usually catches more, and bigger, fish than I do. But the hole we'd started out at had always been golden for me, and moving away from it, downstream and skunked, was more than a little frustrating.

There's a way in which my wife has always been more relentless than me—about the hunt, that is. I used to joke, "I love fishing; she loves catching fish." That the point of the former is presumably the latter I also understood to be a misconception; I just wasn't sure whose misconception it was. Or how. She often says she has to remind herself to look up and see where we are, meaning the beauty of the landscape, the mountain slopes and ridges, the big cedars and the wildflowers; sometimes I have to remind myself that I'd like to catch a fish, too. That hot fishing day before, it was easy to pay attention. But fishing failure begets indolence in me, even a kind of sloth. Until it doesn't. Until the boredom of failure leads to concentration, when you force yourself to pay real attention. Eventually, *not* catching fish while your partner does becomes downright dispiriting. Used to be that sort of dispiritedness made me a hideous, impatient, and ultimately desperate, profoundly shitty fisherman. Not so much now. I think I'm both more philosophical about *not* catching fish and a substantially more resourceful fisher.

So after a desultory while, I moved downstream a ways, while my sweetheart stayed at the hole and landed still more. Might have been *because* she landed more. I walked along and surveyed the river. There were pockets of holding water against the other shore, although the whole river in this stretch is more rightly called a run—shallow and shoaly on the right, a reef of round rock in the middle that the river scooted over in a long, slick, and smooth tongue—but over there, a bit of an eddy under a grassy cutbank and a little depth, too, maybe just over knee-high. *If I were a cutthroat,* I thought to myself, *I'd hang out there and see what might drift by.*

Photo by Robert Wrigley

Robert Wrigley and Kim Barnes fishing together, Idaho.

By that point in my fishing life, this was less a hunch than a calculated surmise based on experience. There are lots of fish in this river, but they're savvy. Fishing pressure is considerable all summer long, and catch and release regulations might well have helped make those cutthroats among the wiliest around. Some days there's a kind of rhythm to everything that you have to get in synch with. Or that I do. Whatever it was about yesterday, today had a new kind of breathing and movement to it, which I had to get aligned with. And having left that good hole with nothing, especially while my wife was hauling them in—well, I was on a mission: There was a fish over there and I meant to catch it.

I put a good amount of line into the air and tossed the beloved Spruce Moth just a few yards upstream of where I figured the trout would be, and, sure enough, on the drift a big gold-green head surfaced just upstream from it, followed a ways, then went back down. Didn't strike, didn't offer. But he was there.

After I took the fly up gently, and after a few more casts toward the same spot, I thought better of it and hauled in. The Spruce Moth's delectability yesterday notwithstanding, I made a decision to tie on something new. If the fish was attracted by those wings, how about more? Something dramatic, say. In this case, that something was a big (#8), blond, "golden" stonefly Stimulator. For this cast I didn't plan on much of a drift but hoped to drop the Stimulator soft as cottonwood fluff right where he'd come up before. Of course, the problem with planning the perfect cast always comes down to execution, but maybe that earlier skunking at the hole helped me bear down some, and sure enough, the fly fell almost straight down onto exactly the right spot and was hardly even in the water when the cutt took it, and I lifted the rod tip and had him on. A couple of minutes of run and reclaim, that sweet and adrenalizing give-and-take, and I netted him. He was eighteen inches, easy, with a broad swag of belly and brilliant red about the gills.

What hole? What skunk? What Spruce Moth?

My sweetheart, Kim, was elated for me. She would have been elated even if she had also been skunked up above, but her elation in this case was accompanied by relief, no doubt. Certainly my own elation also held a measure of relief. She was two or three fish ahead of me still, but now we were both in the game. This suggests that there's something competitive about our fishing, and really there isn't. Or isn't exactly. Fly fishing is something we've always done together, and the other's success is nearly as valuable as our own.

On the one hand, I haul in a pack fly rod in backpacks, as my backpacking pals do, and then, for some reason—we're all men, after all; our love for one another is brotherly and we're overtly competitive—it's more important to us, catching the most or the biggest. Besides, we're usually fishing some high mountain lake and planning to eat a few. On the other hand, my wife and I learned the art of fly fishing at more or less the same pace. She remains more determined and less easily distracted than I am; my casts are longer. And usually, yes, she catches more fish, and bigger ones too. It is less that I prefer this state of affairs than that it just seems to be a safe bet. I have better days, and even better trips, than she does, now and then, but I love to watch her with a fish. The bigger, more impressive ones she likes to talk to. She almost coos. She tells the fish how beautiful it is. A couple of times she has even given an especially nice trout a kiss. Her attachment, and her gratitude, seem a lot deeper than mine. I admire the fish and let it go, usually with all deliberate speed. She dawdles some, and that seems to be just so that she can be in the presence of the trout a little longer.

This is not a ruse. You'll have to trust me on that. To paraphrase the poet James Wright, "Sometimes I feel like half a fish myself."

The river I'm talking about is our home field, our home river. We camp, almost always, in the same spot. We've learned, over a decade and hundreds of fishing days, the best places, and we've learned to leap-frog downriver to give one another first crack at the usually reliable hot spots. She's learned—at my insistence—never to say where this or that photo, and this or that fish, was taken. *Nameth not thine river*, is my commandment. She's generous; I've learned to be stingy. With others, at least. Sorry about that, but as with women, so with fish, as far as I'm concerned. Find your own.

In a way, it's hard for me to imagine better times than we have fishing, and after nearly thirty years of marriage, it's hard to imagine that we would know one another so well if we had not taken up this sport. We hit the water about the same time the terrestrials are getting active. We pack a lunch and fish sometimes for six hours or more, then head back to camp, the sun-shower, a glass of champagne (often with a few huckleberries dropped in), then dinner (salmon or lamb chops or steaks, spuds, grilled tomatoes, a

Photo by Kim Barnes

**Robert Wrigley
with cutthroat
trout, Idaho.**

good bottle of wine). Afterward, we head down to the hole by camp. I've caught half a dozen nice fish right there by camp; she's caught, of course, more. Sometimes in addition to my rod and vest I'll haul down a milk crate and my guitar and, while she keeps fishing, I'll play and sing and watch the river, but mostly I watch her.

Twenty-eight years ago we fled from Idaho to Montana to get married by a justice of the peace in need of a haircut. It was sort of an elopement. We blazed into Missoula just in time to sign the license application, then—facing a compulsory three-day wait (I wonder if Montana still requires that?)—we went on what we still refer to as our "prenuptial backpack." She was twenty-five and I was thirty-two. We weren't fly fishers in those days, but she was still a determined hunter of fish. On our second day at that little lake, I left her in camp and climbed up a nearby ridge to get a few pictures. Of the pictures I took, the only memorable one is the one I snapped surreptitiously, after I'd come back down to camp. She didn't know I was there. She was standing on a smooth stone shelf that extended maybe ten yards out into the lake, casting some sort of a spinning lure and reeling in. She's wearing a pair of blue gym shorts and nothing else. If she'd been sunbathing, say, or just basking, I might not have taken the picture, and she's too far off to be recognized, especially since all you see is her bare back, her reddish hair tied up on her head, and her arms upheld as she reels in a fish. You can see a splash from the fish out in front of her. She and I are the only ones who've ever set eyes on that picture, and there are few pictures of her I love more.

We didn't take up fly fishing seriously until our kids were old enough to be left at home alone, right around the turn of the millennium. Now it's what our summers are all about. Everything else that comprises our lives together must be worked around. We spend four or five days on the river, come home, pay bills, do the other necessaries, then repack and head off again. When we're back at work toward the end of August, we steal away any weekend we can for more, through September and into early October, when the first larch needles are falling and the nights are almost uncomfortably cold. The routines of our fishing trips seem, during the working part of the year, magical, and when we know we're leaving the river for the last time each autumn, we're already thinking of the next July.

The "work" we go back to is two full-time jobs apiece. We write and we teach writing. That means, from late August to early May, sixty to eighty hours per week of reading and reading and writing and reading. We hardly ever write in the summer months; we teach even less (the occasional writer's conference, provided it doesn't interfere with fishing season). I'm a poet; she writes prose.

A good many of my poems are about being in the woods (we *live* in the woods) and occasionally about being on the rivers we frequent. This has led to my being called by some "a nature poet." It's not a label I'm fond of. Actually, I'm pretty much opposed to any classifying label being attached to the noun "poet" when it refers to me, with the possible exception of the word "living." I write about all sorts of things, after all: love and sex; death, biology, and music; culture and history, not to mention the venality of the political world; most of all, I write about my favorite of all the wild animals: the human being. I have no idea what a "general audience" might be, especially for poetry, but such a readership, if it exists, is probably what I'm inclined toward. If I thought I were only writing poems to be read by people with advanced degrees in literature, I'd slit my wrists. Writing about fishing for people who fish is at least as specialized as writing poetry, but all sorts of people fish and, believe it or not, all sorts of people read poetry, too. I've written only a few poems in which fly fishing is mentioned, but when I have, my motive is to get at something more (or other) than the awesomeness of a wild river and its trout.

A few years ago I wrote a poem (which Russ Lumpkin published in *Gray's Sporting Journal*) that probably served in some way as a template for this essay. What got the poem started was its punny title—"Cutthroats in Heaven"—but the aim, ultimately, was to imagine the idea of "heaven"—what, for someone like me, paradise might be. For a fly fisher, such a place would be a trout stream, and for me, it also had to include Kim. Here it is:

Cutthroats in Heaven

I don't mean the big guy, dropper of Job
into an earthly hell of loss and boils,
nor the avengers, the brave rebel fools,
the burners who later burned forever at the stake

themselves. No, this heaven's unchurched at all,
but for the river I would have it be,
its nave of run and hole, congregation
of no one but me and, just downriver,

my beloved, having left our lesser
fleshes for these new miraculous ones,
requiring even in the coldest water
wearing nothing, neither neoprene nor Gore-tex,
able to stand on the beslicked stone backs
of the river's bed barefoot and casting
with more accuracy and floating fall
than ever in our lives for the fish there.

And though the cutthroats shall rise to our flies,
they shall in no way give themselves to us
more easily than ever we sought them
in days past, for each fish shall represent

whatever measure of grace we have earned.
Meaning, as it was in our past lives,
that she still will catch and release bigger and more
most of the time, meaning there will be days

my mind will wander and my eyes look up
from the fly's drift to note how a single
tributary sidestream caresses stones
and enters the cold river of heaven

for the rest of all of time I will live,
which, by such theology as I crave,
shall be forever, with her, in summer mountains,
among the holy trout, our cutthroat gods.

Among the many things I love about fly fishing is that it's so much like writing poems. You go at each of them with a certain array of tools and you don't know, while you're putting out fly line or poetic lines, if you're going to get anything. And sometimes you get something on and you can't land it. I'm talking about the poem here, mind you, not just fishing. When you first started fly fishing, you sucked at it. As with fishing, the more you write, the more competent you get, but neither writing nor fishing is only about competence in the end. Who wants to be a merely "competent" poet? It's not even about netting the fish or finishing the poem. It's about the process. There are a couple of other activities I might mention in the category of "things that make me feel most alive," but I'll stick to writing and fishing. All such activities offer something like the pure attentiveness that comes with casting for and, especially, hooking, playing, and landing a trout. I'd call it almost holy. That kind of attentiveness is rare and in some lives virtually nonexistent. Time spent at such attentiveness is time you are somehow not accountable for but something you are given, time in which your mind and body are in a different and better place. That's what it feels like writing a poem too.

You might notice, by the way, that in the poem the speaker and his beloved have the river of heaven entirely to themselves (they're as naked as the prelapsarian Adam and Eve after all, not so much as a neoprene fig leaf). In real life, Kim and I fish mostly clothed, but we run into a lot of other fishers as well, nearly all of them men. I don't think I'm imagining it, when I say that a good many of those men show something a little like envy in their eyes, when they see us fishing together.

It was probably our second or third trip to the river, in the early 2000s, when Kim caught the biggest fish of her life. I didn't carry the camera then, and that's probably why I do now. She had that particular cutthroat on for a good ten minutes. He'd run downstream and, having made my way to shore, I listened to her reel zing as it gave out line. She'd gather him back and get him close and he'd take off again, upstream or straight across, and all I did was watch and cheer her on. By the time she was able to net him, she was so arm-weary she was groaning with the effort. It was, I admit, very sexy, that noise she made, as I was watching her there, locked-in and battling. She had to tuck the rod under her arm and use both hands to lift the net into the air, with several inches of head and tail stuck up from the tip- and handle-ends. Better than twenty inches, that fish. Massively bodied. Really, a spectacular trout. And the biggest fish I've netted on that river, impressive as it was, was fairly dwarfed by hers.

It would take me another thousand words to describe the enormity and perfection of her smile that day, after she let the fish loose and turned to look at me there, sitting on a rock on shore, smiling back.

This is true. I'm not sure, had I been the one who'd caught that fish, if I would feel any more blessed.

Contributors' Notes

KIM BARNES ("Why I Fish") has published memoirs—*In the Wilderness: Coming of Age in Unknown Country* (1996), a PEN/Jerard Award winner and nominee for a Pulitzer Prize, and *Hungry for the World* (2000), a Borders Books New Voices selection; and novels—*Finding Caruso* (2003), *A Country Called Home* (2008), winner of the 2009 PEN Center USA Literary Award in Fiction, and *In the Kingdom of Men* (2012). She co-edited *Circle of Women: An Anthology of Contemporary Western Women Writers* (2001) with Mary Clearman Blew and *Kiss Tomorrow Hello: Notes from the Midlife Underground by Twenty-five Women Over Forty* (2006) with Claire Davis. A former Idaho-Writer-in-Residence, Barnes teaches at the University of Idaho and lives with her husband, poet Robert Wrigley, on Moscow Mountain.

WALTER BENNETT ("Black Quill") is a retired lawyer, judge, and clinical law professor at the University of North Carolina at Chapel Hill. He's published short fiction in print and online journals, including *The Cortland Review*, numerous articles on the legal profession, a highly acclaimed book, *The Lawyer's Myth: Reviving Ideals in the Legal Profession* (2001), and a novel, *Leaving Tuscaloosa* (2012), a finalist for the Bellwether Prize. He is co-producer of a literary documentary film, *Landscape of the Heart: The Elizabeth Spencer Story* (2012). A Southerner by birth, Bennett and his wife, Betsy, a museum director, divide their time between Chapel Hill, North Carolina, and Bozeman, Montana, where they fish every chance they can.

RUSSELL CHATHAM ("A Set of Tides"), renowned landscape painter and lithographer, writer, independent publisher (Clark City Press), restaurateur, and world record holder (striped bass on a fly), has had more than 400 one-man shows at museums, galleries, and universities throughout America. His writings on art, fly fishing, bird hunting, and food and wine have appeared in many major magazines. His books include *Silent Seasons* (1978, rev. 1988); *Dark Waters: Essays,*

Stories, and Articles (1988), with a foreword by Nick Lyons; the highly acclaimed *The Angler's Coast* (1976, rev. 1990), with a prologue by Thomas McGuane; and a catalogue, *One Hundred Paintings* (1990). Recipient of the 1993 Arnold Gingrich Award from the Federation of Fly Fishers, he supplied forewords to Harry Middleton's *The Earth Is Enough: Growing Up in a World of Flyfishing, Trout, and Old Men* (1996), and *The Bright Country: A Fisherman's Return to Trout, Wild Water, and Himself* (2000). He is featured in the Justin Coupe-Palmer Taylor film, *Rivers of a Lost Coast* (2008). After four decades in Livingston, Montana, Chatham has returned to his native California, where he is writing a memoir of his early angling days tentatively titled *Tide, Wind, and Fog,* while he also continues to paint.

GUY DE LA VALDÈNE ("Remembering Woody"), photographer/filmmaker, writer, conservationist, international sportsman, and gourmand, was born in New York City but raised in France. He is co-director, with Christian Odasso, of the pioneering 1974 cult film, *Tarpon* (released as a remastered DVD in 2008), featuring Jim Harrison, Thomas McGuane, Richard Brautigan, and music by Jimmy Buffett. He is author of three highly regarded nonfiction works on hunting, two of which—*Making Game: An Essay on Woodcock* (1985, 1990) and *For a Handful of Feathers* (1997)—are considered classics in the field, and the other being *The Fragrance of Grass* (2010), as well as a novel, *Red Stag* (2003). De la Valdène, a contributing editor for *Field & Stream,* lives in northern Florida and is working on a book about the natural life of the lake that anchors his Dogwood Plantation.

ROBERT DeMOTT ("Deserve's Got Nothing to Do with It"), Edwin and Ruth Kennedy Distinguished Professor at Ohio University, received six different graduate and undergraduate teaching awards. His many books include *Steinbeck's Typewriter: Essays on His Art* (1996), winner of the Nancy Dasher Award; three poetry collections—*News of Loss* (1995), *The Weather in Athens* (2001), winner of the Ohioana Book Award for poetry, and *Brief and Glorious Transit: Prose Poems* (2007); a bio-bibliography and memoir, *Dave Smith: A Literary Archive* (2000); and edited anthologies, including *Conversations with Jim Harrison* (2002) and *Afield: American Writers on Bird Dogs* (2010). His poems and sporting pieces have appeared in the *Georgia Review, Southern Review, Cimarron Review, Quarterly West, Southern Poetry Review, North Dakota Quarterly, Gray's Sporting Journal, Trout, American Angler, Yale Anglers' Journal, American Fly Fisher,* and *Contemporary Sportsman.* A Federation of Fly Fishers–certified casting instructor, DeMott lives with partner Kate Fox in Athens, Ohio.

CHRIS DOMBROWSKI ("Brainwashing") has chronicled his fifteen summers as a river guide in Montana in *Gray's Sporting Journal, Orion, Outside* magazine, and the *Drake*. His poems have appeared in numerous literary journals, including *Crazyhorse*, *Denver Quarterly*, *New Letters*, *Poetry*, and *Poetry Daily*. His poetry collections include *Fragments with Dusk in Them* (2008); *By Cold Water* (2009), a finalist for *ForeWord's* Poetry Book of the Year; *September Miniatures with Blood and Mars* (2012); and a forthcoming collection, *Fire's Bride* (2013). His awards include the Associated Writing Programs' Intro Award, Alligator Juniper's National Poetry Prize, and a writing fellowship from Wyoming's UCross Foundation. Dombrowski teaches creative writing at Interlochen Center for the Arts, and, with his family, divides his time between Michigan and Montana.

RON ELLIS ("A Lovely Simplicity") wrote the Foreword to the posthumous edition of Harry Middleton's *On the Spine of Time: A Flyfisher's Journey Among Mountain People, Streams, and Trout* (1997). He is author of an acclaimed fictionalized memoir, *Cogan's Woods*, reissued in a tenth anniversary edition in 2011 by Skyhorse Publishing, with a new Foreword by Rick Bass and a Preface by Nick Lyons. Ellis's other books are Of *Woods and Waters: A Kentucky Outdoors Reader* (2005), *Brushes with Nature: The Art of Ron Van Gilder* (2008), and *In That Sweet Country: Uncollected Writings of Harry Middleton* (2010). His essays have appeared in *The Gigantic Book of Hunting Stories* (2008), *Afield: American Writers on Bird Dogs* (2010), and in *Sporting Classics*, *Kentucky Afield*, and *Kentucky Monthly*. Ellis is an associate editor and columnist for the web-based magazines *Contemporary Sportsman* and *Contemporary Wingshooter*. He and his wife, Deborah, divide their time between northern Kentucky and the Tennessee mountains.

JIM FERGUS ("Let's Do It Again Next Year"), peripatetic sportsman, has published on various topics in *Newsweek*, *Harrowsmith Country Life*, *The Paris Review*, *MD Magazine*, *Savvy*, *Texas Monthly*, *Esquire*, *Fly Fisherman*, *Outdoor Life*, *Outside*, *Sports Afield*, and *Field & Stream*. His books include a travel/sporting memoir, *A Hunter's Road: A Journey with Gun and Dog Across the American Uplands* (1992), and a collection of outdoor articles and essays, *The Sporting Road: Travels Across America in an Airstream Trailer with Fly Rod, Shotgun, and a Yellow Lab Named Sweetzer* (1999). His first novel, *One Thousand White Women: The Journals of May Dodd* (1998), won the 1999 Fiction of the Year Award from the Mountains & Plains Booksellers Association, and its French edition, *Milles Femmes Blanches*, was a runaway bestseller abroad. His second novel, *The Wild Girl: The Notebooks of Ned Giles* (2005), is a historical fiction novel set in the 1930s. Fergus lives in Arizona and is at work on a new novel.

KATE FOX ("Life Among the Anglish") was born in Colorado and educated in the Midwest, where she earned her Ph.D. in American literature and creative writing at Ohio University. Her articles have appeared in *Gray's Sporting Journal*, *The Drake, Over the Back Fence, CCCC Journal*, and *Kaleidoscope*. Her poems have appeared in the *Great River Review, New Virginia Review, Valparaiso Review, West Branch*, and *Green Mountains Review*, among others. *The Lazarus Method* (1996), published under the name of Kate Hancock, won Kent State University Press's Wick Poetry Chapbook Prize. She served as Ohio University's publications editor; as editor of *Echoes*, the Ohio Historical Society's newsletter; and, until her retirement in 2007, as the long-standing editor of the *Ohioana Quarterly* book review journal. Fox lives in Athens, Ohio, and currently runs Textual Healing, a freelance writing and editing business, and has completed *This Side of the Afterlife*, a book-length poetry collection.

CHARLES GAINES ("Rivers Owned in the Mind"), widely traveled journalist, novelist, screenwriter, and co-inventor of Paintball®, has published extensively on many different subjects in periodicals ranging from *Architectural Digest* to *Town and Country*. His twenty-three books (three became movies) include the novel *Stay Hungry* (1972), finalist for the National Book Award; the documentary *Pumping Iron: The Art and Sport of Bodybuilding* (1974), with photographs by George Butler; the biography *Yours in Perfect Manhood: Charles Atlas* (1982); and three nonfiction works, *A Family Place: A Man Returns to the Center of His Life* (1994), *The Next Valley Over: An Angler's Progress* (2000), and *Leaper: The Wonderful World of Atlantic Salmon Fishing* (2001), co-edited with his nephew Monte Burke. Gaines has won two Cine Gold Eagle Awards and three Emmy Awards for television writing. A contributing editor at *Garden & Gun*, Gaines divides his time between Alabama and Nova Scotia.

BRUCE GUERNSEY ("A Line in Still-Cold Water"), a native New Englander, is Distinguished Professor Emeritus at Eastern Illinois University, where his long career in teaching was frequently honored for its excellence. A former editor of *Spoon River Poetry Review*, his books of poetry include *Lost Wealth* (1974), *January Thaw* (1982), *The Lost Brigade* (2004), *New England Primer* (2008), and *From Rain: Poems, 1970–2010* (2012). His prose and poetry have been published in the *Virginia Quarterly Review, Flyway, Fly Rod & Reel, Poetry, Atlantic Monthly, American Scholar, Yankee, Afield: American Writers on Bird Dogs* (2010), and elsewhere. He has received fellowships in writing from the National Endowment for the Arts, the Illinois Arts Council, and the Bread Loaf Writers' Conference. Guernsey and his wife, the artist/jeweler Victoria Woollen-Danner, divide their time between Illinois and Maine.

JIM HARRISON ("Older Fishing"), poet, novelist, screenwriter, memoirist, essayist, and gastronome, has published more than forty books since 1965, most recently *The Farmer's Daughter* (2010), a collection of three novellas; *The Practice of the Wild: A Conversation with Gary Snyder and Jim Harrison* (2010); a film originally published in book form as *The Etiquette of Freedom* (2010); *The Great Leader* (2011), a novel; and two books of poems, *In Search of Small Gods* (2009) and *Songs of Unreason* (2011). Since 2003 he has written a quarterly column, "Eat or Die," for the Canadian literary journal *Brick.* Harrison, whose work has been translated into more than two dozen languages, won Colorado's Evil Companions Literary Award (1999) and the Spirit of the West literary achievement award from Mountains & Plains Booksellers Association (2000). He was elected to the American Academy of Arts and Letters in 2007. Originally from Michigan, Harrison divides his time between Montana's Paradise Valley and southern Arizona, where he continues to puzzle out the logic of birds and fishes.

PAM HOUSTON ("In the Company of Men [Redux]"), former river guide and big game hunting guide, is author of two novels, *Sight Hound* (2006) and *Contents May Have Shifted* (2012); two linked short story collections, *Cowboys Are My Weakness* (1992), translated into eleven languages, and *Waltzing the Cat* (1998); as well as a collection of essays, *A Little More About Me* (1999), all published by W. W. Norton. She edited a collection of multi-genre writing for Ecco Press, called *Women on Hunting* (1994), and wrote the text for a book of photographs, *Men Before Ten A.M.* (1996). Her stories have been selected for volumes of *Best American Short Stories, The O. Henry Awards, The Pushcart Prize,* and *Best American Short Stories of the Century.* Houston has won the Western State Book Award, the WILLA Award for contemporary fiction, and Colorado's Evil Companions Literary Award. She directs the Creative Writing Program at the University of California, Davis, and divides her time between northern California and a 9,000-foot-high ranch in Colorado, near the headwaters of the Rio Grande River.

MICHAEL KEATON ("Moving Water"), actor and world traveling sportsman, has a keen eye for well-written scripts. Keaton has garnered popular and critical acclaim for his range of character portrayals in *Mr. Mom* (1983), *Beetlejuice* (1988), *Clean and Sober* (1988)—the latter two for which he received the National Society of Film Critics' Best Actor Award in 1989—*Batman* (1989), *Batman Returns* (1992), and *Jackie Brown* (1997), as well as for his recent voice work as Ken, Barbie's fashion-conscious boyfriend, in the mega-hit *Toy Story 3* (2010). Keaton has been a featured angler with Tom Brokaw, Thomas McGuane, Yvon Chouinard, Lefty Kreh, and others on The Outdoor Channel's widely viewed salt water fly fishing program, *Pirates of the Flats* (2010), and its sequels, *Buccaneers and Bones* (2011, 2012). He divides his time between Southern California and a ranch in Montana's Sweet Grass County.

GREG KEELER ("Sourdough Down"), poet, painter, playwright, troubadour, satirist, and oft-honored teacher (most recently the James and Mary Ross Provost's Award for Excellence) in Montana State University's English Department, has published two memoirs, *Waltzing with the Captain: Remembering Richard Brautigan* (2004) and the incomparable *Trash Fish: A Life* (2008); nine collections of poetry, from *Epiphany at Goofy's Gas* (1991) through *Dead West* and *Lord of Nothing* (both 2011); a novel, *Painting Water* (2011); and a song book, *Forgettable: The Collected Songs of Greg Keeler* (2011), plus numerous music CDs. His essays and paintings have appeared in *Gray's Sporting Journal*, *Outside*, *FlyFish Journal*, *Big Sky Journal*, *Fly Rod and Reel*, and *Distinctly Montana*. His paintings have been exhibited in galleries in Bozeman, Livingston, and Butte; his acrylics are on permanent display at Columbo's Pizza and Pasta, Bozeman. Founder and CEO of Dumbass Press, Keeler lives with his wife, Judy, in Bozeman, Montana, where he wears his many artistic hats.

SYDNEY LEA ("Epic and Idyll") founded the acclaimed literary quarterly, *New England Review*, which he edited from 1977 to 1989. His work has appeared in many periodicals, including the *New Yorker*, *Atlantic Monthly*, the *New Republic*, and *Sports Illustrated*, as well as more than forty anthologies, including *Afield: American Writers on Bird Dogs* (2010). Lea has held Rockefeller, Fulbright, and Guggenheim fellowships and has published ten collections of poems, including *Pursuit of a Wound* (2000), a finalist for the 2001 Pulitzer Prize; *Young of the Year* (2011); *Six Sundays Toward a Seventh: Selected Spiritual Poems* (2012); and the forthcoming *I Was Thinking of Beauty* (2013). In addition to a novel, *A Place in Mind* (1989), he has published collections of outdoor essays, notably *Hunting the Whole Way Home* (1994), *A Little Wildness: Some Notes on Rambling* (2006), and *Now Look* (2012); and a collection of literary criticism, *A Hundred Himalayas* (2012). He lives in Newbury, Vermont, and makes regular hunting-fishing forays to his Maine cabin. In 2011 Lea was named Poet Laureate of Vermont.

TED LEESON ("Donor"), educated on the spring creeks of southwest Wisconsin's Driftless Region, then at Marquette University and University of Virginia, received the Roderick Haig-Brown Award from the Federation of Fly Fishers in 1996 and was designated *Fly Rod & Reel's* Angler of the Year in 2008. He has written *The Orvis Guide to Tackle Care and Repair* (2006), and with Jim Schollmeyer, half a dozen indispensible references, from *The Fly Tyer's Benchside Reference* (1998) to *Flies for Western Super Hatches* (2011). He wrote introductions to The Lyons Press collected edition of Roderick Haig-Brown's *The Seasons of a Fisherman: A Fly Fisher's Classic Evocations of Spring, Summer, Fall, and Winter Fishing* (2000). Leeson edited *A Gift of Trout* (1996) and has written three important, must-read nonfiction works: *The Habit of Rivers: Reflections on Trout Streams and Fly Fishing* (1994), *Jerusalem Creek: Journeys into Driftless Country* (2002), and *Inventing Montana: Dispatches from the Madison Valley* (2009). Leeson, tackle guru and maven at *Fly Rod & Reel*, teaches creative writing at Oregon State University in Corvallis, where he lives with his wife Betty Campbell, a Victorian literature specialist.

NICK LYONS ("Indian Summer of a Fly Fisher"), author, editor, publisher, professor, and all-around fly fishing facilitator, mentor, and ambassador, was born in 1932 in New York City and attended the University of Pennsylvania, Bard College, and the University of Michigan (Ph.D.). He began teaching at the Hunter College of the City University of New York in 1961 and remained there until 1988. He was executive editor of Crown Publishers from 1964 to 1974. In 1977 he created Nick Lyons Books. In 1984 the firm became Nick Lyons Books, Inc. In 1989, with a new partner, it became Lyons & Burford, Publishers. When Burford left in 1997, it became Lyons Press, which during its final full year of production in 2000, published 190 titles. In 2001 Lyons Press was acquired by Globe Pequot Press of Guilford, Connecticut. Lyons has written numerous books on various topics, most prominently on fly fishing, including *The Seasonable Angler: Journeys Through a Fisherman's Year* (1970), *Fishing Widows* (1974), *Bright Rivers* (1977), *Confessions of a Fly Fishing Addict* (1989), *Spring Creek* (1992), *A Fly Fisher's World* (1996), *My Secret Fishing Life* (1999), *Full Creel: A Nick Lyons Reader* (2000), with a Foreword by Thomas McGuane, and *Trout River* (2000), with photographs by Lawrence Madison. He wrote a long-running feature column, "The Seasonable Angler," in *Fly Fisherman* magazine, and has provided countless introductions, forewords, and prefaces for others' angling books. In 2000 he was awarded the Medal of Honor by the The Anglers' Club of New York. He is featured on the American Museum of Fly Fishing's DVD, *Why Fly Fish* (2008). Lyons and his wife, Mari, a painter, divide time between New York City and Woodstock, New York.

CRAIG MATHEWS ("In the Nick of Time"), *Fly Rod & Reel's* Angler of the Year in 2005, has published several noted guides, including *Fishing Yellowstone Hatches* (1992); *The Yellowstone Fly-Fishing Guide* (1997), with Clayton Molinero; *Western Fly Fishing Strategies* (1998); two volumes of *Fly Patterns of Yellowstone*

(1987, 2008), with John Juracek; and *Fly Fishing the Madison River* (2001), with Gary La Fontaine. Mathews contributes a regular "Letter from Yellowstone" to the Anglers' Club of New York *Bulletin*. He has narrated and produced five Telly Award–winning DVDs on fly fishing, and has developed famous fly patterns, including Sparkle Dun, X-Caddis, and Pops Bonefish Bitters. He and his wife, Jackie, own Blue Ribbon Flies in West Yellowstone, Montana, and are co-founders of 1% for the Planet, an environmentally conscious organization of business alliances. Active in riverine stewardship, Blue Ribbon Flies has received numerous conservation and protection awards from Yellowstone National Park (1997), Greater Yellowstone Coalition (2000), Federation of Fly Fishers (2003), Trout Unlimited (2007), and the Madison River Foundation (2008).

THOMAS McGUANE ("Seeing Snook"), recipient of the 2000 Roderick Haig-Brown Award from the Federation of Fly Fishers, and the 2009 Wallace Stegner Award from the Center of the American West at the University of Colorado, Boulder, was elected to the American Academy of Arts and Letters in 2010 and received the Distinguished Achievement Award from the Western Literature Association in 2011. McGuane has published twelve books of fiction, from *The Sporting Club* (1968) and *Ninety-two in the Shade* (1973) to *Gallatin Canyon: Stories* (2006) and *Driving On The Rim* (2010). His screenplays include *Rancho Deluxe* (1974); *The Missouri Breaks* (1976); *Tom Horn* (1980), with Bud Shrake; and *Cold Feet* (1989), with Jim Harrison. His sporting books are *An Outside Chance* (1990); *Some Horses: Essays* (1999); *The Longest Silence: A Life in Fishing* (1999), considered a classic of contemporary fly fishing literature; and *Upstream: Fly Fishing in the American West* (2002), with photographer Charles Lindsay. McGuane was *Fly Rod & Reel*'s Angler of the Year in 2010. McGuane was a featured angler on the salt water film series *Pirates of the Flats* (2010) and *Buccaneers and Bones* (2011). An award-winning horseman, avid upland bird hunter, and working cattle rancher, he lives on the banks of the West Boulder River in McLeod, Montana.

JOSEPH MONNINGER ("A Night on the Kennebago"), former Temple University football player, Peace Corps volunteer in West Africa, and licensed fishing guide, has published eleven novels, from *The Night Caller* (1981) to *The World as We Know It* (2011); three young adult novels, including *Baby* (2007) and *Hippie Chick* (2008), both award-winning books; and three nonfiction works, including the memoirs *Home Waters: Fishing with an Old Friend* (1999) and *A Barn in New England: Making a Home on Three Acres* (2003). He has received fellowships from the New Hampshire Council for the Arts and the National Endowment for the Arts. For several years his family competed in the New England Sled Dog sprint races and ran a small sled dog business in New Hampshire's White Mountains. Monninger teaches at Plymouth State University and lives with his family near New Hampshire's Baker River. In the coming year he will be a visiting professor in Limerick, Ireland, close to excellent trout fishing.

HOWARD FRANK MOSHER ("The Legacy") is the author of ten novels, including *Disappearances* (1977), *Where the Rivers Flow North* (1978), and *A Stranger in the Kingdom* (1989)—all of which have been made into feature films—as well as *On Kingdom Mountain* (2007) and *Walking to Gatlinburg* (2010), plus two personal travel memoirs, *North Country* (1997) and *The Great Northern Express: A Writer's Journey Home* (2012). Mosher has received Guggenheim and National Endowment for the Arts fellowships, an Arts and Letters Award from the American Academy of Arts and Letters, the American Civil Liberties Award for Excellence in the Arts, the Vermont Governor's Award for Excellence in the Arts, the New England Book Award, and, most recently, the 2011 President's Award for Lifetime Achievement in the Arts from the New England Independent Booksellers Association. He lives with his wife, Phillis, in Vermont's Northeast Kingdom, where he writes the literate blog, *The Kingdom Journal.*

JAKE MOSHER ("September 23, 2010"), a former Golden Gloves boxer and college baseball player who grew up in northern Vermont, has worked as a logger, hard-rock miner, fishing guide, reporter, freelance journalist, and nature writer. His nonfiction hunting and fishing pieces have appeared in *Outdoor Life*, the New York *Times*, *Yankee*, the Rocky Mountain Elk Foundation's *Bugle*, John Bryan's anthology, *Take Me Fishing* (2007), and many other publications. Mosher's novels are *The Last Buffalo Hunter* (2001) and *Every Man's Hand* (2002). He lives in eastern Montana, where he directs blasting operations at a large coal mine.

CRAIG NOVA ("A Shell Game"), novelist, screenwriter, essayist, memoirist, and blogger (*The Writing Life*), attended the University of California, Berkeley, and Columbia University, where he received his graduate degree. A recipient of a Harper Saxton Prize, National Endowment for the Arts and Guggenheim fellowships, and the Arts and Letters Award from the American Academy and Institute of Arts and Letters, Nova has published in *Esquire*, *The Paris Review*, *Men's Journal*, and elsewhere. His thirteen novels, including *The Good Son* (1982), *The Congressman's Daughter* (1986), *Cruisers* (2005), *The Informer* (2010), and *All the Dead Yale Men* (2012), have been translated into ten languages. His autobiography, *Brook Trout and the Writing Life* (1999), was released in a revised edition, with an Introduction by Ann Beattie (2011). Since 2005 Nova has been Class of 1949 Distinguished Professor in the Humanities at the University of North Carolina, Greensboro, where he lives with his wife Christina, and dreams often about fly fishing Western rivers and spring creeks.

MARGOT PAGE ("Inside, Looking Out"), the first woman to contribute an article to the New York *Times* outdoor section, has published in *Countryside, New Woman, Fly Rod & Reel, Trout, A Different Angle: Fly Fishing Stories by Women* (1995), and *Take Me Fishing* (2007), and she supplied the Preface to *Uncommon Waters: Women Write about Fly Fishing* (1991). Page's three books include a ground-breaking memoir, *Little Rivers: Tales of a Woman Angler* (1995), *Just Horses: Living with Horses in America* (1998), and *The Art of Fly Fishing: An Illustrated History of Rods, Reels, and Favorite Flies* (2000), with Paul Fersen. Page was editor of the American Museum of Fly Fishing's journal, *American Fly Fisher,* from 1990 to 1996, and is now director of communications for Casting for Recovery, a national nonprofit organization that she helped found, which is devoted to using fly fishing as a wellness program to help breast cancer survivors. She lives in Sunderland, Vermont.

DATUS PROPER ("May"), born in Iowa in 1934, was educated at Phillips Exeter Academy and Cornell University. He was a diplomat with the United States Foreign Service and served in Washington D.C., Angola, Brazil, Ireland, and Portugal as a political analyst until his retirement in 1987. Proper then moved with his wife Anna and two children to the Gallatin Valley on the banks of Thompson Spring Creek (aka "Humility Creek") near Bozeman, Montana, where he began a full-time career as a writer. *Trout* magazine ranked his first book, *What the Trout Said: About the Design of Trout Flies and Other Mysteries* (1982; rev. 1989) as one of the fifteen best books on trout fishing published between 1959 and 1989. *Pheasants of the Mind* (1990) and *The Last Old Place: A Search Through Portugal* (1993) were followed by a selection of fishing pieces, *Running Waters* (2001). "May" is a completed chapter from an unpublished book-length manuscript, variously titled *The Home Place* and *A Wild Place*, left unfinished at his death in 2003.

HOWELL RAINES ("Foreword") was editorial page editor of the New York *Times* from 1993 to 2001, and its executive editor from September 2001 until June 2003. Winner of an individual Pulitzer Prize in 1993 for his article, "Grady's Gift," he is also the author of *My Soul Is Rested* (1977), an oral history of the civil rights movement; *Whiskey Man* (1977), a novel; *Fly Fishing Through the Midlife*

Crisis (1993), a bestselling, critically acclaimed memoir; and *The One That Got Away* (2003), which continues detailing his fishing life and covers aspects of his journalistic career. He wrote introductions to the fifth edition of *The Compleat Angler* (1996) and John Bryan's anthology *Take Me Fishing* (2007). An Alabama native, Raines lives with his wife, Krystyna, a journalist, during summers in Pennsylvania and winters on Mobile Bay. He is currently at work on a historical novel set in the South during the Civil War.

LE ANNE SCHREIBER ("Life After Fly Fishing"), educated at Rice, Stanford, and Harvard, was editor-in-chief of *womenSports* magazine, former sports editor of the New York *Times*, deputy editor of the New York *Times Book Review*, and ombudsman at ESPN. She has published widely in *Life, Glamour, Elle, SELF, Discover, Parabola, O: The Oprah Magazine, The Yale Review*, and elsewhere. As an independent journalist, she has written about science, politics, medicine, literature, media ethics, sports, and the outdoor life. She has received several awards for her writing, including a National Magazine Award for public interest journalism. She is the author of two memoirs in which fly fishing is central: *Midstream: The Story of a Mother's Death and a Daughter's Renewal* (1990) and *Light Years: A Memoir* (1996), both New York *Times* Notable Books of the Year. She has taught in Columbia University's graduate writing program, at the New York State Writer's Institute, and in the English Department of University at Albany–SUNY. Schreiber escaped the Manhattan grind years ago and now lives and writes in rural Columbia County, New York.

PAUL SCHULLERY ("Dithering over Dogs), author, co-author, or editor of more than forty books and hundreds of articles on nature and our use of it, was born in Pennsylvania and educated next state over at Wittenberg University and Ohio University. He holds an honorary doctorate of letters from Montana State University. Schullery was executive director of the American Museum of Fly Fishing in Manchester, Vermont, from 1977 to 1982. His books on the history and culture of fly fishing include the definitive study *American Fly Fishing: A History* (1987), which *Trout* magazine considered one of the fifteen best books on fishing published between 1959 and 1989; *Royal Coachman: The Lore and Legends of Fly Fishing* (1999); *Cowboy Trout: Western Fly Fishing as if It Matters* (2006); *The Rise: Streamside Observations on Trout, Flies, and Fly Fishing* (2006); *If Fish Could Scream: An Angler's Search for the Future of Fly Fishing* (2008); *Fly-Fishing Secrets of the Ancients: A Celebration of Five Centuries of Lore and Wisdom* (2009); and *The Fishing Life* (2012). In 1998 he received the Wallace Stegner Award from the University of Colorado's Center of the American West, and in 2006, the Federation of Fly Fishers presented him with the Roderick Haig-Brown Award. Retired from the National Park Service since 2008, he and his wife, watercolorist Marsha Karle, have collaborated as author and illustrator on five of his recent books, including *This High, Wild Country* (2010). They live in Bozeman, Montana, where Schullery was recently named Scholar-in-Residence at Montana State University's Renne Library.

W. D. WETHERELL ("Local Knowledge") was raised in Garden City, New York, but long ago moved north. His twenty books of fiction and nonfiction include short stories, *The Man Who Loved Levittown* (1986), winner of a Drue Heinz Literature Prize; novels, *Morning* (2002), *A Century of November* (2005), winner of the Michigan Literary Fiction Award, and the forthcoming *The Writing on the Wall*; a Smithsonian Guide to Natural America, *Northern New England: Vermont, New Hampshire, and Maine* (1995); an autobiography, *Yellowstone Autumn: A Season of Discovery in a Wondrous Land* (2009); and a meditation, *On Admiration: Heroes, Heroines, Role Models, and Mentors* (2011). Wetherell has also written a trilogy of highly regarded angling books—*Vermont River* (1984), which *Trout* magazine included among the fifteen best fishing books published between 1959 and 1989, *Upland Stream: Notes on the Fishing Passion* (1991), and *One River More: A Celebration of Rivers and Fly Fishing* (1998). In 1998 he received a Mildred and Harold Strauss Living Award from the American Academy of Arts and Letters. He lives in Lyme, New Hampshire.

ROBERT WRIGLEY ("Fishing Together"), who hails from East St. Louis, Illinois, earned degrees from Southern Illinois University and the University of Montana in Missoula, where he studied with prominent poet Richard Hugo, and where, just as importantly, he fell in love with the Rocky Mountain West. Wrigley has published eight books of poetry, including *In the Bank of Beautiful Sins* (1995), which earned the San Francisco Poetry Center Book Award and was a finalist for the Lenore Marshall Award from the Academy of American Poets; *Reign of Snakes* (1999), which was awarded the Kingsley Tufts Poetry Award; and, most recently, *Earthly Meditations: New and Selected Poems* (2006) and *Beautiful Country* (2010). A former Guggenheim Fellow and two-time National Endowment for the Arts fellowship recipient, Wrigley has published poems widely in periodicals from the *New Yorker* and the *Atlantic Monthly* to *Poetry* and *Gray's Sporting Journal*, and has been honored with numerous Pushcart Prizes. He teaches creative writing at the University of Idaho and lives in the woods near Moscow, Idaho, with his wife, the writer Kim Barnes.